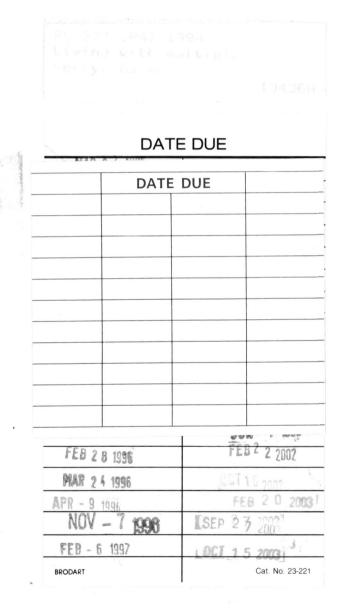

LIVING WITH MULTIPLE SCLEROSIS

To the people with multiple sclerosis who took part in this study.

Living with Multiple Sclerosis

Personal accounts of coping and adaptation

SARAH PERRY
Health and Health Care Research Unit
The Queen's University of Belfast

Avebury

Aldershot · Brookfield USA · Hong Kong · Singapore · Sydney

Published by
Avebury
Ashgate Publishing Limited
Gower House
Croft Road
Aldershot
Hants GU11 3HR
England

Ashgate Publishing Company
Old Post Road
Brookfield
Vermont 05036
USA

British Library Cataloguing in Publication Data

Perry, Sarah
    Living with Multiple Sclerosis: Personal
    Accounts of Coping and Adaptation. –
    (Developments in Nursing & Health Series)
    I. Title II. Series
    362.196834
ISBN 1 85628 893 5

Library of Congress Cataloging-in-Publication Data

Perry, Sarah, 1966-
    Living with multiple sclerosis: personal accounts
    of coping and adaptation / Sarah Perry
        p.   cm. – (Developments in nursing and health care)
    Includes bibliographical references.
    ISBN 1-85628-893-5 : $59.95
    1.Multiple sclerosis--psychological aspects. 2. Adjustment
    (Psychology) I. Title. II. Series.
    RC377.P47 1994
    362.1'96834--dc20   94-14057
                                                             CIP

Printed and Bound in Great Britain by
Athenaeum Press Ltd, Newcastle upon Tyne.

Contents

Figures and tables

Acknowledgements

This book is based upon my doctoral thesis (Perry 1993). The thesis was finished with the help of many people. First of all I must thank the people with multiple sclerosis who took part in this study; without their co-operation this study would not have been possible. I feel privileged to have been entrusted with their stories and am grateful to them for answering what must have seemed an endless stream of questions. I am grateful to the Multiple Scloerosis Society of Northern Ireland for commissioning the project in its final year.

I am also indebted to my colleagues at the Health and Health Care Research Unit of The Queen's University of Belfast for making valuable suggestions and providing advice. To my family and friends, I am grateful for their encouragement during the four years of this study.

Introduction

Chronic Illness

Multiple sclerosis is a chronic, rather than an acute or terminal, condition. It is a disease people live with rather than die from. Like other chronic conditions, multiple sclerosis is, to date, incurable. As chronic conditions become increasingly prevalent in industrialised countries and life expectancies among affected people improve, the social and economic implications of such illnesses and the quality of affected people's lives have become important issues in medical practice. The World Health Organisation (WHO 1980) produced the International Classification of Impairments, Disabilities and Handicaps (ICIDH) in an attempt to identify the consequences of chronic illnesses. The ICIDH is *not* disease specific. It is a three dimensional system which measures degrees of impairment, disability and handicap across different diseases. Impairment is defined as any loss or abnormality of psychological, physiological or anatomical structure or function. Disability refers to any restrictions or inability to perform normal activities. Handicap is defined as social, economic, environmental and cultural disadvantages that arise from impairments or disabilities which prevent a person from fulfilling normal social roles.

There are similarities between the ICIDH's definition of impairments, disabilities and handicaps and academic research which has made distinctions between the concepts disease, illness and sickness (Robinson 1990). Disease, like impairment, is a biomedical construct, concerned with the physical characteristics of biological disorders. Sickness, like handicap, is a social construct, concerned with social roles, status and disadvantage among people with illness. Illness, like disability, is a human construct, although it is more

1

concerned with individual or group perceptions of symptoms and problems rather than the measurement of functional difficulties. This study was guided by these three dimensional constructs of illness.

The Project

This book is concerned with the ways in which people with multiple sclerosis cope with their illness at home and in institutional settings. A semi-structured interview was used to explore personal accounts of illness and psychometric scales were selected to assess the role of stress in adaptation to illness. Results from both techniques were combined to understand the role of perceptions of illness, stress and coping in adaptation to a life with multiple sclerosis. The project focused on everyday problems and needs as well as the participants' own expertise in dealing with multiple sclerosis.

This is a descriptive study of what it is like to live with multiple sclerosis for 40 people in the Belfast and Lisburn area of Northern Ireland. The project was concerned with the perceptions of people diagnosed with the illness rather than the perceptions of informal or formal carers. Personal accounts of multiple sclerosis were studied in terms of the physical characteristics of the disease, personal reactions to the illness and the social consequences of long-term disabilities. The participants in the study were asked to share with the researcher, thoughts and feelings about themselves; their disease; their social lives; their living arrangements; the health care system; and their attempts to manage the consequences of illness.

Stress has been implicated in the cause and course of multiple sclerosis and individual adaptation to the illness (Counte et al 1983; Grant et al 1989; Hickey and Greene 1989; and Warren et al 1991). This project will assess the usefulness of the concept of stress in explaining adaptation to multiple sclerosis. People with multiple sclerosis were asked about the type and number of events that had upset and uplifted them in the last month; how they coped with stressful events; to evaluate their own self-esteem; and to define and rate their own levels of satisfaction with life and health during different phases of their life. Comparisons were made between people with multiple sclerosis living at home and in institutional settings.

The Structure of the Book

The three aspects of chronic illness described above are discussed in the first three chapters of the book. Chapter One details the physical and biomedical characteristics of multiple sclerosis in terms of its classification, aetiology, epidemiology, course, prognosis, diagnosis, symptoms and management. The second chapter focuses on the social aspects of chronic illnesses in terms of stigma, lay and medical concepts of illness and attitudes towards people with chronic illness, discriminatory practices, the patient role, and the policy of care in the community. The third chapter is concerned with subjective perceptions of chronic illness. Two approaches to academic research in this area - the insiders' perspective and the transactional model of stress - are reviewed. The first two chapters provide the context for personal reports of multiple sclerosis. The theoretical basis of the study is encapsulated in the third chapter.

The remaining chapters of the book concentrates on the research project itself. Chapter Four outlines the research design in terms of qualitative and quantitative methods, the research aims, the sample, measures, data collection and analysis. The results are presented in Chapters Five, Six, and Seven. The fifth chapter, consists of excerpts from the semi-structured interviews in which people with multiple sclerosis discussed their experiences of illness. Five themes were identified using content analysis procedures: understanding of multiple sclerosis; consequences of illness; managing illness; the emotional impact of illness; and opinions about care. The sixth chapter addresses the role of stress in adaptation to multiple sclerosis. Statistical analyses are presented in terms of the types and levels of hassles and uplifts reported, preferred coping strategies, ratings of self-esteem and definitions and ratings of satisfaction with life and health. Comparisons are made between people living at home and people living in institutional settings. In Chapter Seven, results from Chapters Five and Six are integrated and common themes throughout the interviews identified. Relationships between the variables are explored further and the meanings associated with adaptation discussed.

Chapter Eight is the last chapter. The main findings are summarised and related to the aims of the research project. The results are compared with the work reviewed in the first three chapters of the book. Shortcoming in the project are recognised and recommendations for further research suggested. Finally, the implications of the research findings are discussed.

1 The disease

Introduction

This chapter will review biomedical and social science literature to investigate the physical implications of multiple sclerosis. Biomedical understanding of multiple sclerosis is as yet incomplete: the aetiology of multiple sclerosis is unknown; classification is difficult; no specific diagnostic test exists; and prognosis is extremely variable and hard to predict. Deciding on treatment or care is problematic in the absence of reliable outcome measures and the above physical characteristics of the illness. Little attention will be given to research concerned with the pathology of multiple sclerosis since this has no direct bearing on people's experience of illness. The chapter will start with a definition of multiple sclerosis and its classification; this is followed by epidemiological information and finally, clinical aspects of the disease.

Definition and Classification

Multiple sclerosis[1] was first recognised as a distinct disease in 1868 by Charcot, an eminent neurologist of the time. 'Sclerosis' means hardening, and refers to the scarring that is the end product of the damage caused to the central nervous system (CNS). 'Multiple' refers to the scattering of these scars/lesions throughout the CNS. The scars cause damage to the myelin sheath which, in turn, affects the transmission of nerve impulses along nerve pathways. Symptoms of the illness generally correspond to the area of the CNS affected.

In the International Classification of Diseases (ICD), multiple sclerosis is categorised as a neurological disease. Within this classification it is identified as a demyelinating disorder, for the reasons mentioned above. However, the evidence collected to date is not conclusive and multiple sclerosis could alternatively be classified as a vascular, metabolic, endocrine or genetic disorder (Graham 1987).

Aetiology

There are two major theories concerning the cause of multiple sclerosis: slow viral infection and auto-immunity. In both theories a viral infection in childhood is claimed to be responsible for the appearance of multiple sclerosis in adulthood. Most of the research into the cause of multiple sclerosis is being carried out in the fields of cell biology, genetics, virology and immunology. However, epidemiological studies suggest that an interaction between environmental and genetic agents is responsible for influencing the occurrence of multiple sclerosis. This has been substantiated by evidence from studies on migration and risk of multiple sclerosis. Migration from high to low areas of risk in early life alters the risk in the direction of the host area. It is likely that the physical effects of climate on daily life, (e.g. through diet), are protective against, or conducive to, the development of multiple sclerosis (Matthews et al 1991). Socio-environmental aspects of multiple sclerosis are less researched. High levels of emotional stress or trauma have been associated with exacerbations of the illness, but there is no conclusive evidence to support this relationship to date (VanderPlate 1984; Warren and Cockerill 1991; McLellan et al 1989; Bauer and Hanefeld 1993).

The bias towards biomedical as opposed to epidemiological and social science approaches to aetiological research seems to rest on two philosophical concepts: that diseases are ontological, and that each disease has a specific cause (Cassell, 1979). As a result, research tends to focus on diseased organs/mechanisms within the body rather than mechanisms/processes outside the body. Although 'biopsychosocial' models of illness are now more commonly postulated than formerly, social and psychological aspects are consistently regarded as "factors" rather than essential parts of causal theory. As a result, they rarely receive the same attention as biomedical models.

The ethics of ploughing such a large percentage of the resources for research into biomedical research at the expense of a more balanced approach, incorporating links between biological, social and psychological research are rarely discussed. Advertisements and media reports often imply that scientists are on the verge of discovering the cause of multiple sclerosis, and with this breakthrough, the potential to prevent or cure the disease. This may offer some hope to sufferers in the short-term, but can lead to despair and disillusionment in the long-term. Indeed, time to wait for a specific cure is a luxury some people with multiple sclerosis do not possess (Cornell 1992).

Epidemiology

Multiple sclerosis is the most common of the demyelinating group of diseases and the second most commonly acquired neurological disorder in young adults after brain and spinal cord injury (Bernat and Vincent 1987). Incidence rates have been associated with sex, age, place of residence and socio-economic factors. Thus, more women are affected than men (one of the most reliable estimations of the sex ratio showed a risk of 1.8 in females as opposed to males (Matthews et al 1991)). The risk of developing multiple sclerosis increases with age from early adolescence, reaches a peak in the early thirties, and then declines until it becomes negligible after the age of sixty years. Two major studies have found a consistent relationship between increasing risk of multiple sclerosis and social and educational advantage (Beebe et al 1967; and Visscher et al 1981). Other studies, however, have found no significant relationship between risk of multiple sclerosis and social advantage (Matthews et al 1991). At the least, evidence suggests that multiple sclerosis is not positively associated with low socio-economic status.

The incidence of multiple sclerosis is significantly related to geographical latitude: risk increases with distance from the equator. Thus, prevalence rates are high in southern Canada, northern and central Europe, and southern Australia but rare in Asia, Africa and Japan (McFarlin and McFarlin 1982).

In terms of Great Britain, the average prevalence rate of multiple sclerosis was calculated at 50 per 100,000 (Matthews 1980), which is equivalent to one person in a population of 2000. More recent surveys have shown a variation in prevalence rate in England and Wales from 99 to 117 per 100,000 population (National Audit Office 1992). The figures are higher still for north-eastern Scotland at 144 per 100,000 (Matthews et al 1991). Northern Ireland prevalence rates are comparable to Scottish figures. The crude prevalence rate was found to be 57 per 100,000 in 1953, 81 per 100,000 in 1961 and 137 per 100,000 in 1988 (Hawkins and Kee 1988). In a population of 1,573 282, it can be estimated that 2155 people have a diagnosis of multiple sclerosis; that is 382 people in the greater Belfast area alone. But prevalence rates of chronic illness and disability are not equivalent. Prevalence of multiple sclerosis and disability within multiple sclerosis have been estimated as 160 per 200,000 and 125 per 200,000 respectively (Anderson and Bury 1988). If this difference is extrapolated and calculated for Northern Ireland

7

figures, the number of people in the Belfast area who are disabled by their condition can be estimated as 285.

Surveys have found that the population of people with multiple sclerosis have a mean age of approximately 50 years; onset of illness usually occurs in the early thirties; and the duration of illness is 15 years (Brunel ARMS Research Unit 1983a; Radford and Trew 1987; McLellan et al 1989; and Bauer and Handfeld 1993). Prevalence rates are usually regarded as conservative estimates. This is because of diagnostic problems, levels of health care and the standard of record keeping. Researchers interested in the prevalence of multiple sclerosis in the Southampton district found that GPs and the local MS Society were the main sources of names (McLellan et al 1989). There is no complete register of people with multiple sclerosis in Northern Ireland. What epidemiological studies do show is that the prevalence of multiple sclerosis in Northern Ireland is amongst the highest in the world.

Clinical Aspects

Course and prognosis

The course of multiple sclerosis is extremely variable and, therefore, difficult to predict. For some it may be practically imperceptible, whereas for others, the disease may cause rapid deterioration and severe impairment within a few years. For the majority of people, the illness is marked by relapses and remissions with increasing deterioration and disability. A distinction is often made between 'prognosis as to life' and 'prognosis as to disability'; in the first case, fatality is calculated; in the second, level of physical ability and employment status are measured. Estimates of average duration of illness in fatal cases range from 13 to 20 years. Poskanzer et al (1963) estimated that men with multiple sclerosis have a life-expectancy reduced by a mean of 9.5 years, and women a reduction of 14.4 years. Multiple sclerosis is rarely a direct cause of death. Causes of death are similar to the general population in approximately 42% of people with the illness. For the remainder, causes of death are generally from secondary infections (pneumonia, septicaemia and loss of protein from bedsores). Recently, Bauer and Handfeld (1993), have reported that suicide was the cause of death in 13% of their cases.

In terms of disability, Weinshenker and Ebers (1987) calculated that for 50% of people with multiple sclerosis progressive development of disability to the extent of requiring walking aids or worse, occurred within fifteen years of diagnosis. Confavreux et al, (1980) estimated that moderate disability occurred on average 3.4 years from onset and with severe disability by 9.5 years on average. The evidence is ambiguous because of the use of different

8

measures of disability and the difficulty of identifying people with multiple sclerosis at the onset of the illness.

Distinctions have been made between benign, mild, progressive, severe and asymptomatic forms of multiple sclerosis or between a relapsing/remitting course and an unrelenting and progressive course of multiple sclerosis. When multiple sclerosis is asymptomatic the lesions are 'silent' and there are no clinical symptoms. When it is benign the illness has a negligible effect and any disability is transitory. The mild type usually starts with remissions with almost complete recoveries to normal functioning, but these improvements gradually lessen with further relapses and remissions. In the progressive form there is steady deterioration with well delineated remissions and relapses; and in case of the severe form, deterioration is rapid and can be terminal within a few months to three years. Phadke (1990), found that between 8% and 17.7% of his sample (of 1055 people with multiple sclerosis), had a severe form of the condition and between 26% and 36.3% had a benign course. A relapsing cumulative course was found in 34% of the sample and 32.8% had a remitting course. These courses are not exclusive of one another (i.e. multiple sclerosis may be mild to begin with, but progressive in later years).

There are many variations within designated patterns of prognosis. The form it may take in the future may be more worrying for people than its present form. Inevitably, severe manifestations of multiple sclerosis are more visible because of the obvious disability caused. Advertisements on behalf of charities also depict multiple sclerosis as a devastating disease which 'strikes at random often with paralysis, impaired sight or speech, and is as yet incurable' (BMP DDP Needam 1993). The Multiple Sclerosis Society presents itself as a 'hope in hell'. The threat of severe disability and consequent dependency is more apparent in these portrayals than maintenance of abilities and autonomy. Worst case scenarios are presented for financial motives. Although the mass media were regarded as an important source of information for learning about multiple sclerosis, people with the disease were concerned with its image in the media (McLellan et al 1989).

Diagnosis

Diagnosis of multiple sclerosis is difficult due to the variable natural history of the disease, the transient nature of early symptoms and the absence of a specific diagnostic test. Magnetic resonance imaging has brought some advances in the detection and monitoring of multiple sclerosis (Webb 1992). Diagnosis is usually based on visible symptoms, documentation of lesions that have occurred on more than one occasion and on more than one site, and taking a medical history which indicates the evolutionary development of multiple sclerosis. Attempts to improve diagnostic accuracy are vital for therapeutic trials, but have had little impact in helping medical practitioners make a diagnosis. Indeed, patients' dissatisfaction with medical practitioners often begins with the diagnostic process; from the identity of the person responsible for conveying the diagnosis; the timing of the diagnosis; and how the diagnosis is made. Each of these features will be dealt with separately.

The source of diagnosis An accurate diagnosis of multiple sclerosis can only be made by a neurologist but this person does not always convey the diagnosis. Three major surveys of people with multiple sclerosis carried out in England (Brunel ARMS Research Unit 1983a and 1983b; and McLellan 1989) and Northern Ireland (Radford and Trew 1987) found that a significant proportion of respondents were given a diagnosis by people other than a doctor (neurologist or GP).[2] Two of these studies consistently found that a small number of people claimed that they had never been given a formal diagnosis.[3] In these cases, people had heard or read about the diagnosis accidentally, but had never received a confirmation from their own doctor, or their doctor used a euphemism (e.g. "inflammation of spinal cord") rather than the proper diagnosis. The Brunel ARMS study (1983b) suggests that a process of 'managed discovery' may account for not receiving a formal diagnosis from a doctor. When this happens the doctor concerned, sometimes with the family's help, postpones making a diagnosis until the patient is thought to be 'ready'. The benefit of such an approach is doubtful.

Another form of discovery is self-diagnosis. In this instance people with multiple sclerosis have already guessed what their illness is, and taken the initiative by asking their doctor to confirm or reject their self-diagnosis. Generally, people with chronic illness are more likely to play an active role in the diagnostic process than people with acute illness (Stewart and Sullivan, 1982).

A report by the British Society of Rehabilitation Medicine (1993), urges that a diagnosis of multiple sclerosis should always be given by a senior doctor and a further appointment should be offered for discussion and counselling. This should include a provisional prognosis with a discussion of the possible outcomes. It seems that doctors themselves are given little help or training in conveying a diagnosis. Such training would be make the task of communicating a diagnosis of chronic illness less painful for both doctors and patients.

Timing a diagnosis A common complaint is the length of time taken to inform people of their diagnosis. After a series of in-depth interviews with people with multiple sclerosis, Stewart and Sullivan (1982) calculated that it took, on average, five and a half years before a correct diagnosis was made. During this time misdiagnoses were common, ranging from other neurological diseases, bone and joint disease to psychiatric disorders. The majority of interviewees were critical about the outcomes of their visits to doctors. In fact, the distress caused by visits to physicians were perceived to be more harmful than the symptoms themselves. Stewart and Sullivan (1982) argue that doctors could be held responsible for causing iatrogenic disorders because over half the people they spoke to reported severe psychological problems before a diagnosis was eventually made (e.g. depression, anxiety, social withdrawal, difficulty falling asleep, weight loss, mental confusion and memory loss, increased alcohol consumption, suicidal thoughts and stomach aches).

Difficulties in making a definite diagnosis are partly responsible for the long time it can take to make a formal or official diagnosis. The difficulties doctors experience in reaching and conveying a diagnosis have already been mentioned. People with multiple sclerosis also play a part in prolonging or speeding up the process of diagnosis. Self-diagnosis is a case in point. Reporting symptoms or avoiding consultation with a doctor are other possible options. Brunel ARMS Research Unit (1983b) teased out some important differences between the onset of illness and the perception of first suspected symptoms, and between discovering a diagnosis and being formally told. Long periods of time may pass before each event. Stewart and Sullivan (1982) also made distinctions between the phases leading up to a formal diagnosis. They referred to the 'nonserious phase', the 'serious phase' and the 'diagnostic phase'. The 'nonserious phase' refers to interviewees' perceptions of symptoms which are viewed, initially, as minor ailments or symptoms of other treated illnesses. In the 'serious phase' respondents began to view their symptoms as more serious and indicative of an acute physical illness. This phase is generally perceived to be the most stressful. In the last phase, diagnosis is made formal.

The impact of diagnosis is not always negative. For many people a diagnosis of multiple sclerosis is a relief, either because worse things had been imagined (like cancer or psychiatric illness[4]), or having a legitimate disease was perceived to be better than living with ambiguity (Brunel ARMS Research Unit 1983b; and Sullivan and Stewart 1982). A common reaction to a diagnosis of multiple sclerosis is grief. Grief has been related to loss of one's former life, body and self (Register 1987) and a tendency to perceive one's present life through the lens of future dependency, vulnerability, weakness, inadequacy, incompetence or loss of control (Duval 1984).

Making a diagnosis is a time of emotional and social conflict for both the doctor and patient. Labels can be valuable (they can legitimise a previously unrecognised illness) but their consequences may be detrimental (in terms of social stigma). To people with multiple sclerosis, their immediate emotional response may be relief, disbelief or grief. How a diagnosis is made can alleviate or magnify the impact of such news.

How a diagnosis is made Criticisms of how a diagnosis of multiple sclerosis is made have focused on doctors' attitudes, their manner, the amount of advice and information given and the level of emotional support offered. As one person with multiple sclerosis writes:

> I know telling someone they have an incurable condition must be difficult, but to follow this with an avalanche of hopelessness seemed cruel. My specialist told me not to join the MS Society as people in wheelchairs would depress me... I was left alone, trying to dress with shaky hands... (Wright 1992)

In contrast, doctors have also been accused of being 'unrealistically optimistic' (Stewart and Sullivan, 1982). Although, a working group organised by the Royal College of Physicians (1990), set up to provide standards of care for patients with neurological disease, states that it is appropriate to err on the optimistic side when discussing the prognosis early on in the course of the illness. Data from Ben-Sira's (1984) investigation of chronic illness, stress and coping, highlighted the significance of doctors' emotional support which was 'the most sought for yet least attainable resource in alleviating distress.'

The most common complaint made against doctors concerns the lack of advice and information given. In the Northern Ireland survey (Radford and Trew 1987), 53.4% of the people interviewed said that the medical practitioner responsible for making a diagnosis, did not explain multiple sclerosis to them at all. Informing people of the sort of care available also appears to be lacking. The National Audit Office (1992) report on health services for physically disabled people, recommended that health authorities 'improve the timeliness, quality and availability of information on services available for physically disabled people'.

To conclude, problems with the diagnostic process can have an enormous impact on how people with multiple sclerosis perceive and manage their illness, ranging from hopelessness to optimism and rebellion to passivity.

There is no perfect procedure suitable for all circumstances, but a basic rule appears to be: listen to each person's story and let this guide professional behaviour. Each story is based on individual experiences and fears - the first is based on the past and the second is based on what is yet to come (or may never come). Both aspects need to be addressed, when timing information and deciding on the nature of advice/support provided.

Symptoms

Common symptoms of multiple sclerosis can be listed as follows: optic neuritis, altered sensations, fatigue, weakness, spasms, paralysis, incontinence, memory and concentration difficulties, numbness, tingling pins and needles, sexual problems, disturbances of co-ordination, problems with balance, pain, speech disturbance, cognitive impairment and emotional disturbances such as depression. Secondary symptoms like constipation, obesity, contractures and pressure sores can cause major discomfort, but can be avoided with careful management. Bauer and Hanefeld (1993) found that secondary symptoms occurred in 90% of their sample over the age of 60 years. Difficulties in walking, fatigue and incontinence tend to be the most frequently reported problems (McLellan et al 1989). Dealing with multiple sclerosis symptoms requires that the person diagnosed is informed of what the symptoms may mean in the first place, and secondly, that the significance of reported symptoms is recognised by others. Problems arise when the affected individual does not associate abnormal feelings with symptoms of multiple sclerosis, or when others misinterpret or fail to recognise the importance of reported sensations.

Invisible symptoms can be more problematic than more obvious symptoms. The "how well you look" comment is often exasperating for people with multiple sclerosis when they feel awful. The assumption that being in a wheelchair means paralysis and no other physical problems, is another common misunderstanding (Gould 1992). Symptoms also tend to fluctuate; they can disappear, reappear worsen or subside for no apparent reason. As a result, personal capabilities and expectations or demands from other people may be at odds with each other. People with multiple sclerosis often feel in a 'limbo' - neither fully functioning and well nor disabled and sick (VanderPlate 1984).

Psychological and psychiatric symptoms of multiple sclerosis (in particular, cognitive impairments and emotion lability), have received much debate in professional journals (Peyser et al 1980; Schiffer et al 1983; McIvor et al 1884; Paulley 1985; Ron 1986; and Joffe et al 1987; McIntosh-Michailis et al 1991; and Rao et al 1992). The MS Society (1987) reiterates that multiple sclerosis 'is *not* a psychiatric or 'nervous disorder", but commentators in academic journals describe multiple sclerosis as 'a disease of the brain and mind' in which 'psychiatric morbidity' is observed (Ron and Feinstein 1992). There is also dispute as to whether depression in multiple sclerosis is a direct product of the disease process itself or a response to illness and the stress it engenders. (Devins and Seland 1987). It is more realistic to view psychological responses to multiple sclerosis as a complex interaction between disease, psychological and socio-environmental variables.

Lastly, a report by the Brunel ARMS Research Unit (1986) discovered differences in the ways people with multiple sclerosis and doctors perceived and explained symptoms. Medical practitioners tend to concentrate on physical abnormalities and clinical signs, whilst people with multiple sclerosis focus on 'the total experience and meaning of living with the disease.' Discrepancies such as these can result in communication problems between professionals and people with the disease. It would be beneficial if current medical perceptions of symptoms relevant to multiple sclerosis were broadened to include those symptoms perceived by those with multiple sclerosis as being related to their disease (Brunel ARMS Research Unit 1986).

Management

The absence of a specific diagnostic test for multiple sclerosis, its variability in terms of severity and duration, and the idiosyncratic nature of relapses and remissions within each individual, make it hard to judge the performance of various treatments. As yet there is no treatment that is known to alter the course of the condition. The hormone adrenocorticotropic (ACTH) can shorten the duration of a sudden relapse, although long-term use of the drug can result in side-effects, such as weight gain, acne and acute psychosis (Matthews et al 1991). A multitude of "cures" or successful treatments for multiple sclerosis have been claimed ranging from yoga, hyperbaric oxygen, acupuncture, diets, reflexology, the removal of dental fillings, and oil of evening primrose to pilgrimages and faith healing. In her book 'Coping with MS', Cynthia Benz (1988) reviews the range of alternative treatments available. She encourages people to get involved with what they think will suit them personally without pushing themselves to exhaustion-point. Melanie Wright (1992) also believes in such an approach:

> I am convinced that my own good health is thanks to the numerous therapies I have tried. They have all helped in different ways - but what has helped most is the feeling of doing something to help my body help itself...

Self-helps groups often perform this function for individual members. As well as providing social support, they are generally founded on the belief that positive action is better than waiting for something to happen.

But alternative therapies and self-help groups do not appeal to everyone. More conventional forms of care (used alone or in addition to other methods), which offer long-term help with rehabilitation and effective treatments for symptomatic complications may be preferred by some. Drug treatment and surgery can ameliorate the effects of many symptoms (e.g. ataxia, spasticity, sexual function, urinary incontinence, fatigue and pain). However, the benefits of drug treatment are limited and the side-effects of some may cause additional problems. Surgical treatment also carries risks and the practical gains of such action need to be clearly considered (British Society of Rehabilitation Medicine 1993).

De Souza, (1990) succinctly lists the hallmarks of good approaches to long-term management of multiple sclerosis as: flexibility, continual involvement, regular assessments, multi-disciplinary teamwork, offering accurate information, encouraging the individual to take an active role in his/her rehabilitation programme and providing emotional and physical support.

Surveys of people with multiple sclerosis and their perceptions of health and social care, provide important information about current shortcomings in service provision (Elian and Dean 1983; Simons 1984; Radford and Trew 1987; McLellan et al 1989; and Bauer and Handfeld 1993). These surveys are remarkably consistent in their findings and can be summarised as follows: physiotherapy was generally perceived to be the most beneficial health intervention, but availability of the service was limited; there was little contact with social workers, but they were perceived to have little relevant expertise; occupational therapists provided aids and equipment, but spent little time on developing life-skills; contacts with clinical psychologists, counsellors, health visitors, speech therapists and disablement resettlement officers were rare; GPs lacked knowledge of the illness; the manner in which neurologists conveyed a diagnosis was often unsatisfactory; information about the illness, relevant services and benefits/entitlements was sporadic; transportation services were often inappropriate; and wheelchairs were frequently uncomfortable. People with multiple sclerosis had mixed feelings about voluntary organisations: they were invaluable sources of information, but many people felt they were for severely disabled people and depressing places to visit. There is little information about day-care services and residential care. The Northern Ireland study (Radford and Trew 1987) is the only study to have assessed the quality of residential care for people with multiple sclerosis. The standard of residential care will be referred to in Chapter Two.

The Royal College of Physicians (1986) also produced evidence of serious deficiencies within rehabilitation services. It recommended that standards of care and audit should be set up for specialist and generic health services and that Regional Disability Medicine Sub-Committees should be developed to review disability services. In response to this report, a survey was conducted in Northern Ireland to find out what services were being provided by the four Health and Personal Social Services Boards (Swallow and Darragh 1991). Some of the results from the survey can be summarised as follows:

1. None of the Boards had a specific individual or team with responsibility for planning and managing rehabilitation services.

2. Only the Eastern Board had set up a Medical Disability Sub-Committee, although membership was limited to the medical profession only.

3. None of the Boards systematically monitored disability services.

4. Disabled people were conspicuous by their lack of representation on planning groups.

5. Information for disabled people and for professionals working in the field was inadequate and uneven.

6. There was a lack of adequate residential and respite care.

7. Medical students in Belfast did not receive specific teaching about the problems of rehabilitation and disability, which was surprising considering the prevalence of chronic illness within the community.

8. Physical disability had a low profile within health care generally.

It was suggested that the Department of Health and Social Services in Northern Ireland should make a formal commitment to improve services for disabled people. To do so required the monitoring of care, the provision of information, the participation of disabled people, staff training, service planning and extra resources.

Standards for rehabilitation services for people with multiple sclerosis are beginning to appear (Royal College of Physicians (RCP) 1990; and British Society of Rehabilitation Medicine (BSRM) 1993). The BSRM report is comprehensive in scope with respect to treatments for specific symptoms, disabilities and complications of multiple sclerosis, ranging from urinary incontinence, oedema, spasticity and erectile impotence to memory and cognitive disorders. Guidelines for imparting a diagnosis are also provided.

However, only passing reference is made to implications of multiple sclerosis on social activities and family life and how to cope with the illness.

The BSRM report concludes with a checklist for an effective medical service which includes: participation of disabled people in the planning and monitoring of services; improving access to buildings; the provision of information; the development of counselling and therapy services for people with multiple sclerosis and their carers; the implementation of a case management system; the introduction of comprehensive care plans and clinical audit; the timely provision of statutory benefits, equipment and modification to dwellings; and the establishment of community-based support teams. The emphasis in rehabilitation is still on providing treatments for specific symptoms rather than support so that people can live independently in their own homes. Multi-disciplinary teams, in real life, often consist of a range of professionals dealing with different aspects of the illness in isolation from one another.

The RCP's report (1990) is more circumspect in making recommendations, considering the under-provision of neurological care at present.[5] The RCP report also emphasises that research into the effectiveness of treatments and aetiology in multiple sclerosis has a 'reputation for [being] poorly conducted and unimaginative'. Bauer and Handfeld (1993) found that out of 200 grants awarded by the MS Society in America only four were related to the problems of rehabilitation. They conclude:

> There is no question that the emphasis on basic and experimental research is justified... It should not be forgotten, however, that MS patients have decades to live with serious impairments and a stressful, often depressing life situation, and that support for them is the major reality in MS today.

There are very few examples of rehabilitation teams in the United Kingdom which meet the standards identified above (Royal College of Physicians, 1986; Beardshaw 1988; National Audit Office 1992)).

There is a danger, however, in professionals believing that rehabilitation is something that is provided by experts for people with disabilities, rather than something disabled people generally achieve with the help of other people. The experience of people with disabilities, and the impact of illness on close relatives should be at the centre of any rehabilitation programme (McLellan 1991). Graham (1987), who has multiple sclerosis herself, suggests ways in which such priorities could influence medical practice:

> if the medical profession would only take a more flexible approach, see each patient as an individual.... Doctors have tended to lapse into

thinking that MS is an incurable and chronic disease so there is nothing they can do.

The WHO Regional Office for Europe (Hermanova, 1991) has identified another aspect of rehabilitation often ignored: the need to change society's attitude towards disabled people.

This chapter has looked at biomedical approaches to multiple sclerosis and how such knowledge is applied in medical practice. Uncertainty underpins many of the physical and clinical aspects of multiple sclerosis. Medical professionals appear to have as much difficulty in dealing with this uncertainty as people with multiple sclerosis. Evidence suggests, however, that individual clinicians generally perceive uncertainty to be a negative and limiting aspect of chronic illness, whereas rehabilitation teams concentrate on more liberating aspects of uncertainty - as a source of hope and encouragement. People with multiple sclerosis experience 'uncertainty' in both these ways at different times. These discrepancies probably reflect unstated differences in agenda setting: individual neurologists perceive diagnosis to be the end-point of consultation; rehabilitation teams perceive their work to be long-term support; and people with multiple sclerosis manage their illness by taking each day as it comes. Absent from the literature are any accounts regarding communication between these three groups.

Multiple sclerosis is like most other chronic illnesses in that it is an illness people *live with* rather than *die from*. Doctors who simply monitor the progress of an illness at yearly intervals, fail to appreciate the detrimental affect this may have on people with multiple sclerosis. The Northern Ireland survey on multiple sclerosis (Radford and Trew, 1987) found that 53.4% of the people they spoke to with multiple sclerosis had not seen their neurologist in the last year and only 12% would like to have more contact with their neurologist. Low contact does not necessarily reflect dissatisfaction with care, but many people did say that 'they felt there was nothing much that any of these people could do for them.' It would not be an exaggeration to conclude that the biomedical perspective of multiple sclerosis, as applied to medical practice, offers little in the way of encouragement to people with multiple sclerosis in Northern Ireland. The experience of illness may, therefore, be one of isolation. This may be reinforced if social attitudes are equally unfavourable.

18

Summary

1. The aim of this chapter was to review biomedical knowledge concerning multiple sclerosis so that the impact of the physical characteristics of the disease on individuals is understood.

2. Uncertainty is characteristic of biomedical knowledge in terms of the definition and classification of the disease, aetiology, diagnosis, prognosis, treatment and care. Epidemiological studies have been more fruitful: incidence is related to geographical latitude, more women are affected than men; onset usually occurs in the early thirties; and prevalence rates between 50 per 100,000 and 144 per 100,000 have been calculated in United Kingdom, depending on latitude. Prevalence rate in Northern Ireland has been estimated at 137 per 100 000.

3. The course of the disease is variable. Distinctions have been made between relapsing remitting, relapsing cumulative, relapsing progressive, and progressive courses with benign, intermediate, mild and severe prognoses.

4. Diagnosis is problematic in the absence of a specific test. Patients are often dissatisfied with the way in which the diagnosis is conveyed. Criticisms concern the source of the diagnosis, timing of the diagnosis and how the diagnosis was made.

5. The symptoms of multiple sclerosis are varied and fluctuate. Secondary complications can be equally problematic. Psychological and psychiatric symptoms of multiple sclerosis are controversial. It is unclear whether depression is a symptom of the disease or a response to illness. Symptoms often have different meanings to patients than they have to doctors.

6. Management of multiple sclerosis was discussed in terms of conventional and unconventional therapies. Shortcomings in rehabilitation services were listed and recommendations for future service provisions were reported. Criticisms of the content and focus of research were discussed. Rehabilitation was perceived to be something that people with multiple sclerosis achieved *with* the help of others, rather than something that was provided by experts only.

Notes

1. The disease has been referred to 'disseminated sclerosis' (in the UK in particular) and 'multiple cerebral sclerosis' (in the USA in particular). Kurtzke (1988) provides a good review of problems in finding a precise definition of multiple sclerosis.

2. Other sources of diagnosis were other medical professionals, members of their own family, friends, or 'other people'. In the Brunel ARMS survey (1983b), 24.3% of sample had not been told of their diagnosis by a doctor (neurologist or GP). The corresponding figure in the Northern Ireland survey (Radford and Trew 1987), is 26.7%, and for the Southampton study (McLellan et al 1989), 9%.

3. 5.1% in the Brunel ARMS study (1983b) and 6.6% in the Northern Ireland study (Radford and Trew 1987). In the Southampton survey (McLellan et al 1989), people who were unaware of their diagnosis were excluded from the sample.

4. Why multiple sclerosis is perceived to be 'preferable' to these two illnesses is interesting because cancer and psychiatric illness are often curable. Sontag (1991) argues that certain illnesses (such as cancer and AIDS) are metaphors for cultural deficiencies and anxieties.

5. The report points out that there are currently 190 neurologists in the UK for a populations of 56.8 million - approximately one per 373 000 people. The British Neurological Society suggests that one neurologist per 200,000 would be more appropriate. There are four full-time neurologists in Northern Ireland for a population of 1,573 282 (The Northern Ireland Census 1991). This is equivalent to one neurologist per 393 320, nearly half the recommended number.

2 Concepts of illness

Introduction

The previous chapter was disease-specific and concerned with the physical characteristics of multiple sclerosis. The chapter outlined the sorts of medical problems people with multiple sclerosis contend with and how these might affect their lives. The impact of multiple sclerosis is broadened in this chapter. The disease is treated as one of a variety of diseases grouped together on the basis of their chronicity. The focus is not on physical impairments, nor personal experiences of illness, but illness as a social condition. Once a diagnosis of multiple sclerosis is made public, relationships between the person with the illness and others are often modified. Illness, therefore, acquires a social definition.

Lay and medical perceptions of illness provide reference points for people with chronic illness. Unfavourable community attitudes towards illness and disability can have a considerable affect on an individual's quality of life. Professional practices limit individual autonomy. The chapter is divided into two parts. The first is concerned with social interactions between relatively healthy and sick people. It starts with the work of Goffman on stigma, before moving on to lay conceptions of health and illness, and finishing with a discussion on the discriminatory practices towards people with chronic illness. The second part is a critique of health care practices and policies. It deals, firstly, with changing professional concepts of people with illness, from deviants to consumers/customers and, secondly, the transition from institutional to community care. Both parts of the chapter place the experience of illness into a historical context. This chapter focuses on the social

...s of chronic illness by looking at the role of social constraints in
...ronic illness.

...s of Illness

...la

Philosophers have distinguished between the material self, the social self, the
spiritual self and the bodily self (James 1950). The nature of the social self
has received much attention in the twentieth century especially. Cooley (1902)
coined the term the "looking-glass self" to explain how a person's perception
of him/herself is influenced by what the individual believes others think of
him/her. Mead (1934) also argued that a person's perception of him/herself
(self-concept) was dependent on and constituted through social interactions.
Through interactions, individuals learn to interpret the world in the same way
as others do, and perceive themselves in terms of the perceptions of the
'generalised other':

> The social-conscious human individual, then, takes up or assumes the
> organised social attitudes of the given social group or community to
> which he belongs. (Mead 1934)

Glover (1988) argues that in the absence of recognition and social
comparison, people become depersonalised - they loose their 'I-ness'. Social
interactions are problematic for people with chronic illness because they are
necessary for developing a sense of identity, but stigmatising relationships
may mean that only negative perceptions of self are consolidated. Symbolic
interactionists were concerned with tensions arising out of social interactions.
Goffman (1963) illustrated such tensions in his essay 'Stigma'. Stigmatised
individuals possessed attributes judged by the majority as socially undesirable
(e.g. physical deformities, character flaws or membership of a minority group).
People with chronic illness and physical disabilities were included in his
analysis of the moral career of stigmatised people along with the mentally ill,
the disfigured, homosexuals, prostitutes and criminals. Goffman suggested
that the stigmatised have to learn to reconcile two opposing processes: firstly,
incorporation of the values of normal people and secondly, an awareness that
they possess a stigma and the social consequences of possessing it.

According to Goffman, the visibility of a particular stigma determines the
way in which a stigmatised individual deals with social interactions. When the
stigma was obtrusive, the individual was automatically 'discredited' by
normals. Discredited individuals had to deal with tensions arising from face-
to-face encounters. They might do this by covering their stigma or minimising

22

its severity. When the stigma was less obvious, the individual was 'discreditable' (the potential to be discredited exists). In this situation, the individual would try to relieve tension by managing information; in other words, deciding whether a stigma should be concealed or revealed. Concealing a stigma - 'passing' as normal - was a common strategy, although Goffman suggested that when concealment was unlearnt and a stigma voluntarily disclosed, a stigmatised individual would be judged as well-adjusted by others. Alternatively stigmatised people might prefer to socially withdraw from the company of normals and seek the companionship of sympathetic others who either shared the same stigma or were 'wise' normals as a result of intimate experience of the stigma. These options are available to people with chronic illness during the course of their disease.

Good adjustment is based on cultural values in which the stigmatised individual is expected to accommodate the prejudices of normals and ease their discomfort in 'mixed' interactions:

> It requires that the stigmatised individual cheerfully and unself-consciously accept himself as essentially the same as normals, while at the same time he voluntarily withholds himself from those situations in which normals would find it difficult to give lip-service to their similar acceptance of him. (Goffman 1963)

Goffman's essay can be criticised for assuming we all share similar conceptions of the social order. Phenomenologists argued that personal meanings of the world are varied, and postmodernists that social realities are constructed, that different people construct different realities and that multiple realities exist and are available to people at different times in their life. Unfortunately there is little contemporary evidence that people with physical disabilities have alternative roles available to them apart from the stigmatised role. Chronic illness and long-term disabilities may represent what Hughes' (1945) terms a "master status" rather than a temporary incumbency. In other words, individuals are identified by others in terms of their illness rather than their own personal characteristics.

Surveys of public attitudes towards disabled people have tended to report societal prejudice against people with disabilities. Tringo (1970) discovered a hierarchy of preference towards specific disability groups. Using a Disability Social Distance Scale, he asked students and graduates for their attitudes towards twenty one different disability groups. He found that chronic illnesses, such as arthritis, asthma, diabetes and heart disease were preferred the most, and mental disorders, addiction, and ex-convicts the least.[1] Among the more preferred disability groups were the three major causes of death and disability (heart disease, stroke and cancer). The relative fatality of different disabilities (and frailty of human life) appears to be less important than familiarity with a condition or aesthetic factors. Tringo found that graduates working in the field of rehabilitation were no more accepting of disabled groups than students. It was concluded that although a hierarchy of preference existed a generalised negative attitude towards all the disabled groups was common.

Similar results were found by Westbrook et al (1993) 23 years later in an Australian study. When health practitioners from different ethnic communities (Chinese, Italian, German, Greek, Arabic and Anglo Australian) were asked to complete a Social Distance Scale, people with asthma, diabetes, heart disease and arthritis were rated as most accepted and people with AIDS, mental retardation, psychiatric illness and cerebral palsy, the least accepted of 20 disability groups. People with multiple sclerosis also scored badly and were perceived to be only more acceptable than the groups 'paraplegia', 'dwarf', 'alcoholism', 'cerebral palsy', 'mental retardation', 'psychiatric illness' and 'AIDS'. The German community reported greatest acceptance and the Arabic community the least acceptance of people with disabilities. The authors suggest that 'individualistic' communities are more positive towards disability groups than 'collectivist' communities,[2] where birth of a disabled child was associated with greater family shame. Cross-cultural similarities, however, are more apparent than differences. The same hierarchy of preference exists not only between communities, but has changed little in the twenty years of research. There is strong evidence that attitudes towards people with disability are not only consistently negative but relatively stable.

Gething (1991) explored the generality or specificity of attitudes towards people with disabilities, and reviewed work in the area. Research studies have associated prejudice with the visibility of the disability, or with specific categories of disability. Thus, distinctions have been made between people with physical disabilities, sensory disabilities and social disabilities; between physical and intellectual disabilities; and between inherited and acquired disabilities. People with physical disabilities are generally perceived more favourably than other disabled groups. However, the wording of attitudes surveys appears to be important: when asked to indicate their attitude towards disability groups, a community sample responded differently to 'epilepsy' than to 'persons with epilepsy' (Antonak and Rankin, 1982). Gething's own research supported the generality rather than specificity of negative attitudes towards disabled people, but found that feelings of discomfort in social interactions were influenced by level of prior close contact with people with disabilities. People with little prior contact with disabled people reported more discomfort during social interactions with disabled people.

In a novel research project, Bogdan and Taylor (1989) focused on the perspectives of non-disabled people who did *not* appear to stigmatise, stereotype or reject people with disabilities. Their study concentrated on agencies that supported children with severe disabilities in natural, foster and adoptive families in their own homes or small community settings. They found that in accepting relationships (i.e. long-standing, relationships characterised by closeness and affection), the 'humanness' of people with disability was maintained, although difference was not denied. The authors identified four dimensions to these non-disabled people's attitudes: that they attributed thought to the disabled person, saw individuality in the disabled person, viewed the disabled person as reciprocating and identified a social place for the disabled person. In accepting relationships, non-disabled people were able to recognise people with severe disabilities as "someone like me" - disability was secondary to the person's humanity. These research findings are informative and could provide guidelines for public education and rehabilitation programmes.

Research evidence indicates, however that negative attitudes towards disabled people are the norm. Disabled people are in a "catch 22" situation: if they socially withdraw from the able-bodied community they run the risk of being further marginalised, but if they attempt to take part in community life they may face social rejection. Safilos-Rothschild (1970) found that interactions between disabled and non-disabled people were generally tense, anxiety-laden, inhibited and stereotyped. Non-disabled people felt uncomfortable with disabled people. They were unsure of how to behave with people who were perceived to be physically or mentally imperfect, deficient or abnormal. Scambler (1984) distinguishes between enacted and felt stigma. Enacted stigma refers to discrimination against people with chronic conditions on the basis of their perceived social inferiority. Discrimination is legitimised through policies of segregation. Discriminatory practices will be discussed later in the chapter. Attention will first be paid to the nature of felt stigma which refers to feelings of shame associated with being chronically ill or disabled. People with physical disabilities become aware of their own abnormalities and the social embarrassment this causes in interactions with others. He argues that felt stigma, especially the fear of enacted stigma, was more harmful than actual enacted stigma. Scambler links felt stigma to perceptions of inferiority. There is also evidence that felt stigma may be related to lay conceptions that people are morally responsible for their own health and illness.

One of the first points to recognise is the importance ordinary people place on health and illness. In his study of human concerns across 14 countries, (developed and developing), Cantril (1965) found that aspirations of good health and fears of ill-health featured consistently among the most important personal concerns. Aspirations and fears which ranked higher than these concerns were standard of living and child welfare. Human patterns of concern were intricately interwoven: good health, a decent standard of living, the provision of child care welfare services, employment and material wealth were perceived to be mutually dependent on one another. In Britain two reports - the Black Report (Townsend and Davidson 1982) and The Health Divide (Whitehead 1988) - have substantiated the link between ill-health and deprivation. Despite health provision for everyone, in the shape of the National Health Service, people at the bottom of the social scale have poorer health than those towards the top.

Despite the strong link between health and material conditions, qualitative studies and community surveys have shown that ordinary people hold beliefs about health and illness which have a predominantly moral basis (Williams 1983 and 1990; Cornwell 1984; Herzlich and Pierrot 1987; and Stainton Rogers 1991). These moral codes are grounded in local folklore, medical knowledge, political allegiances and religious faith. Herzlich and Pierrot (1987) placed the experience of illness into a historical perspective. They found that popular beliefs about illness are relatively permanent, in particular the:

> ancient idea of fate... [and] notions of "sin", "fault," and "responsibility," which throughout the ages has never failed to come into play when illness has struck.

Sontag (1979) argues that illness serves as a metaphor for corrupt and unjust societies, which people must either accept as fate or 'fight' as a potentially lethal enemy. Sontag (1989) believes that every society needs one illness (e.g. TB, cancer, AIDS), which symbolises evil and attaches blame to its victims. This is made obvious in the case of AIDS in which haemophiliac AIDS sufferers are described as innocent victims, which implies that other people with AIDS (i.e. drug addicts, homosexuals and sexually promiscuous people) are guilty or deserving of illness. Illness has become a metaphor for 'mortality, for human frailty and vulnerability.' In chronic illnesses individual infirmity is set against individual will to survive over a long period of time. Physical illness, as a result, becomes a psychological event in which individuals are perceived to be culpable for their own health and by sheer will, responsible for their own recovery. Although multiple sclerosis has not been singled out as a metaphor for social evils, there is a sense of social injustice when the disease is diagnosed. After the initial shock, people with the illness are expected to fight their own battles against the disease. In the absence of a cure, people with chronic illness can expect moral sanctioning or reproach from the community in which they live.

Studies of cultural conceptions of illness among middle and working class communities in Great Britain have made similar observations (Blaxter 1983; Cornwell 1984; and Williams 1990). Eastenders in London felt that people "earned" good health through a life of moderation, virtue, cleanliness, decency and hard work (Cornwell 1984). The cause of an individual's illness was attributed to location (internal-body or external-environment), circumstances (avoidable or unavoidable) and responsibility (whether person was to blame or not). Illness could potentially discredit a person, but an uncomplaining and stoical attitude could restore an ill person's social status. Among working class women Blaxter (1983) found:

> a very stoical, puritanical and at the same time fatalistic view of the occurrence of illness: illness was weakness, 'lying down to it', being functionally unfit, giving in to disease.

The concept 'strength' was also pertinent to elderly working and middle class Aberdonians (Williams 1983 and 1990). Health was related to activity and moral effort. In terms of activity the ability to carry out normal and ordinary everyday duties (employment, housework etc.) was central to people's explanations of good health. In terms of moral effort, illness was regarded as a sign of weakness, but also a test one's faith, providing the opportunity to become a better person through the process of suffering. Williams refers to these two aspects of health and illness as the 'Protestant Legacy'. On the other hand, Welsh mothers were found to be largely fatalistic about health and illness, with only a small proportion reporting lifestyle choices as important factors for future health (Pill and Stott 1985). When lifestyle was regarded as important, however, beliefs about personal responsibility and religious commitment were relevant. The authors also reported that most people were able to hold contradictory theories about health and illness.

Stainton Rodgers (1991) explored the use of multiple explanations of health and illness among academics, health professionals and lay people. She identified eight major accounts of health and illness which were sometimes contradictory, but were selected and used according to the situation or person at hand. Individual accounts reflected political ideologies,[3] biomedical theories,[4] religious beliefs,[5] and psychological theories.[6] Canlan (1987) found that beliefs about health and illness derived from three sources: personal experience and local folklore, sociopolitical values about health and its control, and powerful groups regarded as 'experts' (i.e. medical profession). This is reflected in Stainton Rogers' work.

Ordinary people also make distinctions between "real" and "pseudo" illnesses. Parisians (Herzlich 1973) distinguished between serious/fatal illnesses, chronic conditions, everyday trivial illnesses and childhood ailments. London's Eastenders differentiated between 'normal' common place illnesses that were treated by medicine, 'real' illnesses which were unusual, severe or chronic conditions, and 'health problems', which were linked to individual characteristics, age or lifestyle. In Paris and London, trivial illnesses/health problems were regarded as not real illnesses. Chronic illness were perceived by the general public to be real illnesses, but this did not necessarily mean that people with chronic illness were not perceived to be culpable for their illness.

Evidence suggests that the determinants of health and illness are understood by the public, but there exists a predisposition to moralise illness: the individual is blamed to some extent for his/her weakness and consequent ill-health, and in the case of people with chronic illness, their failure to get well again. Such beliefs can have devastating effects, as prevailing negative attitudes towards people with disabilities demonstrate. Lay beliefs about health and illness and negative attitudes towards chronically ill and disabled people have become institutionalised. Discriminatory practices (enacted stigma) are legitimised through social institutions and passed from one generation to the next.

Discrimination

Work in the area of discrimination has focused on the lives of disabled people. Although disabled people do not necessarily have a chronic illness and chronically ill people are not necessarily disabled, there is a substantial overlap between these two groups. This section relies on the disability literature, in particular the work of a number of academics who identify themselves as disabled (Finkelstein 1980; Asch 1984; Oliver 1990 and 1992; Barnes 1991; and Morris 1991 and 1992). Finkelstein (1980) argues that disability is not an attribute of the individual or a personal misfortune, but an oppressive social relationship between people with physical impairments and society:[7]

> disability as a social relationship can be altered or changed. Once social barriers to the reintegration of people with physical impairments are removed the disability itself is eliminated.

Finkelstein has been criticised for believing that all the problems of disability rest in the environment and for ignoring the very real feelings of personal misfortune and physical and emotional loss among disabled people (see US commentaries on Finkelstein's essay included in the publication (Finkelstein 1980)). Personal experiences of chronic illness and disability will be explored in the following chapter, but the extent to which the social environment discriminates against disabled people will be briefly discussed.

The Office of Population, Censuses and Surveys (OPCS) collected information concerning the prevalence of disability and the financial and employment status of disabled people in Britain (Martin et al 1988; Martin and White 1988; and Martin et al 1989). It has been estimated that 14% of the population have a disability,[8] and that a disability, unemployment and poverty trap exists. The most comprehensive guide to discriminatory practices towards disabled people is provided by Barnes (1991) in his book 'Disabled people in Britain and discrimination.' His aims are made clear:

> Discrimination is not simply a question of specific examples of individuals discriminating against disabled people, although this is not an uncommon view. This book sets out to demonstrate that discrimination is institutionalised within the very fabric of British society. (Barnes 1991)

The infringement of seven basic rights by discrimination against disabled people is discussed by Barnes and can be summarised as follows:

1. *Education* in terms of segregation;

2. *Employment* in terms of unemployment, under-employment and failure to enforce the quota system;[9]

3. *Economic security* in terms of the additional costs incurred by impairments, and the move away from statutory to discretionary awards;

4. *Services* in terms of the small percentage of resources spent on people with physical impairments, the large percentage of money spent on residential care and professional salaries, the lack of information and advice, and problems with technical aids and equipment and availability of personal assistance;

5. *Independent living* in terms of problems with housing, transport and the built environment;

6.   *Culture and recreation* in terms of segregated (e.g. day-centres) and mainstream leisure facilities, social life, lack of financial resources, and the influence of the media;[10]

7.   *Influence* in terms of failure to appear on the electoral register (particularly disabled people living in residential settings), and the role of pressure groups.

Barnes calls for anti-discrimination legislation which enforces policies of integration rather than segregation and emphasises social rights rather than individual needs.

Disabled people, ethnic minority groups, the elderly and single parents have all been described as belonging to an 'underclass', characterised by poverty, unemployment, dependence on welfare, limited access to education and other social services and high levels of health problems. The 'underclass' concept has been used by the left to symbolise social policies which generate inequalities, and by the right to signify the 'dependency culture' or the 'undeserving poor'. Whereas the former portrays people as victims of structural factors, the latter blames the victim. Neither is a particularly encouraging portrayal of the lives of disabled people and other disadvantaged groups. On the other hand, the term does draw attention to the 'entrapment of the poorest and the absence of routes for upward social mobility' (Robinson and Gregson 1992) and provides a powerful critique of current social policies. The second part of this chapter is concerned with health practices and policies towards stigmatised and discriminated groups in particular.

Concepts of Illness in Health Care

Biomedical understanding and management of multiple sclerosis has already been discussed in Chapter One. This section focuses on how health care practices and policies reflect and influence lay conceptions of people with chronic illness and disability. Scrambler (1984) proposes that health care policies and practices towards people with chronic illness and disabilities represent 'official' and culturally sanctioned responses to stigmatising conditions. In contrast, lay attitudes and discriminatory practices towards disabled people reflect 'unofficial' and culturally censured responses to stigmatising conditions. Medical practices appear to reinforce, rather than challenge, lay concepts of stigmatised people. This is reflected in doctor-patient interactions and health care policies.

Professionals as well as lay people are involved in shaping the social circumstances of people with chronic illness. Within health care settings, people with illness become patients. As patients they have been regarded at various times as deviants, partners and consumers. Deviancy theory is grounded in the work of Talcott Parsons (1951). In his analysis of the 'sick role', patients are relatively powerless in the face of the professionals and are required to submit to the ministrations of the doctor who will help him/her to return to normality. In Kleinman's work (1980 and 1988), misunderstandings between doctors and patients are analysed as being due to this very inequality. As a result Kleinman argues that doctor-patient relationships should become more egalitarian, based on working partnerships rather than hierarchical divisions. In many recent health policy statements in Western societies, doctor-patient relationships have been reformulated as 'consumer' relations within health care systems. Such policies have promoted a particular form of individual empowerment and personal responsibility. Power differentials between patients and professionals or their erosion are central to each of these concepts.

Patients' relative lack of control within medical settings contributes to prevailing negative stereotypes of people with illness: that patients lack insight, that they are incapable of making decisions regarding their illness, that they are overly dependent on others or dangerously independent and a risk to themselves. Assumptions such as these influence public conceptions of people with chronic illness and long-term disabilities:

> This has far-reaching negative implications for disabled people, since logic dictates that if they cannot assume responsibility for organising their own lives then they cannot assume the responsibility of citizenship. (Barnes 1991)

The characteristics of these doctor-patient interactions contribute to an understanding of societal responses to people with chronic illness.

Parsons' work has been influential for theory in medical sociology because he recognised that health and illness were social as well as biological conditions.[11] Parsons (1951) believed that health and illness were motivated behaviours. It was the doctor's role to act as an agent of social control to discourage deviant behaviour (illness), and reinforce normal behaviour (health). There are four characteristics of the Parsonian 'sick role': firstly, the patient is not held responsible for his/her illness; secondly, the patient is exempt from normal social obligations; thirdly, the patient is obligated to do what he can to restore health; and lastly, the patient is obligated to seek and accept professional help in order to get well. The doctor, in turn is expected; firstly, to maintain a stand of permissiveness toward the patient; secondly, support the patient; thirdly, remain detached within the relationship; and lastly, reinforce normative behaviour and disapprove of deviant behaviour. The patient's illness is made socially legitimate by the doctor, but only if the patient accepts the responsibilities of the sick role.

Friedson (1961) argued that the Parsonian 'sick role' reflected doctors beliefs about how patients should behave rather than what actually happened in doctor-patient interactions. He suggested that there was in fact a clash in perspectives between doctors and patients. The shortcomings of the model are obvious when applied to doctors' and patients' experience of chronic, rather than acute illness, where: restoration of health is not always possible; professional care is limited to the management of illness rather than treatment of disease; social support from family and friends is often as important as professional support; the patient learns to manage his/her own illness (e.g. self-medication, diet, using prosthetics, testing functioning etc.); the patient becomes an expert in his/her own illness; hospitalisation may have adverse affects on patients (e.g. isolation and institutionalisation); the technical and moral superiority of the doctor may be undermined; the duration and course of illness is uncertain; and patients' values and social resources are important in evaluation of adaptation. (Gallagher 1976; and Hart 1985).

Bearing in mind the characteristics of chronic conditions and long-term disabilities, alternative models have been devised. Safilos-Rothschild (1970) found that doctors and rehabilitation teams held a set of expectations about how patients should behave, which she referred to as the 'disabled role'. In the 'disabled role' patients were: firstly expected to accept their disability and learn to live with it; secondly, they must carry on with their normal roles; thirdly, they must be motivated to regain bodily functioning; fourthly, they must maintain their social responsibilities; and lastly, they must focus on physical recovery. The ideals of the disabled role are very different to the sick role:

> [the patient] must be actively involved in his rehabilitation and in essence be an agent of change rather than a passive object in the hands of the rehabilitation team. (Safilos-Rothschild 1970)

The 'at-risk role' (Baric 1969) was designed to take into account two major issues in chronic illness: health maintenance and risk reduction. Patients were perceived to be responsible for minimising the possibility of further relapses and maintaining control over the symptoms of illness. The 'at-risk role' is not institutionalised; has duties rather than privileges attached to it; has an indefinite time span; and lacks continuous reinforcement from professionals.

In turn, doctors must become participants with patients in the management of illness rather than perceive themselves as an authority on chronic illnesses. On a professional level, chronic illnesses have been described as 'messy' and 'threatening' because they:

> stand out as constant reminders to many specialists of the limits to the therapeutic effectiveness of their procedures and techniques. They mock claim to diagnostic precision and technical power. (Kleinman 1988)

Kleinman (1980 and 1988) suggested that illness had different meanings for doctors and patients. He describes the discrepancies and conflicts between patients' and doctors' accounts of illness and health, which appear to derive from different 'explanatory models'. Patients' knowledge is said to be rooted in the customs of the indigenous population whereas 'healers' derive their knowledge from biomedical theories of medical science. Kleinman relates patient satisfaction and actual health outcomes to the degree of cognitive disparity between doctor and patient. Patients who were more satisfied with health care and reported better health outcomes had physicians who were more attentive to patients' perspectives, their language and cultural differences.[12] Kleinman argues that doctors should encourage patients to talk about their own health beliefs rather than criticise or belittle patients' explanations for their illness. Chronic illness poses a unique set of problems for physicians who have been trained to 'think of "real" disease entities, with natural histories and precise outcomes' (Kleinman 1988).

Doctors may sometimes avoid dealing with people with chronic illness because such conditions represent personal and professional failures. Patients may interpret such evasiveness as rejection from the very people they regard as experts. Kleinman suggests that doctors feel powerless when dealing with chronically ill patients because they have little expertise in dealing with the problems of suffering. Ben Sira (1984) also reports that physicians often fail to recognise the importance of emotional support in their work with patients. Thus, doctors tend to prioritise the treatment or alleviation of symptoms, but patients feel they are more in need of emotional support. Doctors may also view the disability itself as the main problem, whereas patients feel that learning how to cope with the disability was the chief problem.

Conflicts between patients and doctors are bound to arise when doctors perceive themselves as the experts and medical care as the most appropriate solution to a problem. Robinson (1990) also points out that patients need to be realistic about the care professionals can provide in the management of chronic illness. If more doctors perceived themselves as members of a rehabilitation team and incorporated social logic (i.e. those things that are important to a patient's life) along with medical logic (the things that are important to the management of the disease), they would realise that there are many ways in which a patient can be helped and that other professionals may be better equipped to deal with the problems of emotional suffering. When doctors are hesitant to share power with patients and other professionals they compromise patients' personal and social development.

Despite in-depth analysis of doctor-patient interactions and communication patterns across different cultures, Kleinman's portrayal of doctors, like Parsons', is one-dimensional:

> His vision of the impassive professional, always helping, aloof from non-medical influences and interest is however, overly idealised. His theory allows for good and bad doctors, but never develops the implications of the asymmetry in the relationship, the structural underpinnings of doctoring. (Pappas 1990)

Bourhis et al (1989) accept that patients and doctors use different languages in clinical practice (everyday and medical language respectively), but they are more concerned with the purpose behind communication barriers in hospital settings. The authors observed that doctor and nurses were bilingual, but patients were unilingual (i.e. unfamiliar with specialised medical terminology) and from the outset disadvantaged in negotiations with medical professionals. Patients attempted to communicate in medical language, but they, along with nurses, felt that doctors did not reciprocate these efforts by attempting to communicate in everyday language. Nurses were perceived to be 'communication brokers' because they responded to each groups' language preference. Doctors appeared to use communication strategies to maintain power and status differentials between themselves and patients.

Roberts (1985) found that women's opinions about their own doctors ranged from adulation to vitriol. Criticisms of the role of doctors in clinical practice are equally diverse. On the one hand, doctors are accused of being detached and for rigidly adhering to biomedical theory. Yet signs of endeavouring to understand the patient's socio-cultural background and personal experiences have been interpreted as sinister plots to extend medical power and the medicalisation of social problems (Armstrong 1983). Social scientists can be accused of stereotyping doctors as either agents of social control, impartial and sometimes naive scientists, or shrewd entrepreneurs. Their human side is beginning to be appreciated! Thus, Hall et al (1993) revealed that physicians did not remain neutral or detached when interacting with patients - they liked some patients more than others. Male patients and those in better health who were also more satisfied with their care were liked the most. Female doctors with less experience liked their patients the most. These results are important because they point to difficulties in relationships between doctors and people with chronic illness and the possibility that certain patients receive different standards of care.

A study by Miyaji (1993) demonstrated that what doctors say they do and what they actually practice in doctor-patient interactions may be very different. For example, doctors often agreed with the principle of informed consent, but in practice continued to withhold information from patients, by telling them either what they thought they wanted to know, what they thought they needed to know or translating information into terms they thought patients could take.

Physicians were more hesitant about informing patients about the prognosis of their illness than giving them information about treatment options. This point appeared to be linked with the difficulty of balancing basic moral principles, such as respect for the truth, patients' rights and the doctors duty to inform, with the need to preserve hope and honour individual contracts between patients and doctors. The routinisation of giving patients information did not shield doctors from the emotional impact of being frequent bearers of bad news. As a result, doctors often tried to counterbalance bad news with hopeful information or an optimistic outlook. It is emphasised that doctors need to deal with their own as well as patients' emotions and the problems surrounding power differentials.

Miyaji (1993) suggests that no matter what a physician may say, patients' rights in day-to-day clinical reality play a minor role compared to physicians' own emotions, the structural constraints of medical institutions, development of biomedical technology, legal concerns and power relations between care-givers and patients. The appropriate balance between paternalism and autonomy, power and trust, compliance and dependency, rights and responsibilities in doctor-patient relations is vague. Gerson (1976) had also argued that a physician's concern with authoritative control over work was incompatible with a patient's concern for personal independence. When a range of medical services was required, as in the case of chronic illness, patients could become embroiled in professional and administrative disputes. Gerson, therefore, proposed that illness could best be understood as a political process, concerned with the allocation of resources within organisational constraints.[13]

Consumerism within recent health policy statements appears to conform to this political interpretation of patient status. Consumerism is based on the principles of individual choice and individual needs. It suggests that users of health and social services have the right to exercise maximum possible choice about the services they require and that the State, service providers and purchasers are obligated to assess the needs of individual consumers and ensure that services are meeting these needs. Consumerism is also based on viewing transactions between service users and service providers in essentially market terms - buyers and sellers of goods or services. Stacey (1976) was critical of the term 'consumer' when it first became popular within the health service. She argued that the industrial model, from which the term derives, is not applicable to health care because the health service does things to people rather than for people. Patients could be more accurately be described as the 'work objects' of medical professionals. This is particularly the case for stigmatised groups such as disabled people who may find that society offers them, as work objects, to the health care system. Consumerism is a central theme in community care policy, but will be discussed here in terms of empowerment of people with illness. Williams (1991) argues that consumerism is a highly individualistic concept concerned with independence and self-reliance, rather than collective action and greater user involvement in the development of statutory provision. He suggests that disabled and chronically ill people have no more power over their lives as consumers than they did as patients. By concentrating on individual choice the social conditions of people with illness have been avoided. Consumers still have little direct involvement in the development and provision of health care services because service purchasers or care managers are responsible for representing their needs rather than consumers themselves.

The Patient's Charter (1992) could be viewed as an attempt to operationalise consumer choice and power within health care systems. The Charter, which is part of the government's Citizen's Charter initiative, specifies three patient rights to care in the NHS: the right to information on local services, guaranteed admission for treatment within a specific time limit, and the rights to have complaints about services properly investigated. Most of the document deals with the setting of standards rather than legal rights. The charter is also limited to acute hospital services and community services. There is no mention of the rights of consumers of long-stay hospital services and residential care. The Disabled Person's (Services, Consultation and Representation) Act (1986) is a similar piece of legislation which promises much but enforces little.

On the other hand, it could be said the consumerism has drawn attention to the disempowerment of people with chronic illness within management structures and doctor-patient transactions. The setting of service standards is an improvement on vague expectations about care and rehabilitation goals. Although there is limited evidence of consumer involvement in service development, it is accepted that an evaluation of health services must include the opinions of service users. As service users, rather than deviants who rely on the expertise of professional, people with illness have an expertise of their own and provide a unique and valuable perspective on the provision of care. If the charter is adhered to both people with illness and professionals would have a clearer idea about what their rights and responsibilities are and how these can be challenged when a miscarriage of justice occurs or when gaps in service provision exist.

From institutionalisation to community care

This chapter will finish with one of the most controversial areas of health care policy - the segregation of people with chronic illness and severe disabilities from the rest of society. Policies of segregation suggest that disabled people's needs and ordinary people's needs are incompatible and that the needs of some disabled people are best met in long-term institutional rather than community settings. This policy alone has shown that far from caring for vulnerable people, health services have contributed to the problems face by disabled people. Institutions have been shown to be anti-therapeutic and are at the root of many of the negative stereotypes of disabled people that exist today. The shift from institutional to community care has been equally controversial. The evils of segregation have been joined by the evils of neglect in the community (Scull 1977). The Government has been accused of insidiously setting in motion the transition of care in the community to care by the community, where responsibility for disabled people falls onto voluntary services and informal carers rather than the State (Levick 1992). Once again the rights of disabled and non-disabled people appear to be in opposition: support for one group is harmful to the other.

Much of the debate on institutional and community care has concentrated on the experiences of people with mental health problems, people with learning difficulties, and the elderly. Less attention has been paid to the lives of people with physical disabilities. Services for physically disabled people have been described as the 'Cinderella of Cinderella services' (Beardshaw 1988). Care for people with physical difficulties has always lagged behind care for the other groups. The apparent demise of institutional (i.e. hospital) care for people with mental health problems has not been replicated for people with physical disabilities. It could be argued, however, that a different form of institutional care exists - private residential and nursing homes. Indeed, the number of elderly people, physically disabled people and people with mental health problems who live in private homes has dramatically increased since the 1970s (Darton and Wright 1993). This section will provide a brief history of institutional and community care and the impact this has had on the lives of people with chronic illness and physical disabilities. These policies have determined whether people can live in their own homes, work, take part in leisure activities, have sexual relationships and develop friendships with other disabled and non-disabled people.

A 'total institution' was defined by Goffman (1961) as

a place of residence and work were a large number of like-situated individuals, cut off from the wider society for an appreciable period of time, together lead an enclosed, formally administered round of life.

Goffman described how all vestiges of personal control were removed from 'inmates', by the stripping away of previous social identities and 'mortification of self'. Mental hospitals were shown to provide custody rather than treatment. Routines and regimentalisation and the environmental and social poverty of hospital life appeared to create problems rather than alleviate them. Institutionalisation and institutional neurosis became recognised conditions (Barton 1959). Further studies (Wing and Olsen 1979) identified characteristics of hospital life which were particularly harmful:

1.   Social under-stimulation - inactivity and social withdrawal.

2.   Restrictive practices - decreased opportunities for multiple role-playing and exercise of independence.

3.   Depersonalisation - no encouragement to develop personal initiative and identity.

4.   Authoritarianism - emphasised individual's status at the bottom of social scale, allowed no expression of personal taste, and reinforced the fact that all privileges were dependent on the charity of others.

5.   Physical neglect and ill treatment - less common but more serious when they did occur.

These disclosures, along with concerns about cost-effectiveness, provided the impetus for the running down of institutional services and development of care in the community instead. In contrast, the early 1970s saw the building of hospital units, Young Disabled Units, for people with chronic illness aged between 16 and 64 years. By the 1980s, 58 units had been built in England. The growth of such units appear to contradict the movement towards community care and ignore the widespread criticisms of institutional life. These units were built, however, because of the scarcity of specialist services for disabled people. A series of official reports had discovered a significant number of young disabled people living in geriatric wards, mental hospitals and residential homes for the elderly (Beardshaw (1988) and Barnes (1991) provide a history of institutional care for physically disabled people). It was not long before the suitability of residential care for physically disabled people was raised. Unlike people with mental health problems, learning disorders or criminals, people with physical disabilities found that institutions were a point of no return:

> To be admitted to one of these institutions is to enter a kind of limbo in which one has been written off as a member of society but is not yet physically dead. (Miller and Gwynne 1972)

The characteristics of institutional life in the 1980s and 90s for people with physical disabilities are disturbing to read. Hannaford's (1985) report on residential establishments, which included Young Disablement Units and homes run by charities and local authorities, showed that residents had little control over daily activities (e.g. getting up in the morning, what they ate and when they went to bed at night); that there was little contact with the outside world; that staff were paternalistic, making decisions on behalf of residents rather than allowing them to assert themselves; that there was little privacy; that disability was medicalised; that people were forced to abide by hospital regimes; and that troublesome behaviour was explained in terms of the illness, or failure to accept disability rather than problems with institutional life. These features of institutional life match those detailed by Goffman over twenty years earlier in mental hospitals.

Radford and Trew (1987) found that residential care was very often perceived to be a last resort for carers and that people with multiple sclerosis gave the impression that:

> the quality of life was of secondary consideration to the smooth running of the hospital regime. The emphasis appeared to be on well-intentional custodial care, rather than on rehabilitation.

Evans (1982) examined residential care in a chapter titled 'Progress in rehabilitation of multiple sclerosis.'. He discusses two approaches to residential care in terms of the 'horticultural' model and the 'warehousing' model. In the first model individual abilities are assessed and fostered. In the second model:

> residents are there to be got up, fed, clothed, put to bed. They are required to conform to a system which was designed primarily, if subconsciously, for the convenience or the egos of staff... This would sap the residents' individuality so that they became "institutionalised".

Evans recommends resident participation in management of residential institutions, client orientated care, the removal of hospital hierarchies in the form of uniforms and titles, and the promotion of independence among residents.

Enquiries into the conditions of residential care have been conducted in response to concerns about the appropriateness of care offered (Miller and Gwynne 1972; Royal College of Physicians 1986; Wagner 1988). The Wagner report (1988) stated that:

> A distinction should be made between need for accommodation and need for services. No one should be required to change their permanent accommodation in order to receive services which could be made available to them in their own homes.

However, a significant proportion of disabled people live in 'communal establishments. The Policy Panning and Research Unit (PPRU) conducted a survey of the prevalence of disability among adults and children in Northern Ireland (McCoy and Smith 1992[14]). They found that out of the 201,000 adults in Northern Ireland with a disability, 13,000 lived in communal establishments. Seven thousand of these people were found to be severely disabled, but 15,000 people with the same severity of disability continued to live in private households. The most common disability for people living in communal establishments was personal care, followed by locomotion.

Whether moving into residential care was a positive decision or a last resort remains unclear. Residential care (structurally and functionally) is often not designed to cater for the needs of disabled people, particularly those people under the age of 65 years (Beardshaw 1988).

Standards for residential care for people with physical disability have also been documented by the Social Services Inspectorate (Department of Health 1990). The SSI report makes distinctions between quality of life (experienced by residents), quality of care (resources provided by establishments) and quality of management (effective and efficient use of resources). The following values were identified as fundamental to any residential home: choice, rights, fulfilment, independence, privacy and dignity. These values are converted into guidelines against which any home can be evaluated. The report also emphasises that:

> it should be remembered that the disabled person himself has the greatest experience of his own needs and disabilities and will usually be the best person to give advice and teaching about the management of his disabilities. Assumptions should not be made without seeking his advice.

Glouberman (1990) conducted a series of interviews with people who worked in total institutions (i.e. prisons, psychiatric hospitals, long-stay wards for chronically ill and disabled, geriatric wards and hospitals for physically and mentally disabled children were included). These interviews revealed not only the failure of institutions, as perceived by 'keepers' themselves, but the limitations of humanity and relationships between human beings in such places.

The Chronically Sick and Disabled Act (1970), grew out of the growing awareness that community services were unorganised, standards of care were variable and that levels of poverty were high among disabled people. In the Act local authorities were expected to improve services to disabled people (e.g. housing, access to public buildings, and domiciliary services) and to keep local registers. However, the lack of additional resources to meet these improvements meant that the provision of community services continued to be scattered and uneven across different local authorities. The 1986 Disabled Persons (Services, Consultation and Representation) Act was another attempt to better match local services to individual need. As already mentioned above, however, recommendations within the Act have since been curtailed.

Lack of progress in the implementation of care in the community had led to a series of major enquiries (Social Services Committee 1985; Audit Commission 1986: Griffiths 1988; and Wagner 1988). Despite 30 years of debate, Griffiths commented on the huge gap between political rhetoric and reality in the field. Community care was supposed to enable people to live in their own homes rather than be cared for in a hospital or residential home, but it was obvious that one form of residential care (hospital) had merely been replaced by another (private residential homes), funded by social security benefits. Griffiths recommended that services should centre on individual needs and that social service departments should be responsible for arranging services to meet these needs. In order to maximise choice, voluntary and private organisations were encouraged to provide a range of services. He envisaged partnerships

> between central and local government; between health and social services; between governmental and the private and voluntary sectors; between professionals and individuals - to the benefit of those in need. (Griffiths 1988).

Following on from these recommendations, the Government produced the White Papers, 'Caring for People' (1989) and 'Working for People' (1989) which set out the plans for the future management of services. 'People First' (1990) was the corresponding policy document for Northern Ireland. 'People First' incorporated the new language of community care: 'consumerism', 'mixed economies of care', 'care packages', 'case management', 'purchasers and providers' and 'quality control'. The principles were the same as those stipulated in 'Caring for People': services should be flexible and sensitive to the needs of individuals and the relatives and friends who care for them; a range of options should be on offer; services should only intervene to foster independence; and services should concentrate on those with the greatest need.

The shift from institutional care to care in the community is one of the main themes in the Northern Ireland Regional Strategy 1992-1997 (DHSS(NI) 1992). 'Physical and sensory disability' is also identified as one of eight key areas of concern. Reductions in the number of elderly, mentally ill and mentally handicapped people living in hospital are specified and related to targets to be reached by 1997. There is no mention of reductions in the number of people with physical disabilities living in hospital settings. The report simply states that Boards should ensure than no young person with physical disability is inappropriately placed in a hospital or residential setting occupied primarily by elderly people. There is no concept that physically disabled people also face the problems of growing old. There is an assumption that when the problems of old age are added to those of physical disability, residential care is inevitable. In Northern Ireland the number of nursing home places has doubled every two years over the last 6 years (DHSS(NI) 1992). Institutional care has increased for elderly people. It is unclear how many of these people are also disabled.

The implementation of the NHS and Community Care Act was postponed and rescheduled to take place from April 1993. Pressure groups, representing service users, remain sceptical about community care and the future role of disabled people within the Health Service. Institutional care for disabled people in the shape of residential care and nursing homes is still apparent. There is a sense too, that in all the debate about the transfer of care from hospitals to the community and mixed economies of care, that the basic philosophy of community care has been lost - that everyone has a right to dignity, equality and full participation in society. Hall (1990) makes a unique contribution to the community care debate by actually attempting to define the concept 'care'! He identifies four main components to care; these include a set of beliefs (e.g. 'normalisation'); a set of goals (e.g. restoration of function or improving subjective quality of life); a set of practices (relating to personal assistance, vigilance, exchange of information, verbal interactions etc.); and the emotions and feelings which accompany care (e.g. feelings of commitment, warmth, love, guilt, anxiety, frustration, anger and sexuality). Care is portrayed as a mutual process in which 'carers' and the 'cared-for' attempt to develop a 'working alliance'.

Hall provides a more realistic appraisal of the nature of caring by focusing on the reciprocal nature of most human relationships, rather than traditional distinctions between those who are independent ('normal' people) and those who are dependent (disabled people). Neither carers nor cared-for are set apart or stereotyped as 'wonderful', 'brave' or 'sad' cases. Consumerism and community care provides disabled people with the opportunity to become active participants in developing services that meet their needs. The traditional image of dependent and incapable patients could be transformed to one of competent and equally valuable members of society. In this way negative portrayals of disabled and chronically ill people can be challenged and countered with more positive images of people - 'the right to be both different and equal' (Morris 1991).

Summary

This chapter has focused on the social condition of people with chronic illness and physical disabilities by discussing lay and health care concepts of illness and people with chronic illness and disability. The first part was concerned with lay beliefs about health and illness, interactions between disabled and non-disabled people and discriminatory practices. The second part was concerned with health care concepts of patients and illness and how these are presented in doctor-patient interactions and the policies of institutional and community care. Although they have been discussed sequentially, medical and lay beliefs about health and illness have been shown to influence and reinforce one another. The medical profession has both responded to society's unease with disabled people (by providing institutional care, for example), and reinforced negative stereotypes of disability within society (by portraying disabled people as passive and incapable patients for whom decisions have to be made). It has been shown that negative attitudes towards disabled people, held by lay and professional people, are moulded by the moral standards of a community, political beliefs, folklore and claims to expert knowledge within biomedicine. Debates on consumerism and care in the community have questioned the suitability of past health care practices for people with chronic illness and long-term disabilities. Despite the growth of a different form of institutional care (private residential homes), there is potential within current policies for disabled people to develop more positive identities within society.

Cultural concepts of illness and perceptions of disabled people cause problems of their own in adaptation to chronic illness. People with multiple sclerosis may find that outside their circle of family and friends, they are socially rejected and discriminated against (this may happen inside the circle too). Encounters with lay and professional people are often tense, but for different reasons. Lay people are generally uncomfortable with disabled people because they are unfamiliar with the consequences of chronic illnesses.

Doctors' unease, on the other hand, lies more with their willingness to admit the limitations of medicine and their own expertise in dealing with chronic illness and the challenge this poses to traditional doctor-patient relationships. Multiple sclerosis, then, is not only a disease but a complex social, political and economic condition. This chapter has attempted to show that society can cause as many problems as the disease process itself for people with a chronic illnesses. In the next chapter the physical, social and personal aspects of chronic illness are assessed from the perspective of people with chronic illness and people with multiple sclerosis specifically.

Notes

1. The groups included people with addictions, sensory impairments, disfigurements, congenital and acquired physical disabilities, terminal diseases, and mental disorders. 'Ex-convict' and 'old age' were also included. The authors appear to be confusing social disadvantage with disability. The terminology used is also inconsistent; sometimes conditions are defined (e.g. heart disease) and at other times, specific identities (e.g. the term 'paraplegic' is used rather than 'paraplegia'). The findings should therefore be treated with caution.

2. An emphasis on the values of autonomy, self-reliance and independence are characteristic of individualistic communities, whereas duty, conformity, co-operation and sacrifice are emphasised in collectivist communities. The authors also define individualistic societies as more affluent and industrialised.

3. Three types of account fitted this perspective: the 'cultural critique' account was based on a dominance sociological world view of oppression and exploitation and the social construction of health; the 'inequality of access' account was convinced about the benefits of medicine but concerned about the availability of health services to those who need them the most; and the 'robust individualism' account was more concerned with individual rights and the freedom to choose how to live their lives.

4. Two accounts fit this perspective: the 'body as machine' account was based on an assumption that diseases are naturally occurring and biomedicine provides the only effective treatment available; and the 'health promotion' account, which stresses the importance of life-styles.

5. The 'God's power' account argues that health is a product of 'good living' and recovery from illness a matter of regaining spiritual wholeness.

6. In the 'body under siege' account the individual is under threat from germs, interpersonal conflicts and the stresses of modern life. The 'willpower' account suggests that the individual is in control and morally responsible for maintain good health.

7. An issue of the journal Disability, Handicap & Society (Vol. 7, No. 2, 1992) focuses on the role of academic research on disability issues, in particular the relationship between non-disabled researchers and disabled people. An issue of the American Psychologist (Vol. 39, No. 5, 1984) discussed the contribution of psychology in disability research.

8. The figure is slightly higher in Northern Ireland at 17% (McCoy and Smith 1992).

9. All employers with 20 or more employees are required by law to employ three percent of registered disabled people on their work force. Many private and public sector employers avoid this obligation in practice.

10. In terms of the media, under-representation and misrepresentation of disabled people are discussed. Barnes refers to a study by Biklen and Bogdana (1977) in which 10 recurring negative stereotypes of disabled people in the mass media were identified: disabled person as pitiable/pathetic, as an object of curiosity or violence, as sinister or evil, as the super cripple, as laughable, as her/his own worst enemy, as a burden, as non-sexual and as being unable to participate in daily life. The portrayal of disabled people in charity advertising is also discussed. Evidence suggests that the disabled person as pitiable and pathetic is the most common stereotype used by charities (this point has already been noted in Chapter One).

11. For example, Mechanic's (1972) explanation of 'illness behaviour' and pathways to medical care and Scheff's (1966) analysis of the process and consequences of medical diagnosis - 'labelling' theory - can both be seen as responses to and developments of Parsons' work in the sociology of illness.

12. Byrne and Long (1976) had previously suggested that doctor-patient communications could be arranged on a continuum of doctor-to-patient-centred treatment. Doctor-centred interactions were most

common and characterised by interrogation style approaches aimed at gathering and analysing information in the quickest possible time. Patient-centred interactions were characterised by silence, listening, reflecting on and clarifying information. In other words, attending to patients' knowledge and experience. Interactions were also limited by time schedules and doctors were found to deliberately withhold information from patients to protect themselves from detection when errors occurred.

13. The difference between Kleinman's concern with interpersonal interactions and Gerson's concern with structural process reflects the agency/structure or micro/macro dichotomy in medical anthropology. Action theorists, like Kleinman, tend to ignore the relevance of political and social structures, but structuralists tend to ignore the significance of doctor-patient encounters. Pappas (1990) provides a good analysis of the implications this has had on the study of doctor-patient interactions.

14. Equivalent to the Office of Population Censuses and Surveys (OPCS) surveys carried out in Great Britain.

3 Personal accounts of illness and stress

Introduction

The physiological and social aspects of multiple sclerosis have been discussed in earlier chapters. This chapter is concerned with the personal consequences of illness, from the perspective of people with chronic illness themselves. Psychology and sociology have contributed most to this area of research. Two approaches to research in particular have been productive in revealing how individuals perceive and cope with their *own* illness. The first has been referred to as the insiders' perspective (Anderson and Bury 1988), and is concerned with recording the problems people experience in living with, and managing their illnesses. Work in this field is largely investigative and sociologically influenced and uses qualitative methods, such as in-depth semi-structured interviews. The second is known as the 'transactional model of stress' (Lazarus and Folkman 1984), and is concerned with assessing perceptions of stress and coping strategies and their roles in adaptation to illness. Work in this field tends to be more prescriptive and psychologically influenced and based on quantitative methods, such as standardised psychometric scales. These two areas of research provide the theoretical background for this study.

Both approaches share three basic principles: firstly, perceptions of people with illness are regarded as central to an understanding of the impact of illness on individual lives; secondly, both the physiological characteristics of the disease and the socio-cultural context of sickness are taken as integral to personal accounts of illness; and lastly, both are fundamentally concerned with how people manage to live with chronic illness. Despite these similarities

47

there appears to be little communication and collaboration between researchers in the two fields of study. The insiders' perspective deals in problems in living with illness, social roles, normalisation, work and illness trajectories. The transactional model of stress, on the other hand deals in stressors and stressful events, personal and social resources, coping strategies and adaptive tasks. The terminology used might be different but the underlying personal features of chronic illness described by both fields of research are similar. There have been few attempts to bridge the language and academic barriers between the two approaches. One of the aims of this research is to use both approaches to gain a fuller understanding of the ways in which people live with their illness.

Before discussing the insiders' perspective and the stress model it is useful briefly to put such work in context within health psychology as a whole. In this field distinctions have been made between *antecedent variables* (i.e. personality, attribution styles, social support and demographic factors), behavioural variables (i.e. coping, adherence, substance use and abuse, and exercise and other health variables), *provocative variables* (i.e. stress), and *health outcomes* (i.e. the prevalence of disease).[1] As a result, specific diseases have been associated with personality types and behaviour patterns[2] and health preventive behaviours and compliance with treatments/regimens have been related to individual attribution styles.[3]

Four concepts dominate research within health psychology. They are: perceptions of *control* (internal, external or significant other); attribution of *blame* (self or others); personal *commitment* (motivation); and *meaningfulness* of illness (challenge, liberation, loss, threatening, etc.). These concepts also appear in sociological and anthropological studies concerned with lay perceptions of health and illness, as discussed in Chapter Two. It could be argued that these four concepts demonstrate how individuals interpret the experience of health and illness within the values of society. However, these four concepts alone do not do justice to the diverse and complex ways in which individuals respond to their illness. As well as drawing on socio-cultural values and biographical experiences to give meaning to their illness, they develop ways of managing their illness too.

Stainton Rogers (1991) and Pinder (1990) suggest that people are 'weavers' of stories and information - they make sense of the world by drawing on a variety of competing and coexisting theories and discard what they do not want to hear. Stainton Rogers calls this 'account sympatricity', and believes that cataloguing the 'texts' people use is more useful in understanding peoples' perceptions of health and illness than trying to classify personality types and cognitive styles. Texts are more flexible than classification systems and take into account personal development and the evolution of meanings of illness over time. The insiders' perspective was selected in this study for similar reasons; it encourages people with illness to tell their own 'stories'. The transactional model of stress was chosen because it is sensitive to interactions between environmental, biological and psychological variables. Within both approaches, the concepts of control, blame, commitment and meaningfulness inform interpretations of personal accounts of illness rather than provide complete explanations. Although each model has developed separately, the themes underlying each are consistent with one another.

This chapter has two functions; it reviews work within the insiders' perspective and the transactional model of stress and provides the theoretical framework for the study. The origins and development of both models will be described, followed by their application to research on chronic illnesses generally, and then, more specifically, to multiple sclerosis. Lastly, shortcomings in both models will be discussed. The implications of this review for the aims of this research project will be discussed briefly.

The Insiders' Perspective

The development of the insiders' perspective

In Chapter Two sociological theories, such as stigma, sick role and institutionalisation were discussed. These theories offer explanations for patterns of behaviour between people with illness and others. They are based on observations of relationships and interactions between participants within the health care system rather than the subjective realities of people with illness. For this reason, Conrad (1990) refers to sociological theories such as these as the 'outsiders' perspective. The 'insiders'' perspective, in contrast, is concerned with the meanings of illness as described by people with illness, rather than the social roles they may occupy at certain periods in their life, as indicated by terms like 'patients', 'sufferers' or 'consumers'. The insiders' perspective treats people with chronic illness as unique individuals rather than a homogeneous group. However, it is recognised that people with chronic illness do experience similar socio-cultural conditions and psychological problems which influence their own perspective of illness. Thus, two strands of research have evolved; one concentrating on specific chronic disorders (e.g. multiple sclerosis, epilepsy and spinal cord injury), and the different impacts they have on individual lives, the other focusing on chronic disorders in general and the problems they typically cause (e.g. disability and handicap). In both cases, the identification of common themes or problems among people with chronic illness is based on making comparisons between individual life-stories.[4]

Conrad (1990) and Gerhardt (1990) provide commentaries on the origins and development of qualitative research on chronic illness. Gerhardt traces the impact of sociological research on medical practice, from providing a critique of professional dominance and the supposed benefits of medical care, to emphasising the social construction of illness (from the perspectives of formal and informal carers, people with illness, policy makers and people unaffected by chronic illness). With the latter development, qualitative research has provided valuable information on the perspectives of people with illness and their families. Social scientists in the field have become increasingly methodologically self-conscious, aware that both people with illness and researchers are involved in constructing stories out of miscellaneous events, an array of emotions and a variety of perceptions and theories. Gerhardt reviews three lines of research which have all been concerned with recording the insiders' perspective of chronic illness: grounded theory; ethnomethodology/narrative analysis; and biographical research. In all three, research is largely exploratory, involving in-depth personal interviews with people with illness and their families, and aimed at discovering the sorts of problems people experience in living with their chronic illness. Analysis and presentation of data tends to rely on providing verbatim quotes from interviews rather than results from statistical tests. Gerhardt argues that sociologists and medical practitioners both rely on case-related knowledge. Their mutual concern for the patient or individual should, therefore, promote co-operation rather than antagonism.

Conrad, like Gerhardt, provides a historical account of the development of qualitative research within medical sociology. He makes comparisons between earlier academic preoccupations with the sick role to the current concerns with the subjective experiences of illness; between outsiders' and insiders' perspectives on chronic illness; between people as patients and people as clients or users of the health service; and between care in medical setting to care in the community. Conrad believes that social scientists should forge links with 'the arts' (i.e. literature, philosophy and theology) so that the emotional and spiritual aspect of illness can be better understood.

The insiders perspective currently offers a methodological framework for researchers rather than a theoretical model. It has sought to raise awareness of the perspectives of people with chronic illness in order to improve dialogue within the health care system; to identify the social and psychological aspects of chronic illness; to document the expertise held by individuals with illness and their families in managing illness; and to suggest ways in which care can be individualised to meet the needs of people with chronic illness more effectively.[5]

Chronic illness and the insiders' perspective

Anselm Strauss and his colleagues at the University of California are often credited with carrying out one of the first qualitative research projects on chronic illness. In their book 'Chronic illness and the quality of life' (Strauss and Glaser 1975), medical terminology is avoided and the every-day tasks of illness management, carried out by people with illness and their families, are emphasised. Strauss makes comparisons between the work carried out by people in their own homes and the work carried out by professionals in hospitals. In both circumstances the salient features of chronic illness are as follows:

1. long-term;
2. uncertain;
3. requires great efforts at palliation on behalf of patients;
4. multiple diseases or complications are common;
5. intrudes into the lives of patients and their families;
6. requires a wide variety of ancillary services;
7. expensive.

and key problems can be listed as the:

1. prevention of medical crisis;
2. control of symptoms;
3. carrying out regimens;
4. prevention of social isolation;
5. adjusting to changes in the course of the disease;
6. normalising interactions with others and lifestyle;
7. raising funds;
8. dealing with problems in relationships.

Strauss then describes the strategies people with chronic illness use to manage these problems, like enlisting the help of others, keeping to regimens, monitoring and assessing symptoms, and developing organisational skills. Chronically ill people are portrayed as active agents engaged in normalising their lives rather than bearers of spoiled identities. Strauss refers to normalising tactics such as minimisation of illness, passing/concealing their illness, justifying inaction, and social withdrawal, which are illustrated with examples from personal accounts of illness. These tactics were also identified by Goffman (1963) in his essay on stigma.

Hospital and home environments are contrasted by Strauss and Glaser (1975) in terms of their management strategies. On the positive side, hospital environments are controlled and, therefore, less unpredictable and complex than conditions at home. The division of labour is also spread between professional in hospitals whereas at home all the work may fall on people with illness and their carers. Finally, hospital staff are regarded as experienced and knowledgeable, whereas people at home often learn about their illness through trial and error. On the negative side, hospital staff are generally less involved and concerned about care than people with illness and their families and friends at home. Hospital care is usually short-term, whereas care at home entails long-term commitment.

Strauss is critical of the emphasis on doing tasks within medical care, rather than understanding the life situations and biographies of individual people. Unfortunately, Strauss's own work tends to concentrate on the practicalities of chronic illness rather than the emotional consequences of illness. For example, Strauss suggests that adaptation to illness requires 'coming to terms' with illness, which entails accepting lower levels of normality and new restrictions in life. A case history is given to illustrate his point: a family come to terms with the mother's deteriorating condition by moving to different accommodation, sharing out household tasks between family and friends and accepting the curtailment of social activities. These activities all concentrate on behavioural and cognitive adjustments to chronic illness. There is no mention of the emotional adjustments which might occur simultaneously. Strauss's case studies often present people as rational decision makers in control of their lives. There is little evidence of people 'letting off steam', getting angry, 'breaking down', taking risks, or challenging the status quo as they adjust to their illness. The 'work' analogy encourages a bias towards physical tasks rather than emotional expression.

On the other hand, Strauss draws attention to the considerable amount of work involved in managing and shaping illness trajectories undertaken by people with illness and their families. In hospital settings, however, this work is often unrecognised by the professionals:

> since they are not employees of the hospital and have no status as health professionals or as other kinds of health workers, patients are not easily perceived by the staff as actually working. (Strauss and Glaser 1975)

The expertise held by families and friends of people with illness is often disregarded and, whether they like it or not, they are excluded from care activities in hospital. In contrast, families are expected to make important decisions about treatment when patients cannot act for themselves, to take care of legal-administration work and support patients psychologically. Despite this Strauss found that families were often at the bottom of institutional hierarchy of information.

The dichotomy Strauss makes between hospital and home work is a little simplistic. He ignores the provision of long-term care in hospital settings. Hospitals often serve as a reminder to people with illness that physical deterioration or changes in living arrangements could result in permanent institutional care. On the other hand, living at home can be more restricting than hospital life, especially when people are house-bound and socially isolated and daily activities are determined by the availability and flexibility of community services.

Subsequent research on the insiders' perspective has concentrated on the following aspects of chronic illness: common problems associated with living with chronic illness; the ways in which people manage their illness on a daily basis, and more specifically how they deal with their disease in relation to the health care system; the impact of illness on people's perceptions of themselves; stigma; and the work carried out by families in rehabilitation, recovery and management of chronic illness (Locker 1983; Anderson and Bury 1988; Conrad 1990; and Strauss 1990). Particular interest has been shown in people's changing perceptions of themselves as a result of chronic illness.

After interviewing people with chronic illness, Charmaz (1983), concluded that perceived restrictions in life, social isolation, being discrediting and being a burden, were detrimental to people's perceptions of themselves. Charmaz found that feelings of loss, particularly of one's former self, was made more difficult to deal with when there was little opportunity to develop a new and equally valued identity. Later, Charmaz (1987), suggested that people with chronic illness aspire to four possible alternative identities. The first, the 'supernormal identity', entails going to extraordinary lengths to compensate for or hide disabilities from other people. The second, the 'restored self', entails reconstructing one's former self. The third, the 'contingent self', is built on the hope that one's old self will be restored in the future and the fourth, the 'salvaged self', is based on preserving a valued attribute or activity from one's past. Charmaz suggests that people with chronic illness can only maintain a sense of their own worth by sustaining, to varying degrees, their past non-disabled identities.

Yoshida (1993) found that adaptation to chronic illness, among people with spinal cord injury, required more than sustaining aspects of a former self. People with chronic illness also had to integrate aspects of their disabled identities into their total self-concept. Yoshida proposes that people's perceptions of themselves swing back and forth, like a pendulum, from being the same person (disregarding their disability) to feeling totally disabled and then from being supernormal to admitting to some disability. It eventually rests somewhere in the middle, accepting both disabled and non-disabled aspects of themselves and developing an awareness of themselves as part of the disabled community. The middle outcome is achieved by accepting loss, sustaining some aspects of the non-disabled self, integrating non-disabled and disabled aspects of themselves, working on biographical continuity, and achieving personal development and maturation.[6]

These recent studies propose that the best way to live with chronic illness is to negotiate with the disease and its consequences rather than adhere to past convictions and ambitions. Making deals with the illness, then, is more realistic than searching for guarantees, which do not exist (Register 1987). Doctors who advise their patients to "Just live as you did before" are doing a disservice - they deny the existence of the disease and negate the possibility of having a valuable life with illness. Register argues that the extent to which people adapt to their illness is dependent on their conviction that life is worth living no matter what complications arise. Schnurre (1992) helps people in hospital with cancer by encouraging them to 'become a little rebellious, to use their illness to change something in themselves and to live differently'. At the same time, she emphasises that the steps taken are very small and there are always setbacks.

Underlying many of the stories told by people with chronic illness, as reported by researchers, is the importance of preserving personal control, motivation and meaning in life, concepts which have already been established as central in individual and cultural conceptions of health and illness (see above and Chapter Two). The insiders' perspective has shown, however, that these concepts are not limited to people's perceptions of their disease. They are also essential to adaptation to illness and development of alternative, but equally valued lifestyles. Attention will now be given to the relevance of these findings to the experience of illness from the perspective of people with multiple sclerosis.

Multiple sclerosis and the insiders' perspective

The Brunel ARMS Research Unit has made a major contribution to research concerned with the personal and social consequences of multiple sclerosis as they affect people with the illness and their family and friends. Many of the themes discussed here, therefore, derive from the work of this unit, which has combined postal survey techniques with more qualitative work, including semi-structured interviews, autobiographies and diary information. The first report from the research unit ('Talking about MS' 1982) was based on tape-recorded interviews with 10 people with multiple sclerosis. It touched on a number of themes which appear to have been influential in focusing further research. These themes are: personal explanations of illness; diagnosis and responses to illness; uncertainty; management of illness; relationships with family and friends; and identity problems. These themes coincide with concepts identified from the insiders' perspective on chronic illness more generally.

Diagnosis Problems with diagnosis are particularly troublesome for people with multiple sclerosis (see Chapter One for the main issues). The third ARMS report (1983b) teased out distinctions between the onset of the disease, reporting symptoms, discovering the diagnosis and receiving a formal diagnosis. Some people with multiple sclerosis reported that it took over 50 years before a formal diagnosis was given. Approximately one third of the sample had discovered their diagnosis before a formal diagnosis was given. People with multiple sclerosis and their families do not always react similarly to a formal diagnosis. For people with multiple sclerosis, a formal diagnosis may:

> reassert their personal and social credibility in the face of a sceptical response to their claim to sickness.

For family members, though:

> it can be a time when alternative - and perhaps less painful - explanations of the symptoms and behaviour of those diagnosed are demolished. (Robinson 1988b)

Robinson (1988a) concluded that the circumstances under which the diagnosis was disclosed could influence the strategies people with multiple sclerosis and their families used to manage illness. He implied that problems with diagnosis could be detrimental to marital relationships (especially if diagnosis was withheld from one of the parties involved) and turn people away from conventional forms of care, and towards alternative treatments and self-help practices instead.

Explanations of illness Once a diagnosis is known, people with multiple sclerosis often try to make sense out of this new information. In the first Brunel ARMS report, people with multiple sclerosis expressed feelings of guilt: they worried about being in some way to blame for the cause or onset of the disease; they worried that they had used multiple sclerosis as an excuse for anything that went wrong in their lives and for not meeting their responsibilities. Stress was often implicated in explanations of the cause of multiple sclerosis. When Pollock (1984), carried out in-depth interviews with 34 families in which one member had multiple sclerosis,[7] she found that over half the families believed that stress had 'triggered' the onset of the disease and subsequent relapses. Many of the respondents said they tried to avoid stressful situations (e.g. promotion at work) so as not to exacerbate the illness. The characteristics of stress explanations were unique to each respondent. As in the transactional model of stress, specific events in themselves were not stressful; it was how a person perceived, appraised and interpreted an event that determined whether it was stressful. Stress, as an explanation for illness, seems to serve two favourable purposes for people with multiple sclerosis because it:

> reinforces the idea that the individual himself has no responsibility for causing his illness, and even gives him a possible means of exerting a degree of control over its future course, by modifying his attitudes and behaviour in order to minimise the amount of stress he experiences. (Pollock 1984)

As well as dealing with issues of blame, control and uncertainty and consequent perceived responsibility for illness, stress explanations enable respondents to construct 'personal' theories for their illness. Personal theories are generally complex, combining biographical information with scientific cultural and supernatural conceptions of health and illness. Robinson (1988a) observes that people with multiple sclerosis develop a 'personal research strategy' which involves weighing up the pros and cons of medical treatment and the range of alternative therapies available. Awareness of medical knowledge and medical research both encourage hope and dispel fears for the future - it bolsters people's confidence that a cure for the disease or ways of controlling it will eventually be discovered.

Robinson, however, overlooks the negative aspects of information. Some people deliberately avoid access to information because not knowing the consequences of their illness is perceived to be better than getting their worst fears confirmed. Pinder (1990) classified people with Parkinson's disease and their families as either 'seekers', 'weavers' or 'avoiders' of information. Respondents were equally active in each of these strategies and there were benefits and costs to each in terms of managing illness. Pollock found that the processes of constructing meaning, acquiring knowledge and deciding on which treatment/therapies to use, enabled people with multiple sclerosis to avoid the status of patient, which, she argues, is a necessary part of successful adjustment to chronic illness.

Management of illness Robinson (1988a) and Pollock (1984) focus on two basic management strategies. The first strategy has already been referred to and consists of self-care practices (e.g. monitoring symptoms, abiding by regimens, accessing information, trying alternative therapies and joining self-help groups). The second strategy has a more philosophical orientation and consists of mentally 'coming to terms' with illness. Pollock describes how some of the respondents in her study managed multiple sclerosis by treating it as a problem in living[8] rather than a medical problem. Duval (1984) also reports how people with multiple sclerosis describe their illness in terms of psychosocial problems. In this way they were able to distance themselves from the physically destructive aspects of their disease. Pollock called people who were able to do this, 'optimists', and people who were unable to separate their disease from their evaluations of general health 'realists'. It could be said that optimists managed their disease by denying its existence, but Pollock suggests that in separating their minds from their bodies, optimists believed they had some control over their illness, whereas realists did not. As a result optimists were 'fighters', more positive and more inventive in living with their illness than realists, who are portrayed, by Pollock, as people paralysed by their fears, self-pitying, negative and insecure.

The dichotomy described by Pollock between optimists and realists, is similar to the distinctions Robinson (1988a) makes between 'coping' and 'succumbing' to illness or 'fighting' and 'accepting' illness. The first approach in each pair is valued because it involves *active* attempts to deal with illness, whereas the latter indicates passivity and resignation. These 'attitudes of mind' as Pollock calls them, are tied to culturally sanctioned ways of managing illness.[9] 'Fighters' gain social approval whereas 'acceptors' experience social disapproval and impatience. The tendency for people with multiple sclerosis to present themselves as 'fighters' or 'optimists' in terms of managing their illness, may partly reflect conformity to socially acceptable attitudes. Monks (1993) also makes distinctions between positivity and negativity in terms of people's responses to multiple sclerosis. The centrality of positivity in people's accounts of multiple sclerosis is recognised, but Monks also emphasises the importance of negativity in personal account of illness. People with multiple sclerosis reported that it was a relief to be negative sometimes - being positive all the time was hard work! Fighting is not always appropriate and realism/negativity is sometimes necessary to protect oneself from exhaustion. Charmaz (1987) makes a similar point when she discusses the 'etiquette' of chronic illness.

There appears to be a consensus, then, that people with multiple sclerosis have access to culturally sanctioned coping strategies in dealing with their illness. The 'fighting' metaphor is reflected in the work of rehabilitation services, voluntary organisations, self-help groups, and the consumerist approach of recent health policy. In an analysis of autobiographies collected by the Brunel ARMS Research Unit, Robinson (1990) enlarges upon these culturally embedded coping strategies and likens personal stories of illness to dramatic scripts. Using narrative analysis, distinctions are made between progressive, stable and regressive scripts. In progressive scripts, the individual moves towards valued goals. In regressive scripts, the individual moves away from valued goals. In stable scripts, the individual remains on an even keel, neither moving towards or away from valued goals. As can be predicted, the majority of autobiographies were categorised as progressive (52%). Only 10% of the scripts were regressive. The remainder were stable (20%), or did not fit into any one form (18%). Progressive narratives tended to fit either 'heroic', 'detective' or 'comedy' dramatic structures; stable narratives were like 'documentaries'; and regressive narratives were either 'sad' or 'tragic' tales. Robinson concludes that 'personal narratives' indicate each individual's quest for meaning and mastery over the physical course of their disease.

The positive/negative, fighting/accepting, optimism/realism and active/passive dichotomies, are very alike in that the socially approved strategies have a cognitive or problem-solving orientation, whereas the less approved approaches have an affective or emotion-focused bias. It seems, then, that emotional responses to chronic illness are associated with maladjustment, or, at best, represent the private as opposed to public side of managing multiple sclerosis. Emotional responses to multiple sclerosis are rarely treated in a balanced manner; people with multiple sclerosis are either described as being depressed or euphoric. Duval (1984) found that expression of distress was influenced by cultural metaphors of 'vulnerability, weakness, inadequacy, dependency and incompetence'. Even within the insiders' perspective it is rare to find a quote from someone with multiple sclerosis who simply states, 'I hate MS'. It seems that the potentially cathartic benefits of emotional expression are unacknowledged and the 'stiff upper lip' approach to illness is socially encouraged.

Brooks' and Matson's (1977) model of adjustment to multiple sclerosis encapsulates these biases. Although grief and denial were regarded as acceptable reactions to illness, they were associated with the earlier stages of the disease, (referred to as 'denial', 'resistance' and 'affirmation'). People who reached the final stage of adjustment (referred to as 'integration'), were said to have successfully adapted to their condition, because:

> Dealing with multiple sclerosis problems as they arise, with minimal emotion, is characteristic of the patient now. He is spending energy and thought on matters other than his health no matter how serious his disability. (Brooks and Matson 1977)

Like Pollock, Brooks and Matson seem to be suggesting that the most effective way of dealing with multiple sclerosis is to detach oneself from the disease. They suggest that emotional restraint leads to a 'deeper sensitivity to

life's experiences', but this is a contradiction in terms. Sensitivity is
foremost an emotional quality, in which people are responsive to thei
(both joy and sorrow) and are able to empathise with others. Wor
Silver (1989) are critical of the following assumptions underlyin
about coping with loss: the expectation that people will initially be ___
or depressed; that these responses are necessary and failure to experience both
suggests pathology; subsequently, people have to 'work through' the loss;
recovery is expected; and lastly, a state of resolution is reached in which
people have accepted the loss intellectually and emotionally. These authors
found little empirical evidence for these processes of grief, and suggest
alternative patterns of grief in which people either do not show intense distress
or experience distress for longer than is assumed. Nancy Mairs (1988), who
has multiple sclerosis herself, expresses this point succinctly:

> I learned that one never finishes adjusting to MS. I don't know why I
> thought one would. One does not, after all, finish adjusting to life, and
> MS is simply a fact of life.

Wortman and Silver argue that the 'myths' of coping with loss reflect the
needs of 'outsiders' (researchers, practitioners and friends) rather than the
needs of people experiencing loss.

Relationships with family and friends Burnfield (1985), from his own personal
experience of multiple sclerosis, writes:

> MS is not a disease that affects individual people in isolation. When one
> person in the family has MS, then the whole family 'has MS' as well.

Although the arrival of multiple sclerosis can strengthen relationships
within the family there is evidence of higher levels of divorce and separation
among people with multiple sclerosis, compared to the general population
(Brunel ARMS Research Unit 1983b). Robinson (1988b) reported
discrepancies between spouses and people with multiple sclerosis in their
perceptions of functional disability and ability to cope with illness. People
with multiple sclerosis were more optimistic about their functional
capabilities, but more pessimistic about their ability to cope, than spouses.
Women were particularly pessimistic about their ability to cope with multiple
sclerosis, whether they had the disease themselves or were carers of husbands
with the disease. Marriage strains were also reported by people with multiple
sclerosis and their carers in the Northern Ireland survey (Radford and Trew
1987). The most common were financial strains, the amount of care and
attention involved in dealing with the effects of multiple sclerosis, and
difficulties regarding the 'physical side' of marriage[10]. Carers felt that 'family

_motional problems/sufferers' mood swings/depression' were the hardest thing to deal with, followed by restrictions on family life and personal freedom, and watching sufferers lose independence and being unable to help. Unfortunately, people with multiple sclerosis were not asked the same question. However, 17% of carers felt that their partners' multiple sclerosis had made no difference to their marriage.

Multiple sclerosis also affects roles within the family. When the disease is relatively mild, roles (i.e. partner, parent, grandparent, sibling, wage-earner etc.) can be maintained without many problems, but when the disease is more severe, greater dependence on others can threaten a person with multiple sclerosis's position in the family. New roles are also established; the partner without the disease becomes a 'carer', and people with the disease 'cared for'. Carers sometimes resent their partner for being a burden and for not trying hard enough, and people with the disease sometimes resent their carers for not really understanding or for being healthy. Children may feel they miss out on normal family activities and parents may feel inadequate. On the other hand, families are important sources of social support: people with multiple sclerosis and their families get involved in self-care activities, provide each other with reassurance, reciprocate feelings of love and compassion, and share hopes and fears.

The significance of financial strains within families can be related to high levels of unemployment among people with multiple sclerosis (Larocca et al 1985; Radford and Trew 1987). The loss of the role as a wage-earner in the family is important for many people with multiple sclerosis. Consequently, partners of people with multiple sclerosis either face the prospect of restricting their employment prospects because of 'caring' demands, or seek employment out of financial necessity. The psychological effects of unemployment are well known (i.e. depression, anxiety, insomnia and lack of confidence). It is also a threat to identity, as Breakwell (1986) comments:

> A job normally defines a person's status, establishes a network of social interaction with co-workers, provides an area in which competence can be shown and praised, specifies what goals need to be attained, and not least, determines a timetable for the day, giving it structure and meaning.

Identity Loss of self has already been referred to as a consequence of chronic illness. Evidence from the insiders' perspective suggests that people with chronic illness need to incorporate both disabled and non-disabled aspects of their identity in order to come to terms with their illness. There is a fundamental problem in doing this, however, when disability has such negative connotations within society. People with multiple sclerosis, as members of the general public, discriminate between people with different disabilities and evaluate their own disease according to a 'hierarchy of disability' (see chapter two). Pollock (1984) found that people with multiple sclerosis may be more aware of what is it like have a chronic illness, but are not necessarily more accepting of disability in others than able-bodied people. People with multiple sclerosis sometimes labelled themselves as 'useless' and 'crippled'. Such derogatory terms can be used to reassert identity, as Nancy Mairs (1988), explains:

> I am a cripple. I choose this word to name me... I want [people] to see me as a tough customer, one to whom the fates/gods/viruses have not been kind, but who can face the brutal truth of her existence squarely. As a cripple, I swagger.

People with multiple sclerosis have to deal with their disability as well as their disease, as part of their identity. Zola (1993), in an article on the language of disability, discusses how terminology affects people's perceptions of themselves. He illustrates this with the widespread use of the terms 'patients' and 'sufferers' for people with disabilities, although they only spend a limited amount of time under medical supervision and do not automatically suffer from their condition. Zola also criticises the emphasis in medicine on doing things to patients (which connotes passivity), rather than with them (which implies activity/involvement of patients). Similarly, he makes distinctions between the verbs be and have; in the first a person is owned/identified by the disability, whereas in the second case the person owns/possesses his/her disability.

Atkinson (1993), also discusses the implications of language on identity by questioning the popularity of the term sufferer as opposed to patient. Atkinson argues that there is little difference between the two terms; both imply passivity, acceptance and are victim oriented; both ignore the large parts of people's lives in which they do not suffer; and both reflect the beliefs of specific institutions - medical and theological. The political significance of such terms has also been raised by self-help groups (Oliver 1990; and Finklestein 1980).

People with multiple sclerosis, like other disabled people, may lose their identities in other ways too. Problems with maintaining one's femininity/masculinity and sexuality are also reported. Disability can be an assault on masculine characteristics in particular (e.g. physical strength, independence, control and resilience). Disabled women have spoken about difficulties in retaining their femininity, in particular physical attraction (Campling 1981; Saxton and Howe 1988; and Morris 1989). Despite identity problems there is no evidence that people with multiple sclerosis have a lower self-esteem than people without illness, or that more severely disabled people have lower self-esteem than those who are less disabled by their disease (Robinson 1988a).

Gaps in the insiders' approach

This review has concentrated on central themes in the everyday lives of people with chronic illness (identity, management of illness, explanations of illness, and relationships with others). The insiders' perspective has looked at the psychological and social impact of chronic illness on people's lives and personal responses to illness. Areas for future research, such as the emotional impact of chronic illness, have been suggested. What is striking, however, is the dearth of information regarding physically disabled people's experience of institutions. There is no adequate explanation for this considering the number of people with physical disabilities who live in residential care.

A Channel Four television series dealt with experiences of disability in the first half of this century. The book accompanying the series entitled 'Out of Sight' (Humphries and Gordon 1992), charts disabled people's accounts of social rejection and hostility, hopes and fears, ambitions, loves, disappointments and struggles, along with their lives in institutions before the appearance of the welfare state, living on the bread-line in city slums and the appearance of new employment opportunities during the Second World War. The book documents a previously unwritten history. In the series, people with disabilities describe their childhood, adolescence and early adulthood. It is hard to believe that even in the late 1940s a young disabled woman could be found emerging from an institution for 'Crippled Girls' at the age of 25 years with the following perceptions of herself:

* I never dreamt that I'd get married and I certainly didn't think that I'd have children. It's something out of this world to me. Being disabled they made you feel as though you had no use in the world and so why become a mother.

Rules and regulations and uniformity were fundamental to institutional life. John Vaizey's book 'Scenes from Institutional Life' (1986) is a disturbing account of a childhood spent in hospital as a result of osteomyelitis. At the end of the book he concludes that institutions:

impose a pattern on people and detract from their individuality; above all, it seems to me, they detract from their humanity. Institutional life is profoundly limiting; it distorts people's values; above all, it reduces their horizons... all these places do far more harm than good to far too many people.

In a hospital ward in the 1990s, Schnurr (1992) notices that nurses are still taught to leave their emotions outside the hospital. She makes a simple request - that nurses do things now and again that are not part of the hospital routine, like sit on someone's bed and chat with the person. That such things are not automatically part of hospital life demonstrates the limitation of institutional life, for both residents and employees.

In a study looking at the quality of life in long-stay institutions for the elderly, Clark and Bowling (1990) recorded, from observations, many demeaning practices and negative interactions between staff and residents, such as hostility, forgetting residents' names, ignoring needs for help, restraining residents, force feeding, supplying patients with spoons, plastic beakers with spouts or plastic cups at meal times rather than normal domestic crockery, and the removal of cutlery and food before residents had finished their meals. When residents were interviewed, however, they were reluctant to reveal their feelings about these practices. Clark and Bowling conclude that low expectations and fears of repercussions might explain residents hesitancy in criticising institutional environments. Another explanation may be that elderly residents felt that expressing dissatisfaction with a service was tantamount to being a grumbler and no one wanted to be seen in these terms. After interviewing people with multiple sclerosis living in hospitals or nursing homes, Radford and Trew (1987) urge that a more:

> imaginative and positive approach has to be worked out to prevent the infliction (albeit unintentionally) of unnecessary discomfort and indignity of those whose lives are so severely restricted.

Many people with physical disabilities or chronic illness continue to experience institutional life. The perspectives of people with multiple sclerosis living in institutional settings have generally been overlooked. The threat of institutional care for disabled people living at home is also unrecognised. Morris's book 'Pride against prejudice' (1991) is an exception to the rule:

> The possibility of institutionalisation hangs over many disabled people living in our own homes, fuelled by the fear that one day the support which makes our independence possible will disappear, or that an increase in functional limitations will prove too much for whatever resources are available to us.

The worst aspects of institutional life are well known. The advantages of institutional life (although some researchers would argue that there are not advantages to institutional care), are less obvious.

The Transactional Model of Stress

In the second part of this chapter the theoretical basis of the transactional model of stress will be reviewed, followed by its application to the experience of chronic illness, and more specifically to multiple sclerosis. The usefulness of this model in understanding adaptation to chronic illness will be discussed.

Theoretical background

The definition of stress used in this study is based on the work of Lazarus and his colleagues (Cohen and Lazarus 1979; Folkman 1984; Folkman and Lazarus 1985; Lazarus 1986; Folkman and Lazarus 1988; Lazarus 1992; and Lazarus 1993). Lazarus interprets stress as the relationship between individuals and their environment in which the individual judges a situation as taxing or exceeding available resources and, therefore, endangering well-being. Stress is relational (rooted in the interaction between a person and his/her environment) and process-oriented, rather than a stimulus (e.g. life-event) or response (physiological response or subjective distress). The relationship between individuals and their environment is dynamic and reciprocal, thus the origins of the term the 'transactional model of stress'.[11] The transactional model of stress is frequently used to assess causative links between stress and illness outcomes or exacerbations of illness,[12] but the focus here is to assess the usefulness of the model in describing the problems people with chronic illness experience, how they cope with these problems and to explain the role of these processes on adaptation to stressful situations.

The transactional model of stress consists of two basis processes - cognitive appraisals and coping efforts - which are believed to mediate the effects of stress on adaptational outcomes.

Cognitive appraisals There are two major forms of appraisals - primary and secondary appraisals. Primary appraisals entail evaluations of the significance of a transaction to an individual with respect to his/her well-being (i.e. What's at stake?). Lazarus make distinctions between irrelevant, benign and stressful transactions. In the first, transactions are perceived to have no effect on well-being; in the second, transactions are perceived to be beneficial to well-being; and in the third, well-being is either harmed, threatened or challenged. Harm refers to a personal injury or loss; threat to the potential for harm; and challenge the opportunity for personal development. Perceptions of loss, threat and challenge can co-exist. Primary appraisals are influenced by personal beliefs and commitments and the nature of the stressful event (i.e. whether it is familiar or novel and has a clear or ambiguous outcome). Secondary appraisals are assessments of resources available to deal with the demands of stressful situations (i.e. What can I do?). Individuals assess their physical (e.g. health), social (e.g. social support), psychological (beliefs about control and ability to sustain hope, self-esteem, morale etc.), and material assets (e.g. money, equipment, etc.) and how these can help them deal with stress.

Coping Coping refers to cognitive and behavioural efforts to master, reduce or tolerate stressful situations. Although the term implies successful adaptation to stress, coping is not a measure of adaptation. Coping refers to attempts (both effective and ineffective) to manage stressful encounters. Coping has two functions, which are aimed either at regulating emotional distress in the face of stressful situations (emotion-focused coping) or managing/altering the source of distress (problem-focused coping). Folkman and Lazarus (1988) designed a questionnaire, The Ways of Coping Questionnaire, which consists of 67 statements dealing with thoughts and actions which might be used to deal with stressful situations. These statements are categorised into two types of problem-focused and six types of emotion-focused coping strategies. Thus, confrontation and interpersonal, and problem-solving strategies were identified as problem-focused coping strategies, and distancing, escape-avoidance, accepting responsibility or blame, exercising self-control over the expression of feelings, seeking social support, and positive reappraisal were identified as emotion-focused coping strategies.

Lazarus suggests that people use all these strategies to cope with stressful situations. Indeed effective coping requires alleviation of emotional distress before attempts can be made to control the stressful situation. Coping efforts also depend on individual appraisals of control. If a situation is perceived to be controllable, problem-focused coping is predominant, but if a situation is perceived to be uncontrollable problem-focused efforts should be abandoned and emotion-focused coping, aimed at making the situation more tolerable, should be implemented instead. The effectiveness of coping strategies depends on the stressful encounter, individual characteristics and the measurement of adaptation (subjective well-being, social functioning, or somatic health).

Research within the transactional model of stress indicates that adaptation to stressful situations is linked to appraisal processes, (such as the ability of individuals to discover something positive in a negative situation, perceiving a situation to be a challenge, rather than/or as well as a threat, and the creation of new short-term and long-term goals) and the ability to change coping efforts to meet the demands of different stressful encounters (Folkman 1984). Some coping strategies, however, appear to be more stable than others: problem-focused coping is more variable (context-bound) than emotion-focused coping (person-bound) (Lazarus 1992). Lazarus (1986) defines stress as a 'rubric or system of interdependent variables' in which stressful encounters, appraisal processes, coping efforts and stress reactions have reciprocal relationships with one another. Stress reactions are ultimately dependent on appraisal processes. Personal meanings, then, are central to this model. For this reason, life-event approaches to stress are rejected, because they assume that certain situation are perceived as stressful by everyone. Lazarus has shown that this is not the case, and what may be perceived as stressful for one person (e.g. an exam) may be insignificant to another. It is thought that coping efforts influence both short-term reactions and long-term adaptational outcomes, although there is only limited evidence for this.

In his more recent work, Lazarus (1993) focuses on the emotional dimension of stress and concludes that:

> Psychological stress should be considered part of a larger topic, the emotions... Knowing, for example, that in a given encounter... this individual feels angry, anxious, guilty, sad, happy or hopeful tells us much more than knowing merely that he/she is harmed, threatened, or challenged.

Lazarus reinterprets the relationship between individuals and their environments as personal 'stories' or 'plots' which throw up different emotional experiences. For example, feelings of anger are related 'demeaning offence against me and mine'; shame to 'failing to live up to an ego-ideal'; and compassion to 'being moved by another's suffering and wanting to help' (fifteen emotions are identified in total). Like coping efforts, emotional responses are perceived to be dependent on appraisal processes and individual characteristics. Perceptions of failure arouse negative emotions whereas perceptions of success instil positive emotions.

Although other approaches are still used and are being refined, the work of Lazarus and his colleagues has become influential in the field of stress. They have constructed a theory (transactional model of stress) and research instruments to test their theory (Ways of Coping Questionnaire (Folkman et al 1986), to measure coping strategies, and The Hassles and Uplifts Scales to measure the frequency and type of stressful encounters experienced (Kanner et al 1981)). In research terms, they have been prolific, but, perhaps as a result, they are sometimes inconsistent in defining key concepts. For example, Lazarus (1988) refers to two problem-focused and six emotion-focused strategies in one article, but to five problem-focused and three emotion-focused strategies in another article (Lazarus 1992). The same strategies are categorised differently in the two articles. In another article (Folkman 1984) refers to self-esteem initially as a personal resource and later on as an adaptation outcome. Criticisms of the transactional model of stress will be dealt with at the end of the chapter. Much of the research has relied on community samples or student populations and concentrated on the influence of appraisal processes, personality characteristics and the psychosocial environment on coping strategies. (See Pearlin and Schooler 1978; Wheaton 1983; Fleishman 1984; McCrae 1984; McCrae and Costa 1986; Parkes 1986; Aldwin and Revenson 1987; Nowack 1988). The model has also made an important contribution to the area of chronic illness, by attending to the ways in which people with chronic illness cope with their disease.[13]

Coping with the stress of chronic illness

The four aspects of the transactional model of stress (stressful events, appraisal processes, coping strategies and adaptational outcomes) were examined separately to assess the contribution the model has made to an understanding of subjective experiences of chronic illness. This exercise uncovered strengths and weaknesses within the model. For example, much is known about the sorts of coping strategies people with chronic illness use, but less is known about the types of stressors they frequently encounter. When coping is studied, researchers have either concentrated on the relationship between coping and specific stressful encounters or between coping and adaptational outcomes. Surprisingly few projects have examined coping in relation to stressful events and adaptational outcomes without reducing one or the other of these concepts to a one-dimensional construct (i.e. stressful encounter = disease or adaptation = depression score).

Like the insiders' perspective of illness, researchers have either focused on specific diseases or a wide range of different chronic illnesses. Most of the work has concentrated on similarities among different chronic illnesses and favours the ICDHI's definition of chronic illness rather than the ICD's disease specific system.

Stressful events Unlike the insiders' perspective, researchers using the transaction model of stress have paid little attention to the sorts of stressful encounters or problems people with chronic illness experience on a daily basis. Instead, they have treated the disease itself as a single stressor, rather than a complex situation producing a variety of problems with their own coping demands (Auerbach 1989). There is also a misguided assumption that the disease itself is the most stress-provoking event for people with chronic illness. Although this may be the case at the time of diagnosis and during the acute stages of the illness, for the majority of the time the disease may be relatively insignificant compared to employment problems, worries about family relationships, socially embarrassing symptoms, stigma, discrimination and negative social attitudes.

The development of the Hassles and Uplifts Scales (Kanner et al 1981), provided a means of measuring the occurrence of everyday problems and sources of encouragement, as reported by respondents. Kanner and his colleagues emphasised that identifying the types of events reported was as important as calculating the level of stress (i.e. number of hassles) experienced. The Hassles Scale could be used, then, to uncover problems peculiar to individuals or groups of individuals (Chamberlain and Zika 1990).

Unfortunately, researchers using the Hassles Scale generally report mean scores and fail to mention the most frequently reported hassles (Beckam et al 1991; Williams et al 1992; and Pellman 1992). Research suggests that people with chronic illness experience a similar number of hassles and uplifts as people without illness, but there is little evidence about the sorts of hassles and uplifts people with chronic illness experience and how these compare to hassles experienced by other populations (Warren et al 1991). Miller et al (1984) found that the 10 most common hassles for nursing home residents were: worries about physical health; concerns about health in general; being lonely; too much time on hands; declining physical abilities; difficulties seeing and hearing; concerns about news events; friends/relatives being to far away; thoughts about death; and the weather. Their ten most frequent uplifts were: praying; thinking about the past; visiting; phoning or writing someone; feeling safe; socialising; gossiping; getting enough sleep; day-dreaming; laughing; and giving/getting love. Problems with health, personal, family and environmental matters were recurring themes for elderly residents. Uplifts were characterised by moments of personal or private pleasure and involvement in social activities. The absence of certain types of hassles and uplifts point to constraints, deprivation and/or social status, as demonstrated by lack of employment, financial and household events among nursing home residents. Miller et al's study points to possible themes in the lives of people with chronic illness living in institutional settings.

Lazarus (1992) admits that relatively little attention has been given to the role of stressful events themselves in influencing how people cope with and adapt to their illness. He underlines that it is important to know what has gone wrong and right for a person with a chronic illness. One of the advantages of studying hassles, as opposed to life-events, is the potential amenability of hassles to preventive interventions, as opposed to life-events (DeLongis et al 1982). It is a pity, therefore, that so little attention has been given to the sorts of hassles people with chronic illness experience and the effect of different hassles on their lives. The significance of positive events on adaptation has also been largely disregarded. Kanner et al (1978) demonstrated that the

absence of positive events was more strongly associated with a lower e
life satisfaction than the frequency of negative events. They suggest tha
under-stimulation as well as over-stimulation can have poor adaptational
outcomes.

Seyle (1983) coined the term 'eustress' to refer to the benefits of stress.
Eustress is thought to play an important role in adaptation, providing a person
with a welcome break ('breather') from stress, sustaining coping strategies or
restoring damaged resources (Edwards and Cooper 1988). The role of uplifts
and eustress in adaptation is still unclear, but to understand the complexities of
everyday lives among people with chronic illness, the occurrence of positive
and negative events needs to be recorded. Central hassles and uplifts and
recurrent emotions suggest patterns in an individual relationship with his/her
environment. Lazarus (1992) concludes that:

> Intervention should depend on listening to the patient carefully,
> discovering his/her source of threat, harm and distress. This is
> something now almost absent in medical practice, namely, a great
> concern and awareness of the patients' emotional life.

Appraisals

As already mentioned distinctions have been made between primary and
secondary appraisals. Primary appraisals in this case refer to people's
perceptions of their illness, and secondary appraisals to perceptions of the
resources available to manage illness. Lipowski (1970) proposed that there
were eight common ways in which people with illness perceived their
condition: as a challenge; as an enemy; as a punishment; as a weakness; as a
relief; as a strategy; as an irreparable loss or damage; and as a value.
Challenge and value perceptions of illness were associated with constructive
coping strategies, whereas the remaining interpretations of illness were
associated with lack of effort, resistance, malingering, passivity, and feelings
of helplessness, shame, hostility, or depression. The meanings of illness are
influenced by the moral beliefs of a society.

Over twenty years after Lipowski (1970), Schussler (1992) tested the
relevance of these eight concepts of illness to the experience of 153 patients
with chronic illness living in Germany. He found that the concepts were
interrelated (e.g. illness as enemy was closely connected to illness as loss) and
that people held multiple conceptions of their illness. Illness as challenge was
reported most often, followed by illness as enemy. Not surprisingly, illness as
challenge and illness as value were linked to 'favourable' coping strategies
(e.g. cognitive restructuring) and good adaptational outcomes (i.e. lower

69

...pression scores), whereas illness as enemy, punishment or relief ...ated with 'unfavourable' coping strategies (e.g. wishful thinking) ...aptational outcomes (e.g. higher levels of anxiety and depression).

. WHO publication on health promotion and chronic illness (Kaplun ,, Lazarus makes a distinction between three types of stress-provoking ...onic illnesses - terminal, life-threatening, and disabling - which presumably correspond to appraisals of stressful events as harmful, threatening and challenging. Lazarus suggests that these alternative appraisals of illness may be more useful than the ICD classification of diseases in explaining psychological similarities and differences among people with different chronic illnesses. The usefulness of this model has not yet been established, but it does not appear to have any advantages over Lipowski's more detailed analysis of patients' perceptions of illness. Research has shown that perceptions of severity of illness (i.e. disability) and seriousness of illness (i.e. life-threatening) are unrelated to psychosocial adjustment (Roessler and Bolton 1978). A limitation of the stress model is that it concentrates on people's perceptions of their illness according to present day realities and future possibilities. Changes in meaning are tied to specific circumstances (e.g. perceptions before and after medical interventions, or perceptions of chronic illness in childhood and old age). As a result, it is difficult to assess the degree of continuity or change in appraisals of illness over time, from the time of diagnosis.

More attention has been given to the role of secondary appraisals in coping with chronic illness. Many of the concepts discussed within health psychology surface here: attributions of control and blame; self-efficacy; commitment; meaningfulness; hardiness; and social support. Most of the work has concentrated on perceptions of personal and social resources. Appraisals of physical and material assets have been neglected. Again the insiders' perspective and the stress model have different approaches to the problem. In the first, loss of resources (e.g. loss of self and social isolation) is described, whereas in the latter, loss may be recognised, but researchers are more concerned with the usefulness of whatever resources are available, as perceived by people with chronic illness.[14] Research in the area is in general agreement: long-term adjustment to chronic illness is associated with an internal locus of control; perceptions of high levels of social support; maintaining hope; and the sense that life is meaningful.

There are discrepancies, however, about what researchers mean by 'control'. In some reports, control refers to the 'controllability' of the disease (which may be decided by the researcher with reference to medical knowledge); in other reports people's perceptions of control over their illness at present is measured, and in other work, perceptions of control over a variety

70

of life-events is measured. Perceptions of control over the onset of the disease are rarely studied. Despite these inconsistencies, people who believe they have some personal control over their circumstances also report higher levels of well-being. The situation appears to be different for people living in institutional settings. Felton and Kahana (1974) found that among elderly residents, adjustment was associated with an external locus of control (i.e. a belief that staff and others held control rather than a belief in personal control). However, Felton and Kahana were concerned chiefly with control over environmental conditions rather than health or illness. Nine hypothetical problematic situations were used to assess locus of control, representing issues to do with monotony, privacy, conformity, emotional expression, environmental ambiguity, activity, coping with losses, motor control and autonomy concerns. Perceptions of control were related to adjustment in four of the problem areas (privacy, autonomy, environmental ambiguity and emotional expression). The authors concluded that:

> Where opportunities for actual control behaviour are absent, perceptions of oneself as in control may indicate an unhealthy, non-realistic adaptation to institutional life. Perceived external control may also be interpreted as an indication of the need for institutionalised older people to seek out a champion.

When researching the role of control in adaptation, Folkman (1984) advises researchers to ask themselves, 'Control over what?' Generalised beliefs about control are different from beliefs about control over specific situations. Additionally, perceptions of personal control are not always advantageous; for some people an internal locus of control may be at odds with preferred coping strategies (e.g. avoidance), or might even threaten self-esteem if a situation worsens (e.g. relapse). As Folkman states, 'The potential practical, mundane consequences of control are all too often overlooked in both laboratory and field settings.'

The perspectives of people with chronic illness in relation to their physical and material resources have also been neglected. Very often deficits in these areas are perceived as common knowledge. As a result objective indices (disability ratings and socio-economic status) tend to be collected rather than people's subjective evaluations of their own health and material resources. People's satisfaction with services have been studied, but rarely related to adaptational outcomes. The significance of these appraisal processes on adaptation is, therefore, uncertain.

Coping strategies The orientation of early research on coping with chronic illness is demonstrated by Abram's editorial (1974) in the Journal of Chronic

71

Illness. He relates adaptation to chronic illness (measured in terms of depression, over-dependency and non-adherence to treatments) to unconscious defence mechanisms such as regression, denial, and intellectualisation. People with chronic illness are, at best, presented as victims of their own unconscious drives, at worst, hopelessly inadequate. With the rise of cognitive psychology, the importance of conscious, individual interpretations of illness was established. Thus Moos and Tsu (1977) identified the following coping strategies among people with illness: denial and minimisation; information seeking; emotional support and reassurance; learning medical regimens; setting limited short-term goals; preparing for alternative outcomes; and constructing meaning out of stressful events. The development of coping scales enabled researchers to concentrate either on the relationship between these sorts of coping strategies and different types of problems (stressful encounters) or between coping and different adaptational outcomes.

Viney and Westbrook (1982) focused on variables that might influence the way in which people coped with chronic illness. People with different chronic illnesses were asked to answer questions concerning demographic characteristics, lifestyle, illness roles, degree of disability, perceived handicaps and achievement of rehabilitation, and finally, asked how they coped with their illness. The most popular coping strategy was direct action, followed by control, optimism, interpersonal coping, escape, and lastly, fatalism. They found many significant interactions between variables. For example, action strategies were influenced by demographic variables - preferred by men and better educated people with higher occupational status people. Control strategies were influenced by illness variables - preferred by people with little disability and perceived handicap. And fatalism was influenced by a variety of variables - preferred by older, less educated people with lower occupational status, people with little interpersonal involvement and social commitment, few leisure activities, low work satisfaction, more children and social and financial responsibilities and greater perceived handicap!

Vitaliano et al (1990) were more concerned with the influence of different problems on preferred coping strategies. They compared coping patterns among people with either physical health, psychiatric, work, or family problems. They found that people with physical health problems used problem-focused coping more than any other group. In contrast, carers (selected as a group experiencing family problems) used wishful-thinking coping strategies more than any other group. Both carers and people with physical health problems sought social support more than the other two groups and used fewer self-blame strategies. There are, then, similarities and differences between carers and people with physical illness in their preference for different coping strategies. However, the majority of people with physical health problems who used these strategies were both anxious and depressed. Vitaliano et al proposed that the problem situations people functioned in were more important than specific stressors in influencing their use of different coping strategies.

Patterson et al's (1990) study, also revealed the importance of the type of problem in influencing coping patterns, although they emphasised that similar groups of people experienced different overriding problems. Thus elderly people living at home reported a variety of recent life events which were classified by the authors as either role or residence change, other's health, own-health, non-family interactions, death, family or miscellaneous crises. Advice seeking was the most common way of coping with their own health, but wishful thinking was more common when the health of others was of concern. Self-blame was used most of all when role or residence change was experienced, but least by people reporting personal health problems. These results are consistent with those reported by Vitaliano et al above. Patterson et al's study has advantages over Vitaliano's study, however, because of its longitudinal design. When elderly people were asked the same questions four months later, Patterson et al found that people responded to different events in similar ways. They concluded that elderly people used coping strategies that personally "worked for them" and did not necessarily vary coping strategies to suit the type of event.

These research projects show the effects of demographic and illness characteristics and subjective appraisals of illness on the choice of coping strategies. They tell us little, however, about the effectiveness of different strategies on adaptation. Lazarus (1992) pointed out that it is very difficult to distinguish between good and bad coping strategies because coping efforts are constantly changing, according to the type of situation and stage of adaptation involved. For example, avoidance and denial strategies are common before and immediately after an operation and when first diagnosed. These strategies have important short-term advantages; they enable people to distance themselves from their illness, rather than be overwhelmed by it. As time passes, however, denial is generally inappropriate because it prevents people from taking part in rehabilitation activities. On the other hand, information seeking, learning regimens and setting goals are effective coping strategies during rehabilitation (Cohen and Lazarus 1979; and Elliot and et al 1991).

Felton et al (1984) found that the apparent effectiveness of coping strategies depended on the measure of adaptation used. In a study of 170 middle-aged and elderly people with chronic illness, positive affect was related to cognitive restructuring and information seeking; negative affect to emotional expression, wishful thinking and self-blame; positive self-esteem to cognitive restructuring and minimal use of emotional expression, wishful thinking, self-blame; and acceptance of illness to threat minimisation and minimal use of emotional expression, wishful thinking, and self-blame. They concluded that emotion-focused coping is related to poor adjustment and cognitive strategies to good adjustment, although coping strategies only counted for about 11% of the variance in adaptation scores.

Bombardier et al (1990) found that poor adjustment among people with different chronic illnesses was related to emotion-focused coping. They suggest that poor adaptation to chronic illness is associated with an emotion-focused coping 'triad', consisting of wishful thinking, self-blame and avoidance strategies. This result seems to be at odds with a basic premise in stress research: that in the case of uncontrollable situations problem-focused coping should be abandoned and emotion-focused coping, aimed at making the situation more tolerable, implemented instead. Discrepancies such as these may result from sampling problems; samples that include people with different chronic conditions include diseases that vary in terms of their controllability. Lazarus (1992) tentatively suggests that wishful thinking is generally a dysfunctional coping strategy because it inhibits any sort of constructive behaviour. Positive reappraisals, in contrast, seem to facilitate problem-solving behaviour and both are associated with adaptation.

Evaluations of coping strategies are influenced by cultural stereotypes of good and bad coping. Denial, for example, usually meets social disapproval although it is a useful strategy when little can be done to alter a situation. For example, it may be extremely difficult to deny the existence of the disease in the long-term, but it is easier to deny the most negative outcomes of illness. Indeed, denial in the latter case may be encouraged because it avoids confronting people with the reality of the illness and consequent social discomfort. Social unease is also experienced when people with chronic illness express negative emotions (e.g. anger, fear and envy). As Lazarus (1992) observed, people without illness (e.g. friends, colleagues and health professionals) would much prefer it if people with chronic illness downplayed the negative and accentuated the positive aspects of illness.

To summarise, people with chronic illness who develop coping strategies that work for them personally, appear to have fewer problems in adapting to their condition. Difficulties in adapting to illness seem to arise when people either use coping strategies that seem to work for other people, but are not suitable for their own situation, or lose the conviction that coping strategies are of any benefit to them in the short-term or long-term. It is more realistic to recognise that coping alone plays a modest part in adaptation to illness. As already mentioned, however, the effectiveness of coping strategies also depends on how researchers measure adaptation.

Adaptation Cohen and Lazarus (1979) identified a number of adaptive tasks for people with illness. They were: reducing the likelihood of experiencing harmful situations/conditions; learning to tolerate negative events; maintaining positive self-image and emotional stability; and sustaining satisfying relationships with others. Moos (1984) made some additions: dealing with the discomfort of symptoms of illness; managing the stresses of special treatment procedures and of hospital environment; developing and maintaining relationships with medical and other staff; and preparing for an uncertain future. Measures of adaptation generally incorporate these themes and focus on psychological well-being, somatic health and social functioning. The most popular measure of adaptation in the projects mentioned above, was level of depression. There is concern, however, about the suitability of depression as a measure of adaptation. In some neurological disorders it is unclear whether depression is a response to illness or a symptom of the disease process (Devins and Seland 1987). A more accurate assessment of adaptation is gained when more than one measure is used.

Lazarus (1992) outlined the dilemmas faced by researchers when they attempted to measure the role of stress and coping on adaptation (i.e. health status). Firstly, it must be appreciated that health status is affected by a large number of factors. The influence of stress and coping will, therefore, be modest. Secondly, there are conceptual problems in evaluating health. For example, should health be measured in terms of functioning, quality of life or longevity? Thirdly, to assess the impact of stress and coping on adaptation, changes in health status are required. However, health status is usually a very stable variable. Dramatic changes in health status could be a product of the disease process alone. Lastly, longitudinal research is needed to identify consistent stress and coping patterns that may be related to long-term adaptation.

There is considerable evidence that most people, with or without chronic illness, indicate satisfaction with their own health and with life generally (Brown et al 1981). Cassileth et al (1984) found that people with arthritis, diabetes, cancer, renal disease or dermatological disorder did not differ significantly from each other or from the general public on scores for the Mental Health Index (Veit and Ware 1983). They concluded that people with chronic illness showed a 'remarkable' ability to adapt to their illness and that adaptation was independent of specific diagnosis. In light of this evidence, perhaps more attention should be paid to the multiple ways in which people adapt to their illnesses, rather than characterising people in terms of their apparent ability or inability to adapt to their illnesses.

The stress model has been used in multiple sclerosis research to address two major problems: the relationship between stress and onset of illness and exacerbations of illness; and the role of stressful events, appraisal processes, and coping strategies on adaptation. Examples of research in both areas will be provided.

Stress and onset of multiple sclerosis Paulley (1985), Grant et al (1989) and Warren et al (1991) provide reviews of the relationship between stress and the onset of multiple sclerosis as well as reporting on their own research in the field. Autobiographical records, anecdotal evidence, case studies, professional experience, and research studies are referred to as evidence that the onset of multiple sclerosis is preceded by stressful events. Grant et al (1989) used the Life Events and Difficulties Schedule (which entails carrying out detailed interviews concerning the history of illness and the occurrence of difficulties/problems before the diagnosis of illness) (Brown and Harris 1978), to assess the relationship between past events and illness onset. They found that people with multiple sclerosis and 'controls' reported a similar number of events 6-12 months before onset, but a few months before onset, people with multiple sclerosis reported more stressful events than controls. The authors could only speculate that stressful events might have had a 'precipitating' role in the onset of illness. In other words, life events influence the timing of onset rather than cause illness. Onset of illness is not defined in the paper, but it seems to imply the time of diagnosis or the point of contact with hospital services. If this is the case, the meanings people attribute to symptoms before an official diagnosis is known may be responsible for the higher reports of stress preceding onset.

Warren et al (1991) compared people with multiple sclerosis in remission and exacerbation. People in exacerbation were asked to complete the Hassles and Uplifts Scales (Kanner et al 1981) according to their experiences during the three months before relapse. People in remission were asked to do the same, but for the three months before being interviewed. The sample also completed the General Health Questionnaire (to measure emotional stress) (Goldberg and Hillier 1979) and the Ways of Coping Checklist (to measure coping strategies) (Folkman et al 1986). The authors found that taken together, scores on hassles' intensity, uplifts' frequency, the GHQ and reports of fatigue, accounted for approximately 10% of the variance between people in exacerbation or in remission. Coping did not make any significant contribution, although emotion-focused coping was preferred by people in exacerbation. The direction of this relationship is unclear because of the retrospective design of the study. Warren et al (1991) underline that 90% of the variance between people in exacerbation and remission is still unexplained.

Paulley (1985) is less hesitant about the role of emotional stress in the onset of multiple sclerosis. On the basis of clinical practice, he reiterates that 'provocative' stressful events always precede the onset of multiple sclerosis or exacerbations of the illness. Paulley's analysis of the relationship between stressful events and the onset of illness rests in psychoanalytic theory. He argues that failure to overcome threats of separation and engulfment in childhood are responsible for problems in dealing with major life events in adulthood. Multiple sclerosis is perceived to be the somatic response to inappropriate affect (i.e. euphoria and depression), emotional immaturity and the giving-up response. Paulley's confidence in his own theory, unsupported by systematic evidence is disconcerting, especially when it is reported in an reputable academic journal. Despite such conviction, research has shown that the relationship between stress and multiple sclerosis is ambiguous. If an association exists, it is more likely that stress plays a contributory rather than causal role.

The role of stress in adaptation to multiple sclerosis Multiple sclerosis research based on the transactional model of stress has tended to focus on one aspect of the model rather than the 'rubric or system of interdependent variables'. For example, Counte et al (1983) concentrated on stressful events; Wineman (1990) on secondary appraisals; Brooks and Matson (1977 and 1982) on coping strategies; and Hickey and Green (1989) on appraisals and coping strategies. Findings from each of these studies will be summarised.

Counte et al (1983) were concerned with the impact of stressful events (illness and non-illness-related stressors) on the quality of life of people with multiple sclerosis (measured in terms of life satisfaction, self-assessed coping and satisfaction with personnel/facilitates), and the potentially moderating effect of demographic (sex and SEG) and personal (trait anxiety and knowledge of disease) factors. They found that stressful events and moderating variables predicted 20-45% of the variance in well-being: younger people who were less anxious and reported fewer life stressors and hospitalisations were more satisfied with life; less anxious people with fewer hospitalisations and a greater knowledge of their illness believed they were coping better with their illness; and people with fewer life stressors and greater knowledge of illness were more satisfied with their physician and MS Centre facilities. Social class appeared to have no effect on well-being and age only a minor effect in terms of life satisfaction (older people were less satisfied). The authors proposed that informing people about their illness and decreasing their general anxiety may improve their quality of life. No intervention is mentioned in relation to stressful events.

In contrast Maybery and Brewin (1983) found that knowledge about illness, demographic characteristics and severity of illness were not related to adaptation (scores on the General Health Questionnaire and the Self-Esteem Scale). Better adjustment was found among people with multiple sclerosis who had more contact with able-bodied people. No association was found between contact with other disabled people and adaptation. Maybery and Brewin relate these findings to a study by Miles (1979) in which normalisation coping strategies were differentiated from dissociation strategies. In the former, people with multiple sclerosis and their families maintained social relationships with unaffected people and avoided contact with other people with the disease. In the latter strategy, withdrawing contact with able-bodied people was in evidence and a change of address was more common. Miles suggested that families using normalisation strategies coped better with multiple sclerosis than dissociation-oriented families.

Wineman (1990) assessed the role of individual evaluations of illness and personal and social resources on adaptation to multiple sclerosis. She was concerned with the effects of primary (perceived uncertainty of illness) and secondary (functional disability and social support) appraisal processes on adaptation (depression and purpose-in-life scores). Unsupportive interactions were more strongly related to poor outcomes than supportive interactions. Unsupportive interactions were associated with high levels of uncertainty and lower purpose-in-life scores. Wineman suggested that in these circumstances people were particularly concerned about whether they would be cared for in the future. People who experienced more supportive relationships were reassured of their own worth and integration within the community. Demographic variables, supportive and unsupportive interactions, perceived uncertainty and functional disability accounted for 35% of the variance in depression and 33% of the variance in purpose-in-life scores. People who were more severely disabled, perceived their illness to be very unpredictable and experienced negative interactions with others and were more likely to feel that life was meaningless.[15]

Brooks' and Matson's (1977 and 1982) longitudinal study of people with multiple sclerosis provides some interesting information concerning preferred coping strategies and their long-term effects on adaptation. Consistent with other measures of adaptation, they discovered that people with multiple sclerosis had a self-concept similar to people without illness. Findings from the study also indicated that self-concept improved with the duration of illness, but not with increasing physical impairment. On a more controversial level, y concluded that most of the adjustment to illness took place within the first

10 years following diagnosis; after 10 years there was little change in self-concept.

In their first report (Matson and Brooks 1977) 'religion' was the most common coping strategy and associated with a relatively favourable self-concept. 'Accepting it' and 'family' were also popular strategies, but associated with poorer self-concepts. In the follow up study, however, the authors found that the self-concept of people who reported 'religion' as a coping strategy had decreased, whilst the self-concept of those who reported 'family' and 'accepting it' had improved (Brooks and Matson 1982). A possible explanation for this result was that 'accepting it' indicated resignation in the first case, but integration of illness into one's lifestyle in the second. These findings should be treated with caution, however, because the number of coping strategies reported is small and does not reflect the variety of coping strategies people with chronic illness use to manage their condition.

Females and people with higher income, an internal locus of control and fewer relapses also reported better self-concepts in Brooks' and Matson's study. The variable 'living arrangement' also predicted self-concept; the more dependent people were (from 'living alone' to 'in a nursing home') the more negatively they perceived themselves. Although Brooks and Matson maintained that adjustment to multiple sclerosis took place in the first 10 years of illness, in their follow-up study people who had been diagnosed for at least 20 years showed the biggest improvement in self-concept. In contrast, self-concept had decreased for people with an illness duration between 12 and 20 years. It would be more accurate to conclude, from these results, that adaptation is a continuous process.

In the last research project to be discussed, Hickey and Green (1989) studied appraisal processes and coping responses to multiple sclerosis. They measured individuals' coping strategies, locus of control and levels of depression and hopelessness using standardised scales. Higher levels of depression and hopelessness were reported among people with multiple sclerosis than in community samples. Problem-focused coping strategies were used more than emotion-focused strategies. An external locus of control and problem-focused coping were associated with higher levels of depression and hopelessness. There were no noticeable sex differences in scores. The authors conclude that people with multiple sclerosis were using inadequate coping strategies. Unfortunately, they provided little information about the method of coping used (cognitive, behavioural or avoidance) or the sort of stressful circumstances that were referred to when completing the coping questionnaire. For these reasons it is impossible, from this study to assess the appropriateness, or not, of problem-focused coping in managing multiple sclerosis.

It is difficult to draw together the results of these studies because there is little consistency between the measures used. However, the age, sex and social class of people with multiple sclerosis appears to have had only a limited impact on adaptation. When demographic differences were identified in one project, they were contradicted in another project. The severity of illness was significant in two studies; both Wineman (1990) and Brooks and Matson (1977) reported greater difficulties in adaptation among people more severely disabled with multiple sclerosis. In contrast, Maybery and Brewin (1983) found no significant relationship between severity of illness and adaptation. Only Counte et al (1983) observed the impact of stressful events on well-being; higher levels of stress were associated with negative outcomes. Perceived uncertainty and feelings of anxiety seemed to have a negative affect on adaptation. The role of knowledge about illness in adaptation is unclear. Counte et al (1983) associated more knowledge with higher levels of satisfaction, but Maybery and Brewin (1983) reported no relationship between knowledge and well-being. An internal locus of control had favourable outcomes in two of the studies (Brooks and Matson 1982; and Hickey and Greene 1989). Results from the last two studies indicated the benefits of emotion-focused coping over problem-focused coping in adaptation to multiple sclerosis. Lastly, people with multiple sclerosis reported similar levels of well-being as the general population in Brooks and Matson's study, but rated unfavourably with community samples in the Hickey and Green study.

The usefulness of the transactional model of stress in multiple sclerosis research is still relatively unexplored. The results above suggest that stress and coping only play a small part in adaptation to multiple sclerosis. Individual problems in dealing with stress, however, are more immediately accessible to practical interventions than social problems such as prejudice and discrimination and physical problems, such as controlling the course of the disease. Although the focus is on individual problems, understanding these may have important social consequences in terms of developing services that reflect people's needs and challenging negative social conceptions of chronic illness.

Gaps in the transactional model of stress

Problems with the model have been referred to throughout the review. A list of major shortcomings will, therefore, suffice:

1.   Although Lazarus and his colleagues define the major components of the model (stressful events, appraisal processes, coping strategies and

adaptation) there are problems in differentiating between the dependent and independent variables and between appraisal processes and coping strategies.

2. Little attention has been given to the role of stressful events in adaptation to illness. The disease has been viewed as a single stressor. The complex consequences of living with a chronic illness have been overlooked as subsequent stressors.

3. There has been a tendency to simplify the role of coping strategies. Researchers contrast the benefits of one strategy (i.e. problem-focused coping) over another (i.e. emotion-focused coping), rather than observing interactions between both in the management of stress.

4. Retrospective and cross-sectional research designs prevail, but are limited in terms of uncovering the dynamics of everyday life in coping with chronic illness.

Summary

Similarities between the insiders' perspective and the transactional model of stress were outlined at the beginning of the chapter. Both approaches focus on the subjective realities of people with chronic illness and the ways people cope with their own illness. Language, discipline and methodological barriers were suggested as reasons for the lack of communication and corroboration between the two fields of research. However, the following themes are basic to both research areas:

1. Identification of key problems/stressful events that people with chronic illness experience on a daily basis.

2. The meanings/appraisals processes people associate with their illness.

3. Managing illness/coping strategies used by people with chronic illness.

4. Identity changes/stages of coping in the process of adaptation to chronic illness.

Each approach has its strengths and weakness. In terms of strengths, the insiders' perspective has detailed the consequences of chronic illness for individuals' lives. In doing so, it has identified key problems and personalised the experience of illness. The insiders' perspective has also shown that some coping strategies are culturally sanctioned, whereas others are socially disapproved of. The transactional model of stress has concentrated on the numerous ways in which people cope with illness and provided a means of classifying their different coping strategies. The importance of emotion-focused coping as well as problem-focused coping has also been recognised. The transactional model of stress has also turned to the possible significance of positive events (uplifts) in people's lives. In terms of weaknesses, both models have generally neglected the emotional aspects of chronic illness and the experiences of people living in institutional settings. The aims of this project have been influenced by the insights provided by the research summarised in this chapter. This study will attempt to amend some of the oversights of previous research and add to the contributions made by both the insiders' perspective and the transactional model of stress.

Notes

1. Rodin and Salovey (1989) provide a good summary of research within health psychology.

2. For example, individuals with Type A behaviour pattern (TABP) (Fieldman and Rosenman 1974) are said to be more at risk to chronic heart disease; emotionally inhibited individuals are thought to be more at risk to the cancer process (Cooper 1988); and learned helplessness behaviour has been linked to depression (Seligman 1975).

3. There are a range of attribution models: Rosenstock's (1974) Health Belief Model; Wallston et al's (1978) Multidimensional Health Locus of Control scale; Kobasa's (1979) 'hardiness characteristic'; Bandura's (1982, 1989) self-efficacy theory; Antonovsky's (1987) Sense of Coherence model.

4. This approach is similar to narrative and discourse analysis in which single stories are perceived to be reflections of cultural narratives, scripts or texts (Shotter and Gergan 1989). Within scripts each individual constructs knowledge about society from a slightly different perspective. However, multiple-case research of a specific condition (e.g. chronic illness) enables the researcher to pick out each individual's life situation and by comparing different stories, common themes or social constructions of reality are identified. A special issue of the Journal of Personality (Vol. 56, No. 1, 1988), illustrates the ways

in which psychobiography and life narratives can be used in psychology to better understand individual lives.

5.   However, a special edition of the journal Social Science and Medicine addressing qualitative research on chronic illness (where Conrad's and Gerhardt's comments can be found), like other volumes on chronic illness (Roth and Conrad 1987; and Anderson and Bury 1988), can be criticised for failing to address problems in living with chronic psychiatric disorders. A number of social scientists and psychiatrists have studied schizophrenia from the insiders perspective and discovered that people with the disease work hard at managing their illness. This research has challenged medical assumptions that people with schizophrenia are passive victims of their disease (McGlashan et al 1975; Falloon and Talbot 1981; Breier and Strauss 1983; Boker et al 1984; Kumar et al 1989; and Dittman and Schuttler 1990).

6.   Other qualitative studies have found similar processes of adaptation to chronic illness: Linkowski and Dunn (1974) refers to 'acceptance of disability'; Bury (1982) to 'biographical disruption'; Williams (1984) to 'narrative reconstruction'; and Corbin and Strauss (1987) to 'identity reconstitution'.

7.   She also interviewed 34 families in which one member had schizophrenia and 29 'ordinary' families.

8.   Locker (1983) also reports that the 'practical problems of everyday life' were central to people with spinal cord injury experiences of illness.

9.   In the same way that cultural conceptions of health and illness have moral undertones which value independence, self-control, sensible living, hard work and strength of character, as discussed in chapter two.

10. The survey does not define what it means by the 'physical side' of marriage; whether it be the physical strength needed to help people with multiple sclerosis carry out activities of daily living, physical dependency, sexual problems, or perhaps all three.

11. For a review of different traditions in stress research see Vingerhoets and Marcelissen (1988). They list nine approaches to stress research: (1) biological; (2) psychosomatic; (3) life event; (4) transactional; (5) life style and behaviour; (6) group differences; (7) socio-cultural; (8) work and organisational; and (9) intervention and prevention. Eichler et al's (1986) volume 'How to define and research stress' incorporates many of these approaches to stress research, and includes chapters

written by central commentators in the field. Fleming et al (1984) review the 'integrative' approach to stress research, whereas Hinkle (1974) compares biological and social science definitions of stress. The role of individual difference in the relationship between stress and illness is discussed in Janisse's (1988) book 'Individual differences, stress and health psychology' and by Cooper and Payne (1991) in 'Personality and stress: individual differences in the stress process.' Hobfoll (1988) discusses the social context of stress in his book 'The ecology of stress'.

12. Despite the popularity of stress research in this area, only tenuous associations between stress and illness outcomes have been found. Young (1980) and Pollock (1988) provide critiques of the stress-illness theories. They point out that stress research is based on tacit (commonsensical) rather than scientific knowledge, and are critical of the focus on individual, rather than environmental deficits.

13. Fisher and Reason's (1988) book 'Handbook of life, stress, cognition and health' provides a good overview of the sort of work being carried out using the transactional model of stress.

14. For example, Taylor (1983) assessed the role of subjective perceptions of meaningfulness, mastery and self-esteem in adaptation to cancer. Felton et al (1984) concentrated on beliefs about personal control among patients with hypertension, diabetes, cancer and rheumatoid arthritis. Schulz and Decker (1985) examined the appraisals of social support, perceived control and self-blame among people with spinal cord injury. Elliot et al (1991) studied the role of hope in relation to rehabilitation among people with traumatically acquired spinal cord injury. Primomom et al (1990) looked at sources and types of social support among women with diabetes or cancer. Holahan and Moos (1991) tested the importance of self-confidence and easy-going manner among people with depression. Finally, Prosser (1992) discussed appraisals of competence and control among people with physical disabilities.

15. McIver et al (1984) examined the relationship between depression among people with multiple sclerosis and demographic and illness characteristics and social support. They also found that perceived lack of social support (from family and friends) was related to depression. Older and more severely disabled people were more depressed. People in remission or who had experienced remissions were less depressed. There were no significant correlations between sex and length of

illness and depression. Demographic, illness and social support variables accounted for 65% of the variance in the depression scores.

4 Methodology

Introduction

The experience of living with multiple sclerosis and other chronic illnesses has been described from three viewpoints: as a disease, as a social condition and as a personal experience. This project is concerned with personal experiences of multiple sclerosis. The insiders' perspective and transactional model of stress provide the theoretical basis of the study. The benefits of these two contrasting approaches have already been mentioned but will be recapped: firstly, individual perceptions and interpretations of illness are central to both models; secondly, individual perceptions are not taken out of context - biomedical characteristics of the disease and socio-environmental conditions for people with illness are incorporated in both models; and lastly, both are concerned with how people manage to live as normal a life as possible in the face of chronic illness. The two models differ, however, in their methodological approach: the transactional model of stress is derived from and justified through quantitative methods, whereas the insiders' perspective is essentially qualitative. This chapter will start by outlining the key differences between qualitative and quantitative research methods relevant to this project. The aims of the research project will follow. The remainder of the chapter will detail the decisions made regarding the research design and describe the sample, research measures, and the processes of data collection and data analysis.

Qualitative and Quantitative Methods

The dominance of quantitative, as opposed to qualitative, methods in social science and particularly in health care research has been a matter of concern for commentators in the field (Pollitt et al 1990; Waitzin 1990; Roter and Frankel 1992; Henwood and Pidgeon 1992; Pope and Mays 1993). Qualitative research is often perceived to be a "soft" option - used by researchers as a poetic licence to substantiate their own theoretical concepts. Quantitative research, on the other hand, is represented as a "hard" option - a rigorous method for testing theoretical concepts[1]. Figure 4.1 summarises some of the ways in which differences between the two methods have been polarised.

Table 4.1
Some of the hallmarks of quantitative and qualitative research methods

QUANTITATIVE METHODS		QUALITATIVE METHODS
Experimental	vs	Naturalistic
Objective	vs	Subjective
Hypothetico-deductive	vs	Discovery-inductive
Positivist	vs	Interpretive
Measurement-oriented	vs	Representational
Standardised	vs	Flexible
Numeric	vs	Verbal
Universal laws	vs	Cultural patterns
Generalise	vs	Uniqueness
Nomethetic	vs	Ideographic
Explanation	vs	Description
Fixed	vs	Exploratory
Neutrality/impartiality	vs	Reflexivity
Outcome oriented	vs	Process oriented
Survey	vs	Case history
Statistical	vs	Narrative
Psychometric test	vs	Interviews

Qualitative research is criticised for presuming it has direct knowledge of social phenomena (because subjects are encouraged to describe their own experiences), whilst failing to recognise that, like quantitative research, investigation and interpretation processes are guided by methodological assumptions (Hammersley 1990). On the other hand, quantitative research is criticised for failing to capture the meaning of social phenomena by using variables as constraints and reducing relationships to statistical outcomes (Waitzin 1990). For example, Heyden (1993) argues that patient satisfaction surveys based on a set of predetermined questions reveal little about consumer perceptions because consumers are not asked what they think and what is important to them. There are advantages and disadvantages in each methods; trade-offs are sometimes necessary between the breadth (sample size) and depth (detail) of information collected (Daly et al 1992). The way forward in research appears to be in addressing these shortcomings and building on the benefits of each technique. It is not necessary to denigrate one approach to justify the other. Indeed, it can be argued that research projects rarely use either method exclusively. Quantitative research is often based on prior qualitative investigations and vice versa.

Theory and methodology are intertwined in research using the insiders' approach and the transactional model of stress; qualitative methods (e.g. ethnography) are crucial to the former, and quantitative methods (psychometric tests) are customary in the latter. Both approaches are used in the study to complement and inform one another, rather than for 'triangulation' purposes (i.e. as a means of validating data which have been collected using different methods). Qualitative and quantitative were chosen to provide different sorts of information: gathering "how it feels" type of data and local knowledge was dependent on qualitative methods, whereas measuring the severity of specific problems, within and across groups, was dependent on quantitative methods.

Dingwall (1992) and Pollitt et al (1990) provide useful guidelines and standards for qualitative research. For example, Pollitt (1990) suggests that field work should not be completely open-ended; evidence should be checked from a variety of sources; semi-structured interviews should give participants the opportunity to develop their own perspectives; research should consist of four stages - design, data collection, data analysis and explanation; and that procedures should be fully documented. Dingwall (1992) stipulates that good qualitative research should distinguish between data and analysis of data; clarify the ways in which it sets out to test statements proposed on theoretical grounds or previous studies; and recognise the interactive character of social life (including interviews themselves), and deal with people even-handedly.

These criteria acted as precautions in the qualitative part of the study - the insiders' perspective.

The canons of quantitative methods, compared to qualitative methods, are well established and consist of the following steps: identifying the problem, suggesting hypotheses, defining variables, and constructing a research design to test the hypotheses. Instruments used to measure variables are chosen on the basis of their validity and reliability, and subjects are selecting according to a representative sampling design (Nachmias and Nachmias 1981). Deciding on appropriate statistical tests is dependent on the research design (Greene and D'Oliveira 1982). These criteria were important for implementing the quantitative part of the research project the transactional model of stress.

Research Aims

There were two major research objectives: the first was concerned with collecting individual accounts or 'stories' of illness from the perspective of people with multiple sclerosis; the second was concerned with assessing the role of stress in adaptation to multiple sclerosis. The insiders' perspective was used to identify dominant themes in personal accounts of illness and the transactional model of stress to test the role of stressful and uplifting events and coping processes on adaptation. In both approaches information regarding personal details, medical knowledge and social circumstances was collected. The insiders' perspective and transactional model of stress were used to compliment one another and gain a richer understanding of the ways in which people lived with their illness.

The aims of the research were informed by the literature reviews. The qualitative part of the study was guided by research questions rather than hypotheses. The following questions were important: What does multiple sclerosis mean to people with the illness? How do they explain the cause of multiple sclerosis? What have they learnt about the disease? How was the diagnosis conveyed? What problems do people with multiple sclerosis experience most commonly? What are the physical, social and personal consequences of multiple sclerosis? How does their illness affect them emotionally? How do they cope with their illness? What help have they received from statutory and voluntary services and others? What were the reasons for living in an institutional setting rather than at home? How does living in an institutional setting compare to living at home?

The quantitative part of the study was designed to provide descriptive and statistical data. Responses to individual items on questionnaires were treated as having as much importance as total scores. For example, attention was

90

given to both the types of stressful encounters reported and overall levels of stress recorded. One of the aims of this part of the study was to assess the role of accommodation status (home or institutional) on individual scores. The application of the transactional model of stress to research on chronic illness has produced contradictory results. The following research hypotheses, therefore, were made tentatively:

1. People living in institutional settings report fewer hassles and uplifts than people living at home.

2. People living in institutional settings report different types of hassles and uplifts to people living at home.

3. People living in institutional settings use more emotion-focused coping strategies than people living at home.

4. People living in institutional settings have a poorer self-esteem than people living at home.

5. People living in institutional settings are less satisfied with their lives and health than people living at home.

6. High levels of hassles are associated with low levels of satisfaction.

7. Low levels of uplifts are associated with low levels of satisfaction.

8. Coping strategies are influenced by demographic and illness characteristics and the type of problem reported.

9. Problem-focused coping and avoidance coping are associated with low levels of satisfaction.

10. Positive self-esteem is associated with high levels of satisfaction.

The role of demographic (age, sex, marital status), and illness (duration) characteristics in reports of hassles and uplifts, coping strategies, self-esteem and satisfaction with life and health were also investigated.

Research Design

The purpose of the research project was to provide an in-depth study of the everyday lives of people with multiple sclerosis living in institutional settings and at home. Findings unique or general to both groups were examined. A semi-structured interview was constructed to explore personal accounts of multiple sclerosis. Psychometric scales were used to test relationships between hassles, uplifts, coping, self-esteem and measures of adaptation. Resource constraints and time limitations made a cross-sectional design the only viable option.

The sample

The sample was drawn from the day-centre register of the MS Society (Belfast Branch) and from individuals with multiple sclerosis resident at two local residential facilities providing long-term care for disabled people. Forty people with a diagnosis of multiple sclerosis participated in the study. Purposive sampling procedures insured that twenty of these people lived at home and twenty lived in an institutional setting (13 in a hospital and 7 in a residential/nursing home) on a permanent basis. Sampling procedures were used so that men and women were equally represented. The sample is deliberately not representative of the multiple sclerosis population in Northern Ireland; one of the aims of the study was to include people living in institutional settings because they have received little attention in previous studies.

The criteria for selection of the sample were as follows:

a)   a diagnosis of multiple sclerosis made at least two years previously;
b)   able to give informed consent;
c)   able to communicate verbally;
d)   no severe cognitive impairment;
e)   place of residence in the Belfast or Lisburn area;
f)   resident at current address for at least one year.

These criteria were chosen so that the sample included only those people who were familiar with their diagnosis and their current place of residence, thus excluding people who were dealing with a recent diagnosis of multiple sclerosis or a change of address, perhaps as a result of illness. Both of these latter situations have been dealt with by other research projects (Stewart and Sullivan 1982; and Miles 1979). The intention was to concentrate on those people who had a relatively long history of multiple sclerosis since the study focused in part on the question of whether people had adapted to condition, or whether adaptation was a continuous process. Matson Brooks (1977) suggest that nearly all adjustment, as measured by self-conc takes place within the first ten years of the illness. The characteristics of t sample are shown in Table 4.2.

Table 4.2
Characteristics of the sample of people with multiple sclerosis

	Institution	Community	Total
NUMBER:	20	20	40
SEX:			
Female	10	10	20
Male	10	10	20
MARITAL STATUS:			
Married	6	13	19
Separated/divorced	5	2	7
Widowed	4	4	8
Never married	5	1	6
AGE (years):			
Mean	60	56	58
SD	9.7	12.7	11.4
AGE AT DIAGNOSIS (years):			
Mean	37	38	38
SD	10.4	12.9	11.6
DURATION OF ILLNESS (years):			
Mean	24	17	20
SD	10.6	10.9	11.1
LENGTH OF STAY IN HOSPITAL (years):			
Mean	5		
SD	6.6		

Both sexes were equally represented in the home and institutional settings. The majority of people were born in Northern Ireland (34) or had lived in Northern Ireland for most of their lives (37). Their mean age was 58 years (range: 30 - 76 years), with a mean age at time of diagnosis of 38 years (range: 18 - 68 years). The mean duration of illness, from time of diagnosis, was 16 years (range: 2 - 43 years). Women were slightly older than men (mean age for women 61 years, for men 55 years). The institutional group was slightly older than the home group (mean age of 60 years compared to 56 years). On average, people had lived permanently in an institutional setting for five years (range: 1 - 28 years). Nineteen people were married, 21 were single (widowed (8), divorced/separated (7), or never married (6)). Approximately, twice as many men were married as women and half of the single women were widows.

The marital status of institutional and hospital groups differed. The majority of people who lived at home were married (13), whereas the majority of people in an institution were single (14). Of the 7 single people who lived at home, three lived alone and four with relatives, four were widowed, two divorced/separated and one person had never married. Of the 14 single people living in an institution, four were widowed, 5 divorced/separated and 5 had never married.

Twenty-eight people used a wheelchair. For the remaining 12 people, walking was limited; a wheelchair was generally necessary for mobility outside the home or long distances. Nearly all the institution dwellers used a wheelchair (19) compared to approximately half of the home dwellers (9). People living in institutional setting, then, tended to be older, single and more severely disabled than people living at home.

The population from which the sample was drawn was small. The institutional group represents *all* those people known to the researcher who met the selection criteria. Similarly, *all male* attenders of the MS Society in Belfast who lived at home and met the selection criteria were included. Selection of female attenders who lived at home was dependent on a number of additional factors: firstly, whether a person was available for interview at the centre; secondly, their current state of health (those women feeling in bad health were unlikely to attend the centre or if they did attend they often preferred not to take part in an interview); and lastly, whether they had recently experienced a crisis. In this last case, a care assistant would inform the researcher that a person was noticeably distressed and ask if an interview could be delayed until after the crisis had been alleviated.[2] If the timing of some interviews was believed to be inopportune, arrangements were made for a later date, if necessary.

Three people who were approached said they preferred not to take part in the research project, (Two of these three people said they would participate if the researcher really needed their assistance, but their assistance was not required). Two people were excluded from the final analysis because of difficulties completing the interviews.

Qualitative and quantitative measures

This section is divided into two parts; the first part deals with the qualitative measures (the semi-structured interview and overview); and the second part describes the quantitative measures used (Hassles and Uplifts Scales, Method and Focus of Coping Measure, Self-esteem Scale, Satisfaction with Life and Health Scales). Both types of measures were selected to address the aim of the research: to assess the roles of individual perceptions of illness, hassles, uplifts, self-esteem and coping on adaptation, as measured by the Satisfaction with Life and Health Scales.

Qualitative measures

1.   Semi-structured interview

The semi-structured interview consisted of fifteen open-ended questions which explored participants' experiences of multiple sclerosis. The interview was designed to be flexible and gave both the researcher and the participant the opportunity to expand on the fifteen primary questions. The content of the questions was decided upon after a review of the literature both specific to multiple sclerosis and general to chronic illness (see Chapters One to Three). Biographical material and first person accounts, newspaper and magazine articles were also referred to. The following themes, as already mentioned, were prominent:

a)   The diagnosis of MS (Westbrook and Viney 1982; Brunel ARMS Research Unit 1983b).

b)   Knowledge of, beliefs about, and attitude towards, illness (Pavlou and Counte 1982; Maybery and Brewin 1984).

c)   Attributions about the cause of the illness (Taylor 1983; Pollock 1984 and 1986).

d)   Opinions on, and satisfaction with, the services available (Radford and Trew 1987; McLellan et al 1989).

e)   Responses to and coping with chronic illness (Matson and Brooks 1977, 1982; Robinson 1988ab; and Pollock et al 1990).

f)   The meanings of illness (Gould 1982; Charmaz 1983).

g)   Key problems when living with chronic illness (Strauss and Glaser 1975; Conrad 1990).

These subject areas were incorporated into the semi-structured interview, thus ensuring that issues pertinent to people with chronic illness were discussed.

A review of the literature also uncovered neglected areas of research. Relatively little attention has been given to 'feelings' people experience whilst living with multiple sclerosis. Psychological and medical academic texts tend to discuss feelings in terms of 'emotional affect' or 'disorder'. Consequently the emotional aspects of multiple sclerosis are often medicalised as symptoms of either depression, euphoria, hysteria, emotional lability, anxiety or even premorbid personality disorder (Marsh et al 1983; and Rao et al 1992). An alternative interpretation could be that emotional aspects of multiple sclerosis are simply responses to changes in lifestyle caused by the condition.

Register (1987) wrote her book, 'Living with Chronic Illness', after failing to find 'a testimony by someone who had been through the worst and emerged with optimism intact.' and failing to meet anyone who could honestly tell her, 'I know exactly how you feel'. This apparent oversight was addressed in the semi-structured interview in two ways: firstly, by including some questions which were solely concerned with feelings (e.g. What do you fear most about your illness?); and secondly, by following up informational questions (e.g. Could you tell me how you first found out you had multiple sclerosis?) with probes into the feelings associated with particular events (e.g. How did you feel when you were first diagnosed?). The questions were framed in such a way that sometimes participants were asked to provide information, sometimes reflect on their experiences, and at other times, express their feelings.

The interviews started with the informational question, 'How did you find out you had multiple sclerosis?'. This question served many purposes. It was a question most respondents had little difficulty in answering and was useful for putting people at ease. It appeared to be a question people were familiar with. Indeed many participants gave well rehearsed and detailed accounts of the history of their illness without the need of further probes. Informational questions are useful in that they bring the respondent further into the interview and establish a chronology, types of events, degrees of awareness, cast of participants, and the like. (Charmaz 1990)

The beginning of an interview was important in establishing a rapport between the researcher and the participant. The question about the diagnosis of multiple sclerosis encouraged such a dialogue. The researcher learnt how the diagnosis was discovered within the context of people's lives. At the same time participants judged how interested the researcher was in what was being said. In the telling of and listening to stories, participants and researcher were concerned with making sense of the illness experience (Whan 1979; and Reissman 1990). As Miller Mair (1988) explained:

> Our lives are, I think, shaped in the stories we live and the quality of our experience is textured by the stories we tell and the ways in which telling is allowed.

The semi-structured interview was an attempt to allow participants to tell their stories in their own words. Each participant was given the opportunity to discuss issues which were important to them. The structure of the interview, however, ensured that comparisons could be made between responses given to the same questions across the sample. The aim of the interview was to talk about what it is like to live with multiple sclerosis. Erikson (1963) argued that understanding individual stories requires a triple bookkeeping system which takes into account physical characteristics (e.g. biological endowments), individual perspectives (e.g. the ways in which people perceive themselves and their place in the world), and the social context (e.g. family, cultural and historical forces which shape and are shaped by the individual). The semi-structured interview gave participants the opportunity to discuss each of these aspects of their lives.

2. Overview

The overview consisted of eleven general questions which were asked at the very end of the interviews. These questions were a recap on the topics covered previously in the semi-structured interviews and psychometric scales. For example, people were asked whether they felt there was a lot of stress in their lives, how they coped with their condition and whether they felt they had adapted to their condition. The overview was designed to give participants the opportunity to make general comments about their lives with multiple sclerosis. The information collected in this section was used to test the consistency of responses collected from questionnaire and interview methods.

These final questions were also useful for bringing the interview to a close. Particular attention was given to making sure that participants were not distressed; that they had nothing else to add to the schedule; and that they were happy with the content of the interviews.

Quantitative measures

1.   Hassles and uplifts scales

The Hassles scale (Kanner et al 1981) was devised as an alternative to measurements of stress which concentrate on the importance of major life events only. The popularity of the major life events approach seems to be unfounded considering the weak correlations between major life events and health outcomes (Rabkin and Streuning 1976). The Uplifts scale (Kanner et al 1981) was developed simultaneously to test whether positive experience acted in a compensatory way, alleviating the impact of stressful events.

When Kanner et al (1981) administered both the Hassles and Uplifts Scales together with a life events scale to a community sample of middle-aged adults, they found that hassles were better predictors of psychological symptoms than life events scores. They concluded that their approach was

a useful step toward improving and extending the measurement of stress and of sources of satisfaction in daily life, and toward advancing our understanding of stress as a factor in health and illness.

Research since has supported these claims.[3] As a result, projects using the hassles and uplifts scale have multiplied and range from studies as diverse as absenteeism (Ivancevich 1986) to mandibular dysfunction syndrome (Wright et al 1991).[4] Some of these research projects provide useful comparative data for this project. Kanner et al (1981) found that the community sample of middle-aged people reported a mean frequency of 22.4 hassles in the last month and approximately three times as many uplifts (mean frequency = 69.5). Warren et al (1991) found that people with multiple sclerosis reported a remarkably similar number of hassles (mean = 22.1) but fewer uplifts (mean = 46.5) than the community sample. The advantages of using the hassles and uplifts scales appeared to outweigh the disadvantages (e.g. the long time it takes to complete the scales and problems with confounding variables).

The Hassles and Uplifts Scales (Kanner et al 1981) are measurements of minor stresses and pleasures that characterise everyday life. It is designed to be self-administered. The original Hassles Scale consists of a 117 items which cover seven domains: work, health, family, the environment, practical considerations, and chance occurrences. Respondents are asked to identify those hassles which have happened to them in the *past month* and then to rate their perceived *severity*: 1 being somewhat severe, 2 moderately severe and 3 extremely severe. The Uplifts scale consists of 135 items in the same life domains. This time, uplifts which have happened in the past month are rated according to their *occurrence*: 1 being somewhat often, 2 moderately often and 3 extremely often. At the end of both scales respondents are asked to write down any hassles or uplifts missed by the scales. Lastly, respondents are asked whether there has been a major change in their life in the last month that has affected the way in which the scale was answered.

Three summary scores can be calculated for the Hassles Scale: frequency, which is the number of items checked (range from 0 to 117); cumulated frequency, which is the sum of the 3-point severity ratings (range from 0 to 351); (3) and intensity, which is the cumulated frequency divided by the frequency, (range from 0 to 3). The intensity score measures the average severity of perceived hassles. Summary scores for the Uplifts Scale are calculated in the same way.

Some alterations were made to the format of the scales to improve administration. This was necessary because self completion of the scales was difficult for many of the participants and all participants preferred to complete the scales with the aid of the researcher. Thus, items were grouped together into specific life domains (finance, work, environment, chance occurrences, relationships, health, personal and practical considerations). Such ordering helped both the researcher and the participant to focus on certain issues. Additionally, when a certain domain was no longer a part of a person's life (e.g. employment), items in this area could be easily by-passed.

Ordering the items under these life domains gave the scale a structure which encouraged discussions between the researcher and participants. Participants had the opportunity to ask the researcher questions and the researcher could ask participants to explain their answers. In this way not only did the researcher find out which incidents were perceived as hassles or uplifts but *why* they were perceived to be. The meanings behind the replies were recorded and referred to in the analysis of the types of hassles reported.

The content of the Hassles Scale was modified slightly. Fifteen of the original items were combined and reduced to seven items because they were shown to overlap in the pilot study (e.g. item 95 'concerns about inner conflicts' was combined with item 96 'feeling conflicted over what to do' into a single item 'inner conflicts/conflicted over what to do'). Twelve additional items were incorporated into the Hassles Scale.[5] Some of these items were identified as missing hassles by participants in the pilot study. Others were based on readings of personal accounts of illness. The final version of the Hassles Scale consisted of 121 items, four more than the original Scale.

Similar changes were made to the Uplifts Scale. Twenty-eight of the original items were combined and reduced to fourteen items. One additional item was included.[6] The final version consisted of 121 items, fourteen fewer than the original scale.

Modifications made to the Hassles and Uplifts Scale in content, format and administration procedures meant that completion of scales and analysis of data were more time-consuming. Both scales stimulated further conversations between the researcher and participants; useful additional information was recorded as a result. On the other hand, completing the scales with the researcher, could have inhibited some participants or they may have been more inclined to give socially desirable responses. There was no way around this problem apart from assuring participants that their response would be treated as confidential, and that they were guaranteed anonymity in any public reports.

2.   The method and focus of coping measure

Interview assessments, open-ended questionnaires, self-report scales, personality inventories and coping checklists have all been used to measure coping.[7] The last mentioned has gained popularity, however, because checklists incorporate a wide range of possible coping styles and enable standardisation of research procedures. As in the case of studies on stress, there has been a proliferation of research into coping. A diverse range of stressful situations have been studied in order to discover coping styles and coping effectiveness.[8] The role of individual coping styles in medical settings and in influencing health outcomes has received much attention.[9] It is generally accepted that coping has an important contributory role in the improvements of our understanding of the dynamics of mental and physical health (Alwin and Revenson 1987; Vitaliano et al 1990; Hobfoll 1988; Cooper and Payne 1991; and Kaplan 1992).

Billings and Moos have made significant contributions to the field of coping and stress research, (1981 and 1984; Moos, 1974, 1984 and 1986). They devised the Method and Focus of Coping Measure (Billings and Moos, 1981) used in this study. In it, respondents are asked to describe their most stressful event or situation encountered in the last month. They are then asked to indicate "yes" or "no" to nineteen items which are suggestions as to ways in which they might have dealt with the stressful situation.

The items are classified according to three method of coping categories (active-cognitive, active-behavioural and avoidance) and two focus of coping categories (emotion-focused and problem-focused). Method of coping refers to strategies used to resolve stressful events. Thus, active-cognitive strategies are those attempts which manage one's perception or interpretation of a situation (e.g. 'tried to see the positive side'); active-behavioural coping strategies are overt actions directed at dealing with the problem (e.g. 'talked with a professional person about the situation'); and avoidance coping refers to attempts to evade confronting a problem (e.g. 'kept my feelings to myself) or to alleviate tension indirectly by behaviour such as eating, smoking or drinking.

Focus of coping refers to the objective behind coping strategies. In problem-focused coping, modifying or eliminating the *sources of stress* is important (e.g. 'considered several alternatives for handling the problem'). In emotion-focused coping the objective is to manage *emotional reactions* to stress or to reduce distress (e.g. 'prayed for guidance and strength'). Each coping measure is scored by calculating the percentage of items answered "yes". When the measure was used on a community sample, Billings and Moos (1981) found that all the coping categories were used fairly often. Problem-focused coping (49.9%) was used slightly more than emotion-focused coping (38.0%). In terms of method of coping, active-cognitive coping (62.7%) was used the most, followed by active-behavioural (60.9%) and lastly avoidance (24.0) coping strategies. Hickey and Green (1989) only report focus of coping scores, but they found that people with multiple sclerosis also used more problem-focused (73.3%) coping than emotion-focused coping (61.6%).

Internal consistency within categories varies. The correlation between items was 0.80 for active-behavioural coping, 0.72 for active-cognitive coping and 0.44 for avoidance coping (Billings and Moos 1981). Relatively low levels of intercorrelation were found across categories, which suggests that the categories are relatively independent. Internal consistency and independence have previously been tested for the focus of coping sub-categories and found to be satisfactory (Folkman and Lazarus 1988).

The relatively low internal consistency found between items in the avoidance category is related to problems with defining coping categories. For example, Billings and Moos (1981) classify the item, 'prepared for the worst' as an avoidance strategy. However, if a person is faced with a chronic illness, 'prepared for the worst' could be classified alternatively, as an active-cognitive coping strategy. Deciding which category some of the items belong to is an ambiguous process and depends on the nature of the stress being dealt with. Perhaps for these reasons, Billings and Moos neglect to classify two items in terms of method of coping. To rectify this omission it was decided that, 'got busy with other things in order to keep my mind off the problem' was an avoidance strategy and that, 'didn't worry about it; figured everything would probably work out fine' was a active-cognitive coping strategy.

Despite these limitations, the Method and Focus of Coping Measure had certain advantages for this study over other coping measures: firstly, it is relatively succinct and easy to administer; and secondly, the scale has been used successfully with chronically ill people (Hickey and Greene 1989; and Ehmann et al 1990).

3.   Self-esteem scale

Robson (1988) commented, in a review article concerning self-esteem that

> Despite the colossal literature that has accumulated, a clear consensus as to the meaning of self-esteem is still lacking.

The absence of a precise definition has been attributed to three factors: its common-sense appeal; an assumption that everyone has an intuitive understanding of its nature; and a taken-for-granted assumption that it is a separate entity although this has not been established (Robson, 1988). Indeed the centrality of self-esteem is often alluded to in theories of self-concept without actually defining the properties integral to the term (Epstein 1973). As a result, synonyms for self-esteem abound, each adding to its obscurity. Closely associated terms are: self-regard, self-image, self-evaluation, self-acceptance, self-awareness, self-consciousness, self-actualisation, self-appraisal, self-perception, self-control, self-efficacy, self-love and self-determination. Basically, self-esteem is related to feelings of personal worth and social value; in other words, a belief that one is a valuable member in a meaningful universe. It is an enduring quality, although under certain conditions it may fluctuate temporarily. High self-esteem has been associated with optimal functioning and low self-esteem with undesirable traits, symptoms and behaviours (Robson 1988; and Soloman et al 1991). It is unclear whether self-esteem is a psychological resource which influences adaptation (see Delongis et al 1988), or a measurement of adaptation itself (see Maybury and Brewin 1984). The role self-esteem plays in adaptation to multiple sclerosis will be assessed.

Rosenberg (1965) is credited with conducting the first empirical study on self-esteem. His measurement of self-esteem is one of the most widely used of its kind and has been selected for this study.[10] The scale consists of ten items to which respondents are asked to either strongly agree (score of 1), agree (score of 2), disagree (score of 3) or strongly disagree (score of 4), depending on how they feel at the time of questioning. Scores, therefore, range from 10 to 40. In this study, higher score represent positive self-esteem. There is substantial evidence that the majority of people rate themselves as above average on the self-esteem scale (Baumeister et al 1989). MacCarthy and

Brown (1989) found the same among people with Parkinson's disease. Although they used a different measure, Brooks and Matson reported that people with multiple sclerosis have self-concept scores comparable to people without illness. The reliability and construct validity of the scale appears to be reasonable, although there is less evidence regarding its sensitivity to change (Bowling 1991). The advantages of the Self-Esteem Scale are its brevity, compared to other scales (e.g. The Tennessee Self-Concept scale (Fitts 1965) and Self-Esteem Inventory (Coopersmith 1967)), and relative simplicity, in term of administration, scoring and analysis.

4. Satisfaction with life and health

It has been claimed that 'For quality of life there are no greater needs than health and happiness.' (Zautra and Hempel 1984). Flanagan's (1982) study on the quality of life of adult Americans, found that material comforts, work, and health and personal safety were the three most important determinants of overall quality of life. Other contributory factors were participation in active recreation, learning or acquiring knowledge, a close relationship with person of opposite sex, socialising and expressing yourself in a creative way.

In his international study of human concerns (on personal and national levels), Cantril (1965) also found that standard of living, work and health were consistently the most common personal concerns. On the other hand, when correlations were made between satisfaction and objective criteria, income was perceived to be relatively unimportant compared to health and friendships (Campbell et al 1976). Quality of life measures, therefore, tend to include both objective (e.g. socio-economic status and environmental standards) and subjective (e.g. well-being) indicators, which reflect the importance of both standards of living and individual perspectives in gauging quality of life. This study will concentrate on measuring the latter.

Well-being can be defined and measured on many different levels: the presence of physical and psychological symptoms; functional ability; social health; life-satisfaction; happiness and morale.[11] Some definitions emphasise feelings, other perceptions and others physical attributes or personality types. This study decided to concentrate on life-satisfaction. Whatever the emphasis, the measurement of well-being is usually based on subjective evaluations. The reason for this is made clear by Morris (1991):

> As a society we cannot, and should not, make judgements about the quality of other people's lives (or potential lives). When we react to the disability of others, or the prospect of disability in a child, we bring our own subjective experience to the situation.

The assumption is, then, that the individuals themselves are the best judges of their own well-being and health. For example, self-rated health has been found to be one of the best predictors of use of health care services and survival; it has been associated with health promotion lifestyle indicators; and appears to play an important intervening role between objective health problems and life satisfaction (Fylkesnes and Forde 1992).

Although greater attention is being paid to individual perceptions of health and satisfaction with health care, less is known about the relationship between perceptions of health and satisfaction with life generally,[12] and how people with chronic illness define, as opposed to rate, satisfaction and dissatisfaction with life and health. These two issues were dealt with in this study using self-report measures of both satisfaction with life and health.

Cantril's ladder was used as a technique to assess both global satisfaction with life and satisfaction with a specific domain of life, in this case health. The "ladder" was used by Cantril in his study of human concerns already mentioned. Cantril's ladder, as a measurement of satisfaction with life, embodies three features said to be desirable in such measures: firstly, it is subjective; secondly, it includes positive measures; and thirdly, it includes a global assessment of all aspects of a person's life (Diener 1984).

It has been used frequently, although the number of rungs on the "ladder" and corresponding instructions varies between projects. The top rung of the ladder is meant to represent 'the best life for you' and the bottom rung 'the worst possible life for you'. Respondents are asked on which rung of the ladder they would put themselves. The ladder appears to be moderately reliable and although Cantril used it without formal validation, it has been used to assess satisfaction among people with chronic illness and shown significant associations with life events and self-ratings of health (McDowell and Newell 1987). The general public indicate a basic satisfaction, as opposed to dissatisfaction, with their lives (Campbell 1976) and life satisfaction is relatively stable across the life-span (Medley 1980). People with chronic illness also indicate that they are satisfied with their lives, but score a little lower than community samples (Brown et al 1981). When Anderson (1988) interviewed people who had a stroke, 65% indicated that they were satisfied with life, 16% were undecided and 19% were dissatisfied. Harper et al (1986) found that people with multiple sclerosis scored lower than a general populations in terms of physical activity, social and, emotional health, perceived satisfaction and quality of life. On the whole it seems that people with chronic illness make impressive 'psychological' recoveries and differ little to 'normal' populations in terms of life-satisfaction and psychological well-being (Cameron et al 1973; Feldman 1974; and Cassileth et al 1984).

The ladder is a simple instrument to use and can be easily adapted to suit the interests of different projects. In this project, definitions of health and satisfaction were believed to be as important as self-ratings on these two dimensions. Thus, respondents were first of all asked to define what their wishes and hopes for the future were and, following on from that, what would make them happy. They were then asked what their fears and worries for the future were and what would make them unhappy. Their own definitions were then used to label the top and bottom rungs of a ladder, numbered from 0 to 10.

Satisfaction with health was measured using the same principles. Respondents were asked to define what good health meant to them and how they felt when they were well. Similarly they were asked what bad health represented to them and how they felt when they were in bad health. Standardised probes were used if respondents had difficulties expressing themselves. Baumann (1961) asked people with chronic illness and medical students what they thought most people mean when they say they are in good physical condition. She discovered three general conceptions of health relating to feelings of well-being, the absence of symptoms and the ability to carry out activities. The biggest difference between people with chronic illness and students on each of these dimensions was in terms of the feeling orientation. People with chronic illness were more likely to link health with feelings of well-being. However, people with chronic illness most frequently associated health with the ability to perform activities (students associated symptoms, more than any other characteristic, with health). Pollock (1984), in her thesis concerning conceptions of health and illness among people with multiple sclerosis and schizophrenia and their families, found that these three conceptions of health were common. The performance orientation was the most frequent response given, especially among the multiple sclerosis group.

Once definitions had been made, participants were asked to place themselves on the ladder according to how they felt: today; before they had multiple sclerosis; the first years of their illness; and where they hoped to be one year from now. In this way, comparative data were collected in terms of satisfaction levels before and after multiple sclerosis; in the early and current years with multiple sclerosis; and in the remembered past and anticipated future. Cantril's ladder is a self-anchoring ladder, thus relative scores are more meaningful than absolute scores. Participants' past lives (pre multiple sclerosis) can be used to set standards. If satisfaction with current life compares favourably to past standards, relative happiness and adaptation have probably been achieved. Current satisfaction is also influenced by aspirations. High aspirations can be as threatening as on-going difficulties because they are difficult or impossible to attain, resulting in disappointment and feelings of failure. Adaptation depends on personal judgements of individual experiences in the past, present conditions and future aspirations.

The application of Cantril's ladder in this project, yielded both qualitative and quantitative data. In terms of the former, participants were asked to define what would make them happy or unhappy and what good and bad health meant to them; and in the latter, participants were asked to rate levels of satisfaction, (the higher the score (from 0-10) the greater the level of satisfaction). Adaptation was measured in terms of well-being (absolute ratings of satisfaction) and perceived changes in well-being over time (relative scores of satisfaction).

Data Collection

A pilot project was conducted in order to test the instruments and assess the feasibility of the project.[13] As a result, one of the original instruments was removed, three were modified and three additions were made.[14] Interviews for the pilot project began in August 1991. Fieldwork for the main project was carried out between November 1991 and March 1993.

Contact with people with multiple sclerosis was made with the help of the MS Society. Slightly different procedures were involved to gain access to the hospital and community groups. For the hospital group, the MS Society identified two local hospitals which provide long-term care for people with multiple sclerosis and the names of the consultants responsible for their care. Consultants were asked for permission to carry out the study in the hospitals. Once consent had been given, the relevant wards were visited. The process of identifying people with multiple sclerosis who met the selection criteria was a joint task, carried out by the researcher and nursing personnel, usually the sister in charge of the ward. Individuals were then approached by a nurse, informed of the project and asked if they would like to meet the researcher. If interest was shown, introductions were made. In this way individuals were not put under pressure to take part in the study. Interviews were carried out in a separate room or if this was not available, a quiet place (although this was not always possible).

A list of people with multiple sclerosis living at home or in residential/nursing home was obtained from the MS Society's day-centre register. Care assistants helped the researcher with the selection process (bearing in mind the sampling criteria), and made the initial contacts and introductions. Interviews took place in a separate room in the MS Society Centre. One person was interviewed in their own home.

106

After a brief explanation of the project, all participants were asked to give consent in writing or if this was not possible, verbally. Participants were assured of confidentiality. Some basic details were taken, (e.g. date of birth, marital status, date multiple sclerosis diagnosis was made). Participants were then asked if they minded having the interview tape-recorded. If they were agreeable, the semi-structured interview was tape-recorded. The interview schedule began with the semi-structured interview, followed by the Hassles and Uplifts scale, the Coping Scale, the Self-Esteem Scale, the Satisfaction with Life and Health measures and lastly, the Overview. A written record of responses given to questions in the Overview was taken, rather than a tape-recording.

The interview schedule was completed in separate sessions because of its length. Each session was thirty minutes to two hours long. At the end of each session arrangements were made to continue unfinished interview schedules the following week. One hundred and sixty-four sessions were carried out in total. On average, each interview schedule was completed in four sessions (range: 1-10), and therefore took a month on average to complete. The average total time taken to complete an interview schedule was five hours of one-to-one contact. The time taken to complete interviews was largely dictated by participants themselves: some participants were brief or concise in the answers they gave; for others the interview provided an opportunity to "get things off their chest" - either to confess, to enquire, to complain or to get some support. The researcher was responsive to participants who had an agenda of their own set for the interview. In this way the distinction between researcher and researched was often blurred.

The time taken to complete interviews and the manner in which they were carried out was also influenced by participants' perceptions of the researcher. As an young English woman, participants were often curious about my own background and reasons for being in Northern Ireland. Roles were often reversed at the outset, with participants asking me how I felt about living in Northern Ireland! This, in fact, proved to be a good way of easing into conversations about personal lives and aided, rather than restrained, dialogue. There were other advantages to being an "outsider": my relative inexperience of life in Northern Ireland and limited social connections with the community, put some participants at their ease and made them more vocal on issues both associated with their illness and unrelated to their illness. The interviews were educational in many ways!

There were possible disadvantages too; some participants may have felt I lacked experience because of my unfamiliarity with life in Northern Ireland, my age and student identity. As a result some participants may have felt it was not worthwhile spending a lot of time describing to me their experiences of illness. Not being a 'professional' working in the field, I feel was an advantage: I had no axe to grind, and participants could be as opinionated as the wished, concerning their illness and the help they had received, without fear of offending me. I tried to present myself as a someone who appreciated the nature of the disease but was keen to learn more about the personal implications of the illness, and to this end I perceived participants as an authority on multiple sclerosis. As the research project progressed I knew that participants often talked amongst themselves about the research project. Their perceptions of me seemed to change, I had become an expert of sorts, not in a practical or professional capacity, but on a personal level I could appreciate how their individual lives had been affected by multiple sclerosis.

The data collection stage was a learning process. I learnt how to tease out replies to questions participants had difficulty in answering by rewording a question or making up hypothetical situations. With hindsight I wished I could have repeated some of the first interviews. However, such knowledge would probably have changed the content of the interviews at the expense of upsetting the balance between guiding conversations and allowing participants to develop their own stories. Throughout the fieldwork, contact was maintained with all the participants who had taken part in the study. Participants joked amongst themselves and with others that they had given me all their 'juicy' stories and that explained why some interviews had taken longer time to complete than others. Participants asked me what I had found and I would give some general impressions, without mentioning names, which would lead to nods of agreement or surprise. What to do with the results and who would benefit from reading them was also discussed. It was felt that the findings would be useful for other people with multiple sclerosis and for professionals. Participants felt that their experiences of multiple sclerosis would be informative and educational for other people with a diagnosis of multiple sclerosis and for policy makers and practitioners involved in the care of people with multiple sclerosis. I hoped that participants felt that the project was as much their project as mine.

Data Analysis

Qualitative and quantitative data were collected and analysed separately. Data collected from the standardised scales were entered onto the SPSS computer package and conventional statistical tests were computed. The semi-structured interview material was assessed using content analysis.

Statistical analysis

Statistical analysis of the quantitative data was based on procedures used in validated research that had been published in peer journals so that comparable data were collected. In this way similarities and differences across different populations (disabled and non-disabled) and within the multiple sclerosis sample could be assessed in the discussion. Researchers using the scales have tended to apply conventional parametric tests to describe and predict associations between variables. Parametric tests were also used in this study, but with some major reservations owing to the relatively small size of the sample, the skewed rather than normal frequency distributions and the levels of measurement provided by the scales.[15] Equivalent non-parametric tests were, therefore, calculated in order to confirm or question apparently statistically significant relationships between variables.

The following parametric tests were used, with their non-parametric equivalents shown in brackets:

i)   T-test (Mann Whitney and Chi-square test).
ii)   One way analysis of variance (Kruskal-Wallis test).
iii) Pearson product-moment correlation (Spearman rank correlation).
iv)   Multiple regression.

The t-tests and one way analysis of variance were used to assess significant associations between scores on the variables (e.g. hassles, uplifts, and self-esteem) and demographic characteristics (age, sex and marital status), illness characteristics (duration) and accommodation status (institutional and community). Correlations and multiple regressions were used to assess relationships between the variables themselves (hassles, uplifts, coping strategies, self-esteem and satisfaction with life and health). Descriptive statistics were used to provide summaries of the data (frequencies and means). Inferential statistics were applied to identify possible associations between variables. Only statistical tests which reached a 95% level of significance ($p < 0.05$) were reported.

Content analysis

Content analysis was used to evaluate transcripts written from the tape-recordings of semi-structured interviews. Krippendorff (1980) defined content analysis as a 'research technique for making inferences by systematically and objectively identifying specified characteristics with a text'. Content analysis provides a method of identifying themes within a text and counting the frequency with which themes occur (within texts or between subjects). Analysis involves reducing qualitative data to separate coded units of information. Coded units correspond to pre-defined categories identified by the researcher, which are often based on standardised scales (see Viney and Westbrook 1981). Earlier research stipulated that coding categories had to be mutually exclusive, but more recent research has argued for the use of 'fuzzy categories', where categories overlap or include other categories (Scherl and Smithson 1987). A unit can either be a single word or a phrase or a whole paragraph.

Content analysis was traditionally popular in media studies as a method of assessing the content, slant, and frequency of newspaper reports on specific subject matters (see McConkey and Roche 1989). Content analysis is a time-consuming process, although ethnographic software programmes have made the analysis of voluminous reports more efficient (Norbeck et al 1991). More recently, content analysis has been applied to transcripts of audio-taped semi-structured interviews and used to interpret data in a more exploratory and descriptive manner (Viney and Westbrook 1981; Hetu et al 1988 and 1990; Norbeck et al 1991; Flaskerud and Calvillo 1991; and Nuttal 1988).

Content analysis entails the coding, categorising and classifying of texts. Grounded theory (Strauss and Corbin 1990) uses similar procedures to content analysis but differs in how categories are defined: in grounded theory categories should 'emerge' from the data, whereas in content analysis, categories are pre-defined and allocated to instances in the text.[16] Although books are available on the standard procedures for carrying out grounded theory and content analysis (Strauss and Corbin 1990; Krippendorff 1980; and Budd 1967), research projects using either method are often vague about how analysis was actually carried out.[17] The validity and reliability of research findings is, therefore, questionable and appears to be susceptible to investigator bias. To avoid such ambiguities the content analysis procedures followed in this study will be made explicit and broken down into the following five steps:

Making transcripts Tape-recordings of the semi-structured interviews were transcribed by the researcher. All but five transcripts were based on the recordings of full interviews. Four transcripts were based on a combination of tape-recorded material and notes taken during and immediately after the interview[18] and one transcript was based on a written record of an entire interview.[19] Transcripts were written to make easy reading and did not include socio-linguistic conventions such as simultaneous speech and changes in tone of voice.

Defining categories and designing a coding frame A review of psychosocial literature specific to multiple sclerosis and general to chronic illness led to the identification of issues pertinent to personal experiences of illness. These issues were incorporated into the semi-structured interview which consisted of 15 questions. The interview was concerned with participants' knowledge of multiple sclerosis; the physical characteristics of their own disease; diagnosis; the ways in which people's lives were affected by the illness; how they managed their illness; their feelings; and concerns about treatment and health care.

As in the content of the questions, the development of categories was theoretically driven. Thus, participants' knowledge of illness was categorised according to biomedical knowledge and social science research (which makes distinctions between the onset, diagnosis, cause, symptoms, course, prognosis and severity of illness and discusses problems caused by uncertainty and lack of control over the illness). The effects of multiple sclerosis were categorised according to the ICIDH's definition of impairment, disability and handicap. Ways of managing illness were categorised according to Billings' and Moos' definitions of cognitive, behavioural and avoidance coping strategies (which focuses on individual approaches) and rehabilitation literature (which focuses on professional approaches). Emotional reactions were categorised in terms of positive and negative affect (rather than symptoms of depression and euphoria). Concerns about treatment/care were categorised in terms of comments about hospital and community services, formal and informal carers, treatment and therapies, and information and advice.

Categories were refined so that distinctions could be made between participants' accounts of factual information, emotional responses and personal opinions. For example, the category 'diagnosis' was further categorised in terms of the person who made the diagnosis, self-diagnosis, and other diagnosis (factual information); problems with diagnosis (personal opinion); and reactions to diagnosis (emotional response). At this stage, the number of categories was kept to a minimum so that the coding of transcripts would not be too complicated. Codes were assigned to each category and a coding frame drawn up. The coding frame provided clear definitions/descriptions of each category and their respective codes.

Reading and coding transcripts Each transcript was read by two raters - the researcher and a psychology student on placement. The psychology student had no previous involvement with the research project. The coding frame was tested out on transcripts from the pilot study. When both raters felt adept in using the coding frame transcripts from the main study were analysed. The raters worked independently. Each transcript was read and coded repeatedly until the raters were satisfied with the precision of their own analyses. The first ten transcripts were compared to assess the inter-rater reliability of the coding frame. High levels of consistency were found between the raters: the mean percentage agreement between the raters was 87.6%. However, agreement fell to 71% when text coded by one rater but missed by the other was counted as a measure of disagreement. Oversights by either one of the raters were more common than actual differences in the way texts were coded. When disagreements occurred, justifications for the chosen codes were discussed until a consensus was reached.[20] When the raters could not agree both codes were excluded from the final analysis. The final version of transcripts included those codes which had been agreed by each rater.

Refining the categories and counting frequencies Each coded unit was copied onto a index card. Each index card was identified by the relevant coding category. Participant's serial number, accommodation status and sex and the page number reference for each coded unit were also written on each card. This system enabled easy access to the units in the original transcripts; identified the source of the quote; and enabled coded units to be sorted into piles according to accommodation and sex group criteria for comparison purposes.

Responses contained within each category were further classified in terms of the direction and content of the remarks made. For example, responses in the 'aetiology' category were sorted into separate piles; firstly to distinguish between those who gave explanations for the cause of multiple sclerosis from those who gave no explanation; and secondly, to identify the different causes of multiple sclerosis reported. Separate piles represented new sub-categories. Sub-categories were combined when there were similarities between the categories. For example, two reported causes of multiple sclerosis - 'shock of cancer' and 'pregnancy' - were initially sorted into separate sub-categories, but later combined to form a new sub-category defined as 'triggers'. Multiple causes given by individual participants were easily identified by sorting cards into piles according to serial number.

The card index system was a useful means of delving into the data and investigating connections between coded units by making constant comparisons within categories and between participants. Whereas the original categories were defined by validated theories, sub-categories were based on participants' own descriptions and explanations of illness. Finer grained analysis of the data was a process of moving from data towards theory and from theory back towards the data.[21] The 'aetiology' category above demonstrates this process: the category was defined by theory, lists from the data defined sub-categories and the rationale for combining certain sub-categories was based on theory.

Sub-categories were the units of measurement for frequency counts. Frequencies were based on the number of participants reporting a theme rather than the actual occurrence of themes within the transcripts. The most frequently reported themes were interpreted as dominant themes for the sample. However, less frequently reported themes were also included in the results (rather than treated as aberrant), because they illustrated the complexity and variety of issues raised.

Presentation of findings Results from the above processes were presented in terms of five broad themes:

i)   understanding of multiple sclerosis;
ii) the consequences of multiple sclerosis on participants' lives;
iii) management of illness;
iv) the emotional impact of illness;
v)   opinions about care.

The first theme, 'understanding of multiple sclerosis', included the following coding categories: aetiology, onset, diagnosis, course, prognosis, severity, impairments, secondary symptoms, control and uncertainty. The categories 'impairment' and 'secondary symptoms', were separated from the other consequences of illness (disability and handicap), because they were integral to participants' descriptions of their disease. The second theme, 'consequences of illness', included the categories disability, handicap and opinions about carers. The last category was included here because it was often directly linked to participants' accounts of the ways in which disability affected their lives. The third theme, 'management of illness', included the categories which defined personal approaches to coping with multiple sclerosis only (cognitive, behavioural and avoidance strategies). Service approaches to managing illness (the categories 'services', 'equipment' and 'regimens') were reported in the fifth theme because they were closely related to opinions about care. The fourth theme, 'emotional impact of illness' included the categories positive and negative affect and fears about illness. The last theme, 'opinions about care' included the categories opinions about staff, hospital and community services, treatment, information and advice, and, as already mentioned, service approaches to managing illness.

The five main themes were described and interpreted using a limited number of excerpts from the transcripts rather than quoting examples from the entire sample. Nevertheless, all the participants are represented in the excerpts selected. Pseudonyms are used to disguise the identity of participants. Themes derived from content analysis were then compared to results from the

113

quantitative measures (hassles, uplifts, coping, self-esteem and measures of adaptation) to explore the links between perceptions of illness and stress in adaptation to multiple sclerosis. Findings from both methods are presented in Chapter Seven.

Summary

Qualitative and quantitative research

This chapter began by distinguishing between qualitative and quantitative research methods and their respective advantages and disadvantages. Both approaches were used in the study in order to assess the role of perceptions of illness, stress and coping on adaptation. Theory and methodology were intertwined: the insiders' perspective is grounded in qualitative research, whereas the transactional model of stress tends to use quantitative research. In line with these orientations, semi-structured interviews were designed to record personal experiences of illness and psychometric scales were used to measure hassles, uplifts, coping strategies, self-esteem and adaptation (satisfaction with life and health). Both methods were used to identify factors important to people with multiple sclerosis in the process of adaptation to illness.

The aims of the research

The aims of the research can be summarised:

i)   to investigate personal accounts of multiple sclerosis from the perspective of people diagnosed with the illness;

ii)   to assess the role of hassles, uplifts, coping strategies and self-esteem in adaptation to illness;

iii) to compare people with multiple sclerosis living in institutions with people with multiple sclerosis living at home on points (i) and (ii);

iv)   to integrate findings from (i) and (ii) to give a more detailed understanding of the ways in which people with multiple sclerosis manage and adapt to their illness.

The sample

Purposive sampling procedures were used to select people who were not newly diagnosed and had not experienced any major stressful life events in the last year. Equal proportions of men and women were selected. Most importantly, purposive sampling ensured the inclusions of two equally represented groups - people who lived in institutional settings and people who lived in their own homes. Little research has been carried out with the first mentioned group. The average age of participants was 58 years. The mean age at diagnosis was 38 years and the mean duration of the illness was 16 years. On average, people had lived permanently in an institutional settings for 5 years. The sample consisted of married (19 people) and single (21 people) individuals. The majority were severely disabled - 28 people used wheelchairs indoors and outdoors. People living in institutional settings tended to be older, and were more severely disabled than people living at home. People living in institutions were more likely to be single, whereas people living at home were more likely to be married.

Measures

The semi-structured interview was designed to collect personal accounts of illness. Psychometric scales were used to measure stress, coping, self-esteem and adaptation. The overview was designed to collect participants global evaluations of the topics covered in the interview before hand. The content of the semi-structured interview was based on a literature review of personal experiences of illness. Psychometric measures were selected on the basis that they had been used on people with chronic illnesses and met validity and reliability standards.

Data collection

A pilot study was carried out to test the suitability of the research measures. Some alterations were necessary before the final interview schedule was drawn up. The interview procedure was described. The role of the researcher in influencing the nature of interviews was discussed.

Data analysis

Statistical analyses were carried out on the quantitative data. Content analysis was applied to the qualitative data. The rationale and steps involved in both were described.

Notes

1. Pollitt et al (1990) comment on the unfortunate preference to do no research in health policy, (although when research is carried out economic models are preferred to ethnography), and the tendency to use 'practitioner theory' - i.e. solve a problem by talking to experienced practitioners in the field.

2. Crises at home were often associated with the health of another member of the family. However, the researcher often found during the course of interviews that many women were experiencing crises at home of which the care assistants at the MS Society were unaware or were so accustomed to the problem, that it was no longer perceived to be a crisis.

3. Chamberlain and Zika (1990) Holahan et al (1984) and Delongis et al (1982) all found that 'hassles' were better predictors of psychological symptoms than major life events. Monroe (1983) found this to be the case even when initial symptom status is controlled for statistically. Burks and Martin (1985) and Eckenrode (1984) devised different measures of daily stressors but also found that everyday problems were more effective than life events in predicting psychological symptoms. Critics of the Hassles Scale, however, believe that the items in the scale are confounded with outcome measures such as number of psychological symptoms, (Dohrenward and Shrout, 1985). In response to this criticism, Lazarus (1985) subtracted suspected confounding items from the Hassles Scale, but still found hassles to be a better predictor of psychological symptoms than life events.

4. The Hassles and Uplifts Scales has also been used in the following subject areas: parenting across early childhood (Crnic 1991); dual earner and no-dual earner women (Alport and Culbertson 1987); postpartum depressed mood (Powell and Drotar 1992); globus pharyngis (Deary 1992); rheumatoid-arthritis (Beckman et al 1991); widowhood (Pellman 1992); caring for a family member with dementia (Kinney and Stephens 1989); nursing home residents (Miller et al 1984); hospitalisation and out-patient visitations (Williams et al 1992): 'burnout' within nursing (Hildman et al 1991) an urban African-American community (Roamo et al 1991); the urban poor and lower classes in Pune, India (Lepore et al 1991) and of course students (Blankstein et al, 1991). Comparisons have also be made between older and younger men (Ewedemi and Linn 1987); elderly men and women (Holohan et al 1984); and elderly people, mothers with young

116

children, older students and a cross-section of the community (Chamberlain and Zika 1990).

5. The twelve additional items are as follows: routines, lack of privacy, visitors not turning up, meeting doctor, socially isolated, being a burden, feeling ignored/not listened to, excluded from decision making, mental health, feeling vulnerable, possibility of moving and being restricted.

6. The additional item included was 'routines'. This item was also perceived to be a hassle by some people.

7. The following are examples of the various methodological approaches: (1) interview assessments have been used by Pavlou and Counte (1982), McGlashan et al (1975), Boker et al (1989); (2) open-ended questionnaires and self-report inventories by Pearlin and Schooler (1978), Fleishman (1984), Brooks and Matson (1977 and 1982), Viney and Westbrook (1982), Dittman and Schuttler (1990) and Falloon and Talbert (1981); (3) personality inventories by Nowack (1988), Wheaton (1983); and Vallient (1977); (4) coping checklists by Folkman and Lazuras (1980, 1985 and 1988), Parker and Endler (1990), Billings and Moos (1981), Vitaliano (1985), Aldwin and Revenson (1987), McCrae and Costa (1986).

8. For example, coping with: marital, parental, household economics and occupational strains (Pearlin and Schooler 1978); major life events and chronic strains (Wheaton 1983); caring for a child with severe learning difficulties (Quine and Pahl 1991); severe accident victims (Bulman and Wortman 1977); time of war (Milgram 1986); domestic violence (Mitchell and Hodson 1986); and rape (Ruch and Leon 1986).

9. A special series appeared in the Journal of Consulting and Clinical Psychology entitled "Coping with Medical Illness and Medical Procedures" (Vol. 57, no. 3). Articles included dealt with chronic illness, pain, loss, radiation therapy and the health care setting.

10. More recent examples of the use of the self-esteem scale are the Euridiss project (1990), a major European research project aimed at elucidating the quality of life of people with chronic illness; and the Oldenburger Study (Walstz and Bandura 1990), a national study in Germany, looking at male cardiac patients, their wives and medical doctors in order to assess the relationship between social support and successful adjustment to chronic illness.

11.   Of the most widely used, The Nottingham Health Profile and Sickness Impact Profile are examples of measurements of subjective perceptions of physical symptoms and health; The General Health Questionnaire and Minnesota Multiphasic Personality Inventory for psychological symptoms; The Index of Activities of Daily Living and Expanded Disability Status Scale for functional ability; The Social Support Questionnaire and The Social Adjustment Scale for social health; The Life Satisfaction Index and General Well-Being Schedule for life-satisfaction and The Bradburn Positive Affect Scale for happiness and The Geriatric Center Morale Scale for morale.   Most of these instruments and others are reviewed by Bowling (1991) and McDowell and Newell (1987) in books on measuring health.   Argyle's book, The Psychology of Happiness (1987), mentions life-satisfaction and morale measures and for ratings of functional disability see Kurtzke (1983).

12.   In a review article on the relationship between subjective well-being and physical health, Zautra and Hempel (1984) found that there was an association between the two variables but that methodological problems made it hard to estimate the extent of the relationship. Campbell et al (1976) found that although health was rated as the most important factor in happiness, satisfaction with health was only the eighth strongest predictor of life satisfaction.   Medley (1980) found that Life Satisfaction was more dependent on Health Satisfaction in late middle age (ages 45-64) and late adulthood (ages 65 and over) than in early adulthood (ages 22-34) and early middle age (35-44).

13.   The pilot project involved nine subjects: five of whom lived in a hospital setting (three women and two men), four at home (two men and two women). Five people had multiple sclerosis. Four people had schizophrenia.   The intention was to test the applicability of the interview schedule across different chronic conditions.

14.   The Nottingham Health Profile (Hunt et al 1981) was used to assess participants' perceptions of their own health.   It is a popular measurement of general health but proved to be inappropriate for this project because only negative aspects of health are covered (e.g. pain, social isolation, physical mobility, emotional reactions, energy and sleep). It gives no indication of good health or well being, apart from the absence of problems. The Self-Esteem Scale and Satisfaction with Life measure were introduced to the schedule as alternatives.   The Overview was also added to improve on the way in which the interviews were concluded.   Modifications made to the Hassles and Uplifts Scales have already been discussed.   Lastly, the number of

rungs on Cantril's Ladder were changed from 0-6 to 0-10 because people were more familiar with rating things 'out of ten'.

15. Strictly speaking scores on the scales represent ordinal measurements (e.g. agreement or disagreement). However, it is common for ordinal scales to be alloted numbers (e.g. 1 to 4), which are treated as if they represent equal numerical intervals, enabling the use of parametric tests.

16. Although it is sometimes difficult to distinguish between the two methods when grounded theorists appear to make a priori assumptions about the data and content analysts in turn, appear to work from data to theory. For example, Blaxter (1983), in her study of women's explanations of the cause of disease, states that content analysis was 'imposed' upon the data, but later on refers to allotting text to 'data-derived categories'. It is often unclear how categories are defined.

17. For example, Kenealy's findings (1989), concerning children's strategies for coping with depression, are based on content analysis of data but we are left in the dark as to how these strategies were identified. She simply says 'The data was subjected to Content Analysis using a set of inductively derived categories, which are grouped under the nine broad headings shown'.

18. In these instances one participant asked for the tape-recorder to be turned off when he disclosed particularly intimate information; two participants were softly spoken and the tape-recordings were of poor quality in places due to the limited sensitivity of the tape-recorder; and in one instance the batteries of the tape-recorder ran out during the course of the interview, making note taking essential.

19. In this case the participant preferred not to be tape-recorded.

20. Disagreement usually involved one or two codes in particular. For example, the category 'problems with diagnosis' (DIA/Pr) was often confused with 'opinions about staff' (OAC/S). Both codes were often appropriate.

21. See Henwood and Pidgeon (1992) for an informative commentary on qualitative research and psychological theory. They refer to an 'constant interplay' between ideas and research experience.

5 Living with multiple sclerosis

Introduction

This chapter provides excerpts from personal accounts of multiple sclerosis as recorded in the semi-structured interviews. Tape-recordings of the interviews were transcribed and analysed. Five themes were identified: an understanding of multiple sclerosis, the consequences of illness, managing illness, the emotional impact of illness and opinions about the care received. These themes were defined by content analysis procedures. In this chapter each theme will be dealt with separately, although, in 'real life', they converge, diverge, appear and disappear as people become familiar with the nuances of their illness.

The interviews concentrated on the sorts of problems participants faced, but drawing up lists of problems or areas of neglect was avoided. Such lists do not capture the complexity and substance of people's lives and are dispiriting to read. Each theme is illustrated with participants' own accounts of their illness, which comprise descriptions, explanations, chronicles and opinions. Frequency scores play a secondary role; they are used to indicate the extent of certain perceptions across the sample. This chapter does not use conventional statistical methods to report findings. Instead common themes are illustrated and interpreted using excerpts from the transcripts. Differences between participants who lived at home and in institutional settings were not obvious in individual accounts of illness. The exception to the case was reference to institutional life, of which half the sample had direct experience and the other half lived with the prospect of being cared for in such places. The second results chapter will provide statistical information concerning the role of hassles, uplifts, coping and self-esteem on adaptation. The third results chapter will incorporate both interview and questionnaire data. Both methods are used to better understand the interplay between physical, psychological and social aspects of multiple sclerosis on adaptation.

For the majority of people in the study, participation was based on altruistic motives; a belief that they had important stories to tell which would be of some benefit to others (i.e. people with multiple sclerosis, carers, the general public, professionals and policy makers). Participation itself was perceived by participants to be a constructive exercise. It is hoped that the following report conveys this message.

Understanding Multiple Sclerosis

In chapter one, biomedical theories about the causes of multiple sclerosis were discussed, along with its diagnosis, prognosis, common symptoms and treatment. In the semi-structured interviews, participants were asked to give their own perspectives on these areas.

Aetiology

The majority of participants (62%) suggested possible causes for multiple sclerosis. These causes tended to refer to personal history rather than underlying pathology. One woman said:

I must have taken it when my youngest child was born for I never felt well after it. I was a very healthy person, never had any bother until then. But I never felt well after she was born... I think it was childbirth. It must have been... Maybe I should tell you, my sister older than me had MS too.

Few people believed there was a single cause for their illness. Multiple factors were often reported in which individual susceptibility and stressful 'triggers' were believed to be jointly responsible for causing the disease:

There is something in us and if it gets cock-eyed or off balance, whether its cold or flu... it will start working on you. Most of the body defences keep it... the majority of us have the protection from it, but sometimes these things breakdown, like cancer. I think something triggers something off in the body.

Like this was probably in my system and I was getting lesions you can't see... [but] if it had been allowed to take its course it mightn't have gone so quick, you know. Now definitely that myelogram made a mess of me.

122

You look for things to pin it on but you can't get anything. The only other thing I can think of, when I was twenty-six I took chicken pox and was very ill...

Only one other person mentioned a virus as being a causative factor, and in this instance personal circumstances were included:

They say a virus or something like that. I mean I had very bad chicken pox when I was fourteen. And then apparently when I was a child I had measles in the family. I was very ill with that. My husband died suddenly you see and... the breast cancer was the shock of that. And then of course the MS followed after that. Whether all those things are connected, I don't really know.

The causes participants attributed to multiple sclerosis can be divided into vulnerability factors, over which people had little control, and stress factors, related to lifestyle or unusual incidents. Vulnerability factors were tied to early childhood, whereas stress factors were more recent and closely associated with the onset of the illness. Place of birth, climate, illness, inherited disease, poor family relationships, and inadequate diet were all mentioned as childhood circumstances which might have had made people more vulnerable to multiple sclerosis in later life. Stress, trauma, accidents, alcohol, work environment, childbirth, medical interventions, and "overdoing it" were all connected to the onset of illness.

Diagnosis

As already mentioned in Chapter One, the onset of multiple sclerosis does not generally coincide with a formal diagnosis. For 78% of the sample, recognising that something was amiss, seeing a doctor and receiving a diagnosis was a lengthy process, and could take up to twenty years:

When I was walking along the street and there's a slight rise in the footpath, my toe would catch and down I would go, but as soon as I was down, I would just bounce back up again before anyone came to help me up. This happened quite often. The knee was giving out on me all the time. And then I went to see the doctor and told him about it... and then he sent me to the specialist, and it was about two years after that before he told me what I had.

As other studies have found (Brunel ARMS Research Unit 1983b; and Radford and Trew 1987), there were many criticisms about the way in which a diagnosis was made. Complaints fall into five categories, relating to: the length of time taken to make a diagnosis, the manner in which a diagnosis was made, not being given any explanation, the use of euphemisms, and never being formally diagnosed. The following descriptions fall into each of these categories:

The specialist knew for two years, but I didn't. I didn't know what I had. He kept examining everything and kept me going back and seeing him again, and eventually he told me.

He said, "This is indicative of MS" to his students. He didn't say it to me. Well this was when I was fairly sure I had MS. But nobody ever put it down on paper, that I had MS.

He said "You've got multiple sclerosis, just try and be happy" and walked away and left me. That's the way I was told.

So he never lifted his head, he was writing away, he says You'll be interested to know, you've got multiple sclerosis.

'I want you to treat yourself as if you've got a bad heart.' And I said 'What?' And he said 'No you haven't got a bad heart but your illness is equivalent to what a bad heart is.'

And then I was told I hadn't MS... after I went home my insurance doctor told me I had MS. I was never diagnosed properly.

Three quarters of the sample were given their diagnosis by a doctor (neurologist or GP); 10% found out by chance (e.g. reading medical notes, overhearing conversation, informed mistakenly by other medical personnel) and the remainder had never been given a formal diagnosis or could not remember exactly how they found out their diagnosis. One man explains how he found out his diagnosis:

So the doctor wrote me a letter and I took it over to the health centre and handed it over to the receptionist. I said "I've come from the hospital and they told me I was on tablets for the rest of my life." She looked at me and said "You're not on tablets - there" and she handed me the card. I read multiple sclerosis. Now I never knew what multiple sclerosis was.

Eighteen percent of the participants reported that they had been misdiagnosed before a proper diagnosis was confirmed. Varicose veins, a touch of polio, torn ligaments, tennis elbow, kidney infection, bad heart and mental disorder were all wrongly diagnosed. Participants themselves (35%) also attributed their symptoms to other disorders, these included stroke, cerebral palsy, tumours, arthritis, paralysis, athelete's injury, heart-attack and cancer. Twenty percent of the sample had made a correct self-diagnosis of multiple sclerosis before confirmation was given. As one woman recalls:

I said, 'Do I have MS?' and here, he said, 'Oh we don't tell people if they have MS.' I said, 'I don't care what you tell people, I want to know if I have it or not. Do I have it?' He said to me 'We are expecting a big break through in about ten years time.' I started to laugh, I said, 'Doctor, I'll be pushing up the daisies by then! So I have MS?' He said, 'Unfortunately.' He didn't know what to say.

For the majority of people the final diagnosis came as a shock:

I was awful taken back when he said that. I just never said a thing. I said 'Oh' and I looked at the doctor just like that, 'Oh, that's not too bad.'

Well the bomb went boom. It took me completely by surprise.

When a terminal illness had been suspected, the diagnosis was a relief:

I was relieved. As long as it wasn't the "Big C", I was quite happy.

Relief was also experienced by those people who preferred knowing what their illness was than living with suspicion:

I said 'Well thank God you have told me what it is, because it was so abnormal to be like this.' I could say to myself it's not laziness, you know.

For a small number of people a diagnosis of multiple sclerosis was meaningless:

Now MS to me was just two letters. It was like me saying you have AB. I didn't know what MS was.

Satisfaction with the care received from doctors generally, will be discussed later in the chapter, but very often these initial contacts influenced the character of further interactions.

Prognosis and course

In clinical terms, the prognosis of multiple sclerosis is judged by combining the degree of disability with the duration of the disease. Moderate disability ten years after onset is accepted as being an indicator of severe form of the disease. Duration of illness in this study was calculated from time of formal diagnosis rather than onset and ranged from two to forty-three years, with a mean score of twenty years. All the participants had at least moderate disability. In clinical terms, then, the participants could be categorised as having a 'severe' disease.[1] Participants were asked how severe they thought their illness was. Judgements were generally based on social comparisons which often referred to degree of disability:

> Well it can't be that severe 'cos I've seen a lot of patients who are worse off than me. I think I'm very fortunate. I'm able to get out of the house and I think I've got a quick enough mind, you know, to keep up with this MS.

> I could be a lot worse indeed. I see other ones in here far worse off than myself, so I do.

Comparisons were also made between multiple sclerosis and other diseases, between respondents who were of different sexes, of different marital states and between those had been diagnosed with multiple sclerosis at an early or late age in life. Most people were able to make a favourable prognosis of their own illness within one of these comparisons. This strategy entailed minimising the severity of illness. Minimisation was also achieved by concentrating on abilities, rather than disabilities, or by localising illness to one part of the body:

> I have my neck, and I have a good mind, eyesight, and speech.

> Well, I wouldn't say it was all that severe. Its only that one leg.

> I had multiple sclerosis of the right leg, still do have.

Distinctions have been made between a relapsing and remitting or a progressive course in multiple sclerosis. The majority of participants (88%) believed that their illness had gradually deteriorated:

> I wasn't in the wheelchair immediately, it was over time. It grew to more and more. I mean I'm gradually going down. It's not absolutely stable.

> I've got slower, walking and doing things.

> It's not there all the time. It kind of keeps coming and going.

The course of multiple sclerosis was also perceived to be influenced by the appearance of other illnesses. Just under half the sample (42.0%) referred to additional problems with their multiple sclerosis and the presence of other problems such as asthma, diabetes, arthritis, angina, hernia and hysterectomy. Considering the mean age of the sample (58 years) this is not surprising, since prevalence of disability increases with age and is highest amongst the elderly. It is also a reminder that a diagnosis of multiple sclerosis does not exclude the occurrence of other unrelated health problems.

Symptoms

Starting with the most common, the ten most frequently mentioned symptoms related to problems with: tiredness/fatigue, vision, sensations, incontinence, spasms, pain, weakness, control of movements, balance, and memory:

> *It's called the MS tiredness. It's hard to explain but you have energy for nothing. You sometimes have no energy to live but you have to get on with it. The tiredness is unbelievable.*

> *There's awful fatigue, everyone's like that. Some people have never wakened up right.*

> *I'm incontinent so I don't like going out. You're afraid of going to the toilet all the time. I'm all right in the house, well sometimes I have a mishap.*

> *I always have cold feet and legs. It's a symptom of MS you know.*

> *I have a sensation in my legs, like pins and needles.*

> *The weakness was very severe, even in the early stages.*

> *First of all it affected by eyes - my vision became blurred.*

> *The first thing that really struck me was the loss of balance.*

> *I have spasms - it started in my legs and ended up in my stomach.*

> *My memory gets bad now too.*

> *My muscles didn't seem to co-ordinate properly.*

Speech problems, hearing, having a "dull mind", sexual problems, headaches and "bad nerves", breathlessness, sleep disturbance and trigeminal neuralgia were also reported. Pain often resulted from the latter symptom:

> *I had awful pain. I couldn't have borne my lips touching, it was so severe. I couldn't talk. I couldn't do anything. I would sit and wait until that pain went away. It was awful.*

Sometimes infections, bedsores, drowsiness, weight gain, loss of appetite, vomiting, circulatory disturbance, impotence, posture problems and contractures, were the main problems reported. These might be described as being secondary symptoms arising from medication, certain treatments or wheelchair use, but they were often more severe than those of the primary disease, multiple sclerosis itself:

I have sores on my bottom. Can't get them cleared up. That's been going on for two years now. I've had everything done, tried everything, and still can't get them cleared up. They sort of way clear up, then all of a sudden just breaks down again. The wife copes with everything. Any dressings I have to get done she does.

Whenever I'm sitting in the wheelchair my legs are bent and whenever I'm lying in bed my legs are bent, so they're never straight. I can feel the tightness and that's when the pain comes at the knee. I would say 'Straighten the knee but take it easy.'

To conclude, participants' understanding of multiple sclerosis was founded, essentially, on personal experience and contact with people with multiple sclerosis. As in biomedical knowledge and clinical practice, uncertainty played a crucial role in participants' perception of multiple sclerosis:

They say that MS can be inside you for a long time without you knowing and it can happen any time. It's an uncertain illness because it can either go slowly or fast. You can't be sure, only there's no cure for it. People do have remissions, which is a strange thing. It means I'll never work again and that I don't know when the end's going to be, you know, how long you've got.

Multiple sclerosis continued to be a 'mysterious' and unpredictable illness, in terms its cause, course, prognosis, treatment and cure, for 78% of the sample.

Another pervading theme was control over illness:

Well, I've no control over it taking away my ability to do things. I've control in as much as it's not going to be my boss. It's got my body, but I hope it won't run away with my mind. As a patient, as I am at present, I have no control. I am living, I'm eating, I get along, I get by.

When participants were asked whether they felt they had any control over their illness, 70% felt they had no control over multiple sclerosis, 15% felt they did have some control, and a further 15% were unable to answer the question.

The accounts above reveal that uncertainty and lack of control were not necessarily negative factors. Uncertainty was both a source of distress, as illustrated above, but also a source of hope and optimism:

> *I just hope it's going to improve. I hope when I'm in the nursing home to be able to write.*

> *It's burnt out more or less. I hope it has any rate.*

In terms of control, distinctions were made between having physical, psychological and social control over multiple sclerosis. Whilst the above example shows that mental control over illness was perceived to be a personal accomplishment, control over the physical characteristics of the illness was relinquished. The disease was blamed for the individual's physical status and the medical system for the individual's lack of social status. Individuals were able to maintain a sense of self-worth and competence by absolving themselves from responsibility over their physical and social circumstances, but crediting themselves with psychological control over the illness.

Consequences of Multiple Sclerosis

The WHO's classification of impairments, disabilities and handicaps (ICIDH) has been discussed already. The consequences of multiple sclerosis on participants' lives were assessed using this framework. The impact of impairment was covered in the previous section, in terms of common symptoms. The nature of 'disability' and 'handicap' will be analysed here.

Disability

Disability, according to the ICIDH, refers to restrictions or inability to perform normal activities. In the study, the five most frequently reported disabilities were in relation to: mobility, self-care, activities/hobbies, housework and movement.

Mobility All the participants described problems with walking, standing and not falling, as one woman said:

> *I can't walk fast. I can't walk in a straight line. I was able to walk but I could feel this staggering you see. That has all happened in the last four or five years, in the wheelchair and all the rest of it.*

Self-care Sixty-eight percent of the sample referred to problems in dressing, washing, eating and toileting. The frustration this can cause was expressed clearly by one man:

> *It's the little things, Sarah, they seem unimportant to you and to most people. To be able to lift a cup up or feed myself with a spoon. To have to sit here, to have someone treat you like a baby. It can be degrading, having other people to do what you took for granted so long ago.*

Activities/hobbies Not being able to take part in once valued interests, leisure pursuits and pastimes was another consequence of illness, as one woman relates:

> *When they were up dancing you know, you see them all dancing. It's wee things like that there, that I can't do. Or say going down to the shops or going to town. Just wee simple things like that. I miss that. Although, don't get me wrong, I still do them, but I can only do them to a certain extent now. I can't go the whole hog since I had MS.*

> *Not being fit to drive a car, that is one of the things I miss most of all.*

Housework Both men and women, and people living in hospital and at home referred to difficulties in performing housework:

> *I was very fond of housework and I couldn't do the things that I used to be able to do.*

> *I couldn't clean windows. I couldn't climb on a chair, can't go upstairs. Just everyday things that you realise you can't do.*

Movements Restrictions relating to movements are implicated in all the above categories, but very often limitations in this area were made explicit:
> *Fine movements are hard to do. Like writing is difficult to do, trying to hold a cup, hold a fork even.*

Striking about these experiences of disability was the significance of simple, mechanical and often spontaneous activities. The consequence of such restrictions was dependency on others, which was perceived to be one of the worst aspects of disability for many people:

> *It's a living hell, you are so dependent on other people to do everything for you.*

Having to depend on people, what you never had to do in your life before, you know. It gets you down realising you have to depend on people.

Taking care of personal needs, as a result of disability, often meant relying on 'carers'. The detrimental affect this had on family relationships was a source of concern:

As I say, I hate the thought of ever restricting him. I hate being away from home [but] I like to give him a break.

My husband does everything in the house anyway but he gets cheesed off.

MS doesn't just affect the person who has it, but the whole family. My son used to hide the wheelchair so his friends wouldn't see. The girls couldn't do enough for you [but] you don't want to impose too much because they've got their life.

Jane's not able to look after me. She would like to have me at home, you know. She thinks she's letting me down [but] it causes her more problems with me being home.

On rare occasions, dependency was felt to have a positive affect on the family:

Nothing's too much trouble for them. They've got used to it like. It was hard to begin with seeing my family was so young. It's brought me closer to everyone in the family. The family is stronger.

Unfortunately, for six people in the study the appearance of multiple sclerosis was held responsible for marital break-up. The demands that disability factors put on participants and their families can not be over-emphasised:

Whenever I took the MS everything went all right for a while with my marriage. Then my wife, she felt she was going to dominate everything. She was getting attendance allowance and I wasn't. None of it was being spent on me. It didn't matter what I was doing, it was always wrong. Bantering all the time about money. If it wasn't money I wasn't driving the car right. Always telling me to do this and to do that... I see her now and again. It's lonely living on your own but it's better living in peace. I still maintain 'til this day, if we hadn't been separated I would have been in a wheelchair four or five years ago.

According to the ICIDH, handicap can be defined as socio-cultural disadvantages which result from impairment and disability. However, handicap is often an outcome of external/environmental factors, over which individuals have little influence. The five most frequently reported handicapping problems were related to: employment, environmental restrictions, stigma, social role and long-term hospital/residential care.

Employment Becoming unemployed as a result of illness was the most common outcome faced by participants (68%). Unemployment was not always related to disability. In some cases, participants had been given notice by their employers once diagnosis had been made public:

> *I just waited until someone said 'Have you got MS?' and someone did, and I said 'Yes, that's what I have.' So, I wasn't in the job long after that. I just had to give up the job. It was a sorry thing too.*

A number of participants had taken the advice of their doctors and left employment:

> *He just said 'You have MS, no more work for you. Stop working.' I had to give up the business. I had to sell it.*

Loss of employment was nearly always a source of regret:

> *I really loved my career. If there was this miracle cure, I'd probably be straight back to it you know.*

> *The fact I can't work anymore, which I loved doing. The fellas out of work come up and sit and chat with me and bring back memories to me - that's even worse.*

Environmental restrictions The majority of participants related how physical barriers within the environment prevented them from taking part in many social activities:

> *Well I'm terribly isolated because I'm in a flat, a multi-storey flat, believe it or not, I'm ten floors up.*

> *You can't do what you want to do, you can't go where you once went. The only travelling I do now is with my eyes.*

> *Well I always worked all my life, I loved working, and then all of a sudden you're imprisoned. You can't get out anywhere.*

I haven't been on a bus in years, socialising very little.

Stigma A particularly painful aspect of multiple sclerosis was dealing with negative social attitudes towards people with illness and being discredited. "Does he take sugar?" incidents were often recalled:

People's attitude with you are quite different. If there's someone with you they talk to that person, instead of asking you what you think. The attitude that because you're in a wheelchair you're mentally deficient.

Complaints about lack of awareness, ignorance or just plain thoughtlessness were also referred to:

A bloke came out to see me and said "Oh, you're unemployable.

I was unsteady and everyone thought you were drunk.

Very few will come to help you. I think it's fear of the unknown, so they shy away from it.

We came up in the wheelchairs and they said that's for customers only. He said you can't sit there.

They say well it's good you can accept it, but what can you do. People would say 'You wouldn't know you have MS.' I said 'Well you don't have a sign sticking up.' People you know say 'Och, you wouldn't know you have MS, you always look the same.' but looks aren't everything, you know.

You're trying to eat and someone's pointing to you, so you stop going out. There's lots of restaurants and bars where you're not accepted.

Negative attitudes and prejudice were especially noticeable for wheelchair users. When the symptoms of multiple sclerosis were less visible, people's lack of understanding was more an issue. One man concluded:

They need educating. You don't want to be patronised. You don't want people to feel sorry for you.

Stigma had a negative affect on participants' perceptions of themselves - their identities were damaged and often felt to be not repairable.

Social roles As already mentioned being "unemployable" for many was an unwelcome new role. New, unwanted identities affected participants' perceptions of themselves:

I very seldom go [to the shop] during the day 'cos... I'm self-conscious. I would think when I'm walking up the road, they're laughing.

I might be feeling all right, but at the same time I'm useless.

Your expectations are a lot lower than the normal person.

Well it's hard to accept. In a wheelchair you're just a cripple. That's all. I'm just a cripple, that's all.

It's just a different way of living, it's a way of life. You don't feel normal. That's rotten isn't it?

Important family, friendship and relationship roles are also affected:

You can't be a normal mum, which is what I had, oh such plans for, you know.

You lose a lot of friends when you take ill like this. My friends make a lot of promises but don't bother a lot of time. That's it, you never see them.

Ordinary relations with people of both sexes. Things you would take some bother with people. That's what I hate about it - restricting your relationships with people. Things I would have like to have done but couldn't. That's the big disappointment.

Although half of the participants perceived loss of social roles to be a consequence of multiple sclerosis, an equal proportion of people were able to link their condition with positive role changes:

I never talked so much in my life since I took MS. I never could have got into a crowd and talked the way I do now. From when I took MS, there's nobody I don't talk to.

Well there's one good thing - I find I can help other people a lot. Other people would come to me and ask for confidential things and are kind of way trusting. It does something for you like. Listening and giving advice, it's not always right but at times you can do it.

When you're able-bodied you don't think of things. I've found I can see things from both sides now.

MS is good in that it introduces you to other [MS] people

Long-term hospital/residential care One of the most obvious consequences of multiple sclerosis was having to leave home and live in communal establishments:

> *So a social worker came to me and she said there was a couple of homes that suited me. So I said for the convenience of the family, I would go to 'x'. The following night I was lying there and I couldn't take it in. I had a feeling I was out of my house for good. I just thought there was nothing I could do about it.*

> *It's life, me in here separated from my family. Although my family come up here, I'm not with them as much as I should be. I would prefer to be at home but this is the next best thing. I'd like to be fit and at home.*

> *It was near wrecking her back, lifting me about, her back was killing her. She said 'I can't work with you anymore. I have to get you in somewhere.' So that's when she got me into hospital.*

For some participants living at home, the prospect of living in a hospital or residential home was a constant threat. One man confided that his biggest worry was his marriage breaking up, resulting in him being "confined" to a "welfare home". In contrast, another man, living in hospital, reflected that his life at home had been "ruled by the care and carers" when nurses came "at any time between half-seven and nine" at night to put him to bed. Three quarters of the sample agreed that life with multiple sclerosis had disrupted family life, employment prospects, relationships with friends and changed their attitude to life. How people coped with these changes is the subject of the next theme.

Managing Illness

Integral to participants' reports of illness were their attempts to manage their illness. The measurement of coping included in the study was used as a guide to identify the ways in which people managed their illness. Accordingly, methods of coping were categorised as either cognitive, behavioural or avoidance. Nineteen cognitive, 18 behavioural and 15 avoidance coping strategies were recorded. They are listed below:

> Cognitive - Perseverance/Maintain control, Accept it/Face facts, Maintain independence, Fight it, Take one day at a time, New perspective, Get on with things/Get used to it, Self-blame, Positive thinking/Bright side of life, Faith, Adjust and learn to live with it,

Minimise, Humour, Social comparison, Careful planning/be prepared, Discipline, Set standards/example, Maintain hope, and Talk to self.

Behavioural - Ask for help/advice, Write about experience, Exercise, Fund-raising, Self-help, Try alternative therapies, Read/Collect written information, Monitor illness, Stopped going to doctor, Stopped taking medicine, Attend day-centre, Design tool/aid, Talk to other people with illness, Special diet, Take rests, Talk to relative, Keep to routine and Smoke.[2]

Avoidance - Keep feeling to self/contain feelings, Fate, Pass illness off, Don't ask any questions, Let illness take over/Nature take its course, Put illness to back of mind/Don't think about it, Give up, Avoid contact with other people (with or without illness), Get drunk, Avoid family discussions, Try not to think about future or/and past, Wishful thinking/Escapism, Keep busy, Deny that illness is really happening and Think about other things.

The list consists of many strategies not included in the scale devised by Billings and Moos (1980). For example, discipline, setting standards/example, fight it and self-help:

I wanted to discipline myself and also I wanted to discipline my children. I didn't want them to see me as just someone lying around the house.

I just think MS is the sort of thing... if you don't work with it, it takes you over. If you don't fight it, it takes over.

We have formed a group now. It's a self-support group. Everybody on the committee has MS and we do our own thing for our own selves. We give each other moral support.

Each participant used a variety of strategies. For example, the statement below made by one man, consists of seven different coping strategies (accept it/face facts, talk to self, positive thinking, humour, social comparison, get on with it/get used to it and adjust/learn to live with it):

I made up my mind early that this thing was getting me and there were certain things I couldn't do. I've said to myself, I'd make the best of this what ever happens. I'll just live and laugh at life if I can. There's people that go out in the morning and they're perfectly healthy. They go to their work and there's an accident and they're maimed for life. I got time to get used to my illness, little by little, and I'm more fortunate than they are. I've sort of like taken a course on how to get along with a handicap.

Interestingly, all of the strategies mentioned in the above statement are cognitive. An example of behavioural strategies is provided by another participant:

I do believe that reflexology helps MS. I'm monitoring it. I'm studying it now, along with the girl that applies it. I've tried acupuncture. I think a good diet is good for everybody because, in a sense, it's your own treatment. If ever there was a treatment to come along in years to come, I would like to be as fit and healthy as I can for that.

Try alternative therapies, monitor illness, read/written information, and Special diet are all behavioural strategies covered in the above example. Avoidance strategies also take many forms:

I don't go out of my way to find out what's wrong or anything like that there, partly because I'm scared.

All I want is just to live my life, just as long as I'm left alone, all I want is peace and quiet. I've given up, you know, the fight with the MS. Where's the sense. I just want to be left alone.

Don't ask questions, avoid contact with other people and give up, appear in these two reports.

No one strategy or combination of strategies appeared to be preferred over another within the transcripts of the sample. The exception to the case, however, was when faith became an important way of coping with illness. For seven people in the study, faith not only helped them manage their illness, it gave meaning to their lives as a whole. For some people faith was a very personal or private source of support. It represented the development of a personal relationship/dialogue with God:

You get angry and you ask yourself 'Why?' but you don't know why. Now I've got faith about God I've got a different perspective. There's a reason for it somewhere. You just have to accept it and someday I will walk. I know if I'm good enough to go - to be with Him - I'll not be in a wheelchair. I'll be sitting beside Him or holding onto Him.

I don't like complaining about MS because I say my God has been good to me. He's been really good to me. If I had no faith I don't know what I'd do. If I had no faith I don't know what I would do! I just thank God everyday that he gives me every breath to breathe. I thank God for it.

137

For other people faith helped because it offered an important source of social support:

I've a very caring church. At the weekend two of the members come out, one on Saturday to get me up and then there's one comes on Sunday morning to take me to church. It's important to me. I know that they pray for me regularly at the prayer meetings and sometimes you can feel the benefit of all that. When I go to church they all shake hands and genuinely ask how I am and all. If I miss a Sunday there's nearly a court enquiry as to why, you know, if I'm not well or what! I seldom miss church. I'm very fortunate that way. Even if the weather's bad, I still go.

For one person faith was a means of sustaining a strong identity in the face of illness, but it also tormented him:

Well you get people saying 'Keep your head up. Keep your chin up.' They can't tell you why. Everybody asks 'Why?' but there is no answer. 'Oh, it's for a greater purpose' they say. 'What purpose?' I say. They say 'It's God's love. He loves you.' But If this is love, what's hate?... Well it does help you to see what is important in life... you can have tons of money and everything but you can't take it with you... To me there's only one God and doesn't matter what way your religion is, but I'm still proud to be a Protestant.

A clearer picture of coping preference was found when participants were asked in the Overview 'Generally, how do you cope with your illness?" Fifteen different responses were identified and classified:

Cognitive - Accept it/Face facts, Adapt/learn to live with it, Fight it, Faith, Positive thinking, Humour, Social comparison, Take one day at a time, Set standards, and Maintain hope.

Behavioural - Ask for help/advice and Exercise.

Avoidance - Put illness to back of mind/Don't think about it, Keep feeling to self/Contain feelings and Keep busy.

The five most common strategies were:

Keep feeling to self/Contain feelings	(25.0%)[3]
Put illness to back of mind/Don't think about it	(22.5%)
Positive thinking	(22.5%)
Ask for help/advice	(20.0%)
Accept it/Face facts	(17.5%)

138

Each of these strategies is equally frequently used. Out of the fifty coping strategies identified however, these five seem to be the most prominent. All, bar accept it/face facts, are included in the Method and Focus of Coping Scale. This scale is, therefore, measuring the most general coping strategies used by the sample.

Emotional Impact of Illness

The emotional consequences of chronic illness have been relatively neglected in research terms. The tendency to medicalise emotional reactions as symptoms of depression has already been mentioned in Chapter Three. More is known about people's beliefs and attitudes concerning illness than about the feelings involved. The interview gave participants the opportunity to express both their thoughts and feelings, if they so desired. A wide range of emotions were reported from fear, anxiety, hopelessness, shame, sadness and frustration to contentment, hope, pride, happiness, relief, and compassion. Three major emotional consequences of illness identified in the analysis were fear, hopelessness and sadness. On the positive side, pride and contentment were common. Reports on fears were a response to a direct question in the interview. Emotional responses were tied to many of the themes already presented.

Fear

Fear was connected to deterioration in illness, greater dependency, mobility, children's health and pain:

What I do fear was if I was to deteriorate to a degree in future years. I would hate to be completely bedridden.

I would fear losing my tongue. I would fear losing my eyesight and hearing, all my senses.

I fear in case I can't use my hands and my speech goes. I fear that very much.

That frightens me, only that I have to be taken care of by others and I can see how difficult it is for them sometimes.

I have an awful fear of falling. I have another fear of breaking bones. I wouldn't walk for them (doctors). The fear was terrible.

Is Simon (son) going to get it? That is the one fear, real fear I have.

Pain - haven't what you call a very high pain barrier.

Fear of needing a wheelchair was also common for those people still mobile with walking aids:

I fear the wheelchair.

What do I fear? I never thought I would be in a wheelchair.

I hate the thought of being in the chair. I wouldn't be happy in it.

Whether wheelchair users or not, the appearance of a wheelchair symbolised both greater dependency and physical deterioration. It was a significant 'landmark' in participants' personal histories of their illness:

I didn't want to go into a wheelchair. Thought if I beat the thing, but anyway, I went into a wheelchair.

The prospect of needing an electric wheelchair left some participants in a turmoil: it offered greater independence, in terms of mobility, but at the expense of greater physical dependence:

I could go down to town in an electric chair but then different people say once you get in an electric chair you start to depend on them, you lose the power in your arms altogether.

A different fear - of getting infections - was very troubling because it signified the fragility of people's lives:

One thing I fear, a lot of people fear with illness, is getting an infection because that can kill you.

The threat of death and the process of dying was a deep concern for 25% of sample:

[I fear] I just wouldn't waken some morning. I'd slip away during the night and die.

One man spoke of euthanasia:

I fear being left like a vegetable without having the right to end my life - where you aren't able to do anything about it or not have the means to do anything... [I would like] to be able to use the means before I reach that stage. I would like to have the right to make that decision myself.

Fears about death were closely associate with feelings of hopelessness.

Twenty-seven and a half percent of the sample felt that life was hopeless. Five people (all men) confided that they had seriously contemplated suicide. Some of them had not spoken of it to anyone before:

I've wanted to do away with myself a couple of times.

When I've had my bad days I wished that the Lord would take me and totally finish with it altogether. I get that, ah, feeling at regular times when I'm on my own. I've never thought of talking to anyone, I don't know whether I could or not. There's some days just when I'm up in the room on my own and it comes into my head. I've never done anything about it, like maybe it's just a thought that comes into my mind.

There's even times now where you wouldn't care if you tried to end it.

Multiple sclerosis was described as a "living death" for others because:

Well that's it. I'm finished now. I'm good for nothing.

There's not much pleasure in living. You have nothing to look forward to. It's never ending, it's very disheartening.

I hadn't the heart to go and look for another job. The heart was knocked out of me. I didn't even try.

I've got to the stage I couldn't care less.

It's a living hell. Everything is hopeless without health.

It's got worse. Now it's hopeless.

Hopelessness often led to feelings of frustration, anger and self-blame:

It annoys me because you can't do anything.

It's so frustrating. It's just bloody awful.

I can get very cross with myself, very cross with myself.

It does make you bitter.

Sadness

Twenty-eight percent of the sample also reported feelings of sadness, sorrow and regret. This was particularly associated with the early period of illness:

> *I cried with him. 'Why did I let you marry me? You can get divorced if you want.' He hates to see me crying. At times I was really upset.*

> *If you'd come in I would have just burst out crying.*

Sometimes participants referred to depression:

> *I sort of went into the depths of depression.*

> *There's times when you get depressed by it.*

Sadness was also expressed as feeling "down" or worthless:

> *It really does get me down.*

> *It really gets me down. It made me feel very low. It didn't do anything for my confidence.*

> *I don't know how I manage to keep my spirit up. Now and again I would weep.*

> *It's a cruel, cruel disease dear. It is well and truly a cruel disease. What hurts me most about MS is when I see a man with MS - a big strong man and just cut down. It really hurts me. I cry about it. It really hurts.*

Sadness for some was part of the grieving process. Eighty-eight percent of the sample felt they had lost something as a result of their condition. Participants felt they had lost the following:

> home, family life, intimacy, marriage, financial security, employment, physical abilities, independence, social life, self-respect, reason for living, role in life, interests and leisure pursuits, normality, health, liberty and dignity.

Pride and contentment

Although participants frequently reported their fears and feelings of sadness and hopelessness, positive feelings were not excluded from individual accounts of illness. Twenty-five percent of the sample had reported feelings of pride and contentment:

I wake up in the morning glad that I'm alive. I kind of look at it that I've got used to it. I don't know why it should matter to me that I'm alive, but I just want to be around. The positive thing is, you could be a hell of a lot worse off than you are. The desires I've had all my life are still there.

I'm happy with my life. I always said that if I could see my children grow up I would be thankful. I've seen my children grow up so I'm quite happy. I have seen my wish fulfilled.

I have too much to live for. I have my three grand-daughters and I think they're wonderful. I would hate to give up.

The way I look at it, when I can do it I want to do it. It makes me feel well when I can do things. I just like doing things for yourself.

I have a routine: I iron on a Monday, I wash on a Tuesday. Then a Wednesday, it's my free day, I can do what I want. I iron on a Thursday to be cleared up to come to the MS Society on a Friday. I work, as I still class it, I work on a Monday, Tuesday, Thursday and Friday and Saturday. And I still have my wee drink on a Saturday night. I live for my Saturday night. I've set my life out. I know what I'm going to do. If I can do that I know I'm winning.

A sense of achievement appeared to underpin feelings of pride and contentment - participants were proud with their own achievements or those of their family and friends. Hope and happiness were also associated with feelings of contentment. However, positive feelings were often overshadowed by a sense of resignation, stemming from recurrent fears and feelings of hopelessness and sadness. When participants spoke about their feelings, they often entrusted the researcher with their most private concerns. The process of confiding was both upsetting and uplifting at times, for the researcher and participants.

Opinions about Care

The semi-structured interview did not include specific questions dealing with people's opinions about care. The opinions recorded below were volunteered by participants themselves during the interviews. Dissatisfaction with medical personnel, particularly doctors, and with health and social services was predominant. Many references were also made to the MS Society (most of the respondents were members of the Society).

143

Dissatisfaction with doctors

Participants were unhappy with the care they received from general practitioners and neurologists. Seventy-seven percent of the comments made about GPs were negative and concerned their lack of competence and unfamiliarity with multiple sclerosis:

I went to the doctor and he didn't know anything about MS.

He would say, "If there is anything I can do for you, you tell me, for I don't know".

There are a lot of GPs too who need to learn about MS.

I'm disillusioned with the medical profession. I feel everything, even if it was a broken arm, it was put down to my MS.

Of the comments made about neurologists, 65% were negative and were connected more to their apparent abrupt and uncaring manner:

"I'm your doctor" he said, "But I can do nothing for you, you know." Well when one of them says they can do nothing for you, except prescribe medicine for you, that was it.

I don't bother going near doctors. I can't be bothered with doctors. I just feel they don't want to know and that's the gospel truth. I went to see the doctor two or three times and he turned around and said to me, "The way you're using that stick your arm will never heal." That's all he said to me. I told myself, what's the point in going to doctors.

Every time I went in, he would say "Walk around that table." I would walk around the table and he would say "Oh, you wouldn't know there was anything wrong with you." I says, "I don't know about that." But he was making me worse every time I went in. I went up to him about my lightness, he said, "Och, it's your imagination." I says "Don't be like that. I should know what's happening to me".

Lack of information and advice was an issue for 58% of the sample:

When I went back to my consultant he says "Go home, don't tire yourself out." But they didn't give me much information. My own GP, he nearly ran out of the door once giving me the information. He just said 'You've MS, ah, sort of take a wee break.' and away he went.

It's like the tax-man, they don't tell you anything. You have to find out about it.

I had no one to advise me on anything. The occupational therapist didn't really know much about me, whether I was living on my own. She told me she didn't think I could ever manage on my own.

From when I took the MS, that's over twenty years ago, I didn't really know what it was. I didn't seem to get any help off anyone. No one told me what to expect or what it consisted about or anything and I was very ignorant of it. I didn't ask. I never asked any doctor about it. I felt if no one was going to tell me that was it. The nurse said maybe the doctor thought it better not to enlarge on it. He knew how ignorant I was about it, I'm sure, I'm certain.

One person suggested that:

A good consultant will say that the MS person knows more about it than he does. But having said that, some of them will say, you know more about it than me, away home. But a good consultant will say, you know more about it than me, tell me. So what I would say is get your consultant to listen. A doctor should listen and learn.

Dissatisfaction with community and hospital services

Some participants felt that they were fighting against the system rather than being helped by it:

If you don't open your mouth you get nothing. You have to beg, you have to get down on your hands and knees and beg for everything.

I had to make a nuisance of myself, pleading and fighting for the service [physiotherapy].

Complaints were also made about the paucity of services (particularly physiotherapy), in the community:

I feel MS people should have physiotherapy everyday but physiotherapy departments in Northern Ireland don't think that way. It's that hard getting it. We got so much hassle I was just ready to forget about it. They couldn't provide physio. You definitely need some.

I get nothing. I don't even get a home-help. I have a social worker but I never see her. I'm living on my own and there's days I can't light the fire. There's days I couldn't stoop down to it. I was asked did I light the fire and could I drive a car. I said I was still able to drive the car and sometimes light the fire, so I wasn't entitled to a home-help. I get a meals on wheels on a Thursday, but other than that, as far as the National Health is concerned, I get nothing.

You don't get treatment 'til you take ill again. They put you on a course of tablets and that's it - see you in four months. You don't have treatment until you take ill or are taken into hospital.

A number of people said that one of the reasons for living in hospital/residential home was the unavailability of facilities in the community:

There were things I could do in hospital - going to the OT and going to the physio and getting exercise - I wouldn't have had at home. So that was the reason, that was what made me think that I'd come to the right decision in going into hospital.

That's one advantage here, there's always staff here to help you. I get physiotherapy regularly. You stiffen up if you don't get this. If I was at home I wouldn't get it.

Access was a problem inside and outside people's homes:

I think the doors could be a bit broader. If I could get into the working kitchen I could do my wee bit of baking.

The powers that be don't consider people in wheelchairs. On the Stoke Road there's only one place where I've seen a recess and that was a pedestrian crossing.

In shops things are in your way. I've found that Texas was the only shop I could get in.

Participants living in hospitals or residential homes were grateful for full-time care and appreciated that services were more obtainable. On the other hand, lack of privacy, unappetising food and lack of activities were severe drawbacks:

You sit and do nothing, you'll be let go like a vegetable.

Not a thing going on. People sleeping. It's very depressing. The nurses haven't the time.

The food's terrible in here. Some days I don't eat it. Lizzy [wife] brings me up my supper. You wouldn't eat it, I'm not joking.

He [owner of residential home] takes us out in the car sometimes. They're all old people. There's one old bloke who seem to have all his faculties, he's the only one I can talk to sensibly.

They haven't got enough nurses. I think if I hit that buzzer it would be five or ten minutes before anyone came up.

Oh it's very good here I must say but it seems to be getting worse off for staff.

One participant living in an institutional setting gave a description of a typical day in his life:

Waiting to get up in the morning and sitting here [in the corridor] to dinner time. Then you go up there and get your dinner in the dining room and then back down here again. Then you're sat here to about twenty-five past one or so and they take you and put you to bed again. That's you in bed for the night, for the day and night, you know, right to next morning. If you hadn't the wee TV in there, you'd have nothing to look at nor to do, you know.

None of the institutional settings in which people lived were designed specifically for the needs of disabled people. In one of the hospitals visited, much of the surrounding grounds were inaccessible to wheelchairs, the dormitory also served as a dining room and living room, and the hospital routine encouraged people to go to bed after lunch where they stayed until the following morning. Two people who lived in residential homes for the elderly were below 60 years of age.

Favourable comments about community facilities were associated with the MS Society. Companionship with people in a similar situation seemed to be the main advantage of this service:

The MS Society was the first place that did help me. I don't know what I would have ended up like if I hadn't this help.

Here you can speak openly and everybody's more or less the same symptoms. So it's the company plus the physio.

I look forward to every Tuesday to come to this [MS] centre, I really do now, 'cos I was sitting looking at four walls before I came here. It was no good. It was awful.

I love coming here [MS centre] because you're sitting with people that have the same things and you're still learning about MS.

Negative remarks emphasised the disproportionate use of funds raised by the Society for biomedical research:

My opinion is that if they spent x thousands upon thousands of pounds on research and they've got nowhere, they should be doing something to make life a wee bit more comfortable for patients now.

Well the thing that annoys me is that the MS and Action MS Societies collect an awful lot of money for research. They spend millions on it. Well they spend millions on research and pennies on patient comfort.

The biomedical concept of rehabilitation is remarkably absent from all these observations, although participants reported that they had received a variety of services; from neurology clinic, Disabled Living Centre, urological service, occupational therapy, physiotherapy, social work service, Housing Executive, home-helps, respite care, day-centres, Twilight scheme, Crossroads service, district nurse to meals on wheels. However, there were some noticeable gaps: only one person had approached a Disablement Resettlement Officer (now known as Disabled Employment Advisory Officer), one person had an appointment with a psychologist, one person had seen a counsellor, one a gynaecologist and no one mentioned use of an educational service. The services received were vital but tended to be concentrated on physical problems and practical needs only.

Summary

This chapter has presented the results of content analysis on the transcripts of semi-structured interviews with people living with multiple sclerosis. The five themes which transpired were: an understanding of multiple sclerosis, the consequences of illness, managing illness, the emotional impact of illness and opinions about care. Each theme has been authenticated with participant's own accounts of their illness. The first theme, 'understanding of illness', demonstrated the efforts people made to make sense out of a disease notable for being unpredictable. Participants often felt let down by the medical profession during the diagnosis period. Two concepts, control and uncertainty, framed people's understanding of illness.

In the second theme, 'consequences of illness', the most common forms of disability (mobility, self-care, activities/hobbies, housework and movements) and handicap (unemployment, environmental restrictions, stigma, social roles and institutional care) were reported. The corollary of disability was dependency on others, in particular carers. Handicap was experienced as altered and often depleted relationships with others and environmental

148

constraints. The illness continued to be a major cause of disruption in people's lives.

'Managing illness' was the third theme to emerge from analyses. This theme is important because it features participants' attempts to deal with illness. People with multiple sclerosis find their own ways of coping with illness, independent of professional rehabilitation services. The effectiveness of different strategies (cognitive, behavioural and avoidance) will be evaluated in the final results chapter. Faith was a strategy used by some people to give meaning to their lives as well as help them manage their illness.

The topic for the fourth theme was the 'emotional impact of illness'. A wide range of emotions were reported but fears, hopelessness and sadness/happiness were most common. Bad feelings were more apparent than good. Fears derived from participants' insecurities (uncertainty, lack of control, dependency and disadvantage). Hopelessness and sadness were tied to loss of health and associated lifestyle. Positive feelings were mostly related to maintaining a sense of pride and achievement. For many, present lives compared unfavourably with previous attainments and aspirations.

The final theme looked at participants' opinions about health care. Interactions with doctors were generally perceived to be disappointing. Community services appeared to be scarce and long-term residential care environments were impoverished. There was little evidence of constructive goal-oriented rehabilitation programmes.

The interviews were concerned with participants' interpretations of multiple sclerosis and how illness had affected their lives. The next results chapter has a different focus: the role of stress and coping on adaptation to the illness is evaluated using standardised instruments.

Notes

1. Phadke (1990) discusses criteria for categorising the prognosis of disease.

2. *Smoke* was categorised as a behavioural strategy rather than an avoidance strategy because in the single example reported, the participant smoked one cigarette a day to ward off severe spasms - smoking was not used to indirectly relieve emotional stress.

3. Percentage figure refers to percentage number of people who used this method to cope with their illness. On average, each participant identified two general coping strategies.

6 Stress, coping and adaptation

Introduction

The life-stories of people with multiple sclerosis are further described in this chapter. The previous chapter was concerned with personal accounts of illness. This chapter broadens the scope of study and looks at daily events, both stressful and uplifting, coping strategies, individuals' sense of personal worth, and satisfaction with their own lives and health. The role of everyday life experiences and individual resources on adaptation will be explored.

The data provided in this chapter were obtained from the instruments outlined in Chapter Four, excluding the semi-structured interview. Results will be presented in the following order: the levels and types of hassles and uplifts reported, preferred coping strategies, ratings of self-esteem and finally, definitions and ratings of satisfaction, with life in general and health in particular. Comparisons will be made between people living at home ('community' group) and people living in long-term residential care facilities ('institution' group). Relationships between the variables will be statistically analysed.

Previous research studies involving the scales in this chapter, have used parametric tests to describe and assess differences in scores between populations. Conventional parametric tests were used in this study to ensure the collection of comparable results. Non-parametric tests were also calculated because of reservations about the nature of the data collected (the relatively small sample size; skewed rather than normal frequency distributions; and the fact that the scales provide ordinal rather than interval levels of measurement). Only results from parametric tests are provided.

However, findings are reported only when significant statistical differences were confirmed by both parametric and non-parametric tests. In fact, parametric and non-parametric tests produced similar findings throughout the study.

The Chi-square test, Mann-Whitney test, t-test, Kruskal-Wallis test and One-way analysis of variance were used to assess whether any statistically significant associations existed between scores on the variables and demographic (sex, age, marital status and residential status) and illness (duration) characteristics. Pearson correlation coefficients and multiple regression analyses were used to assess the relationship between hassles, uplifts, coping and self-esteem and each of the two satisfaction indices. The SPSS+ PC statistical package was used for data analysis.

Hassles and Uplifts

Mean levels and standard deviations of hassles' and uplifts' frequency and intensity scores are given in Table 6.1. There is a significant difference in mean scores between the institution and community groups in terms of perceived *intensity of hassles* (t = 2.12, P < 0.05 (two-tailed)). Hassles were perceived to be more severe for the community group than for the institution group. Other significant differences were as follows: between single[1] and married participants - single people reported fewer *uplifts* than married people (t = 2.47, p < 0.05 (two-tailed)); between older[2] and younger people - younger people reported more *hassles* (t = 2.04, p < 0.05 (two-tailed)) and of greater *intensity* (t = 2.23, p < 0.05 (two-tailed); and between those with shorter and longer duration of illness[3] - people with illness duration under ten years reported more *hassles* (F = 4.72, p < 0.01). There appears to be a tendency for people who have many hassles to also have many uplifts.

Table 6.1
Means and standard deviations of hassles and uplifts frequency and intensity scores by multiple sclerosis groups

| | HASSLES | | | | UPLIFTS | | | |
| | Frequency | | Intensity | | Frequency | | Intensity | |
	X[a]	SD	X	SD	X	SD	X	SD
MS-TOTAL (N=40)	20.6	12.6	1.96	0.44	27.0	11.9	1.77	0.31
MS-Institution (N=20)	17.6	9.0	1.82	0.41	24.6	12.6	1.72	0.33
MS-Community (N=20)	23.6	15.1	2.10[b]	0.43	29.4	10.99	1.81	0.29

[a] X = Mean.

[b]   Significant difference between institution and community groups, $p < 0.05$ (two-tailed).

Table 6.2 lists the most frequently reported hassles in the total multiple sclerosis group and in the community and institution samples. The most frequently reported hassles were distributed across five life domains: health, environment, practical, family and personal matters. Health concerns predominated in all the groups (declining physical abilities, not enough energy, physical illness, difficulties seeing/hearing, concerns about weight and bodily functions).

TOTAL MS GROUP (N=40)	%[a]
Concerns about weight	57.5
Declining physical abilities	55.0
Not enough energy	52.5
News events	50.0
Being a burden	50.0
Having to wait	50.0
Trouble reading, writing etc.	47.5
Physical illness	42.5
Difficulties seeing/hearing	42.5
Being restricted	40.0

MS - INSTITUTION (N=20)	%	MS - COMMUNITY (N=20)	%
Declining physical abilities	60.0	Concerns about weight	70.0
Noise[b]	55.0	Being a burden[b]	65.0
Not enough energy	55.0	News events	60.0
Trouble reading, writing etc.	50.0	Feeling ignored[b]	55.0
Having to wait	50.0	Difficulties seeing/hearing[b]	55.0
Troublesome residents[b]	45.0	Declining physical abilities	50.0
Bodily functions	45.0	Not enough energy	50.0
Concerns about weight	45.0	Having to wait	50.0
Regrets over past decisions[b]	45.0	Being restricted[b], Wasting time, Trouble reading, writing etc., Weather[b], Misplacing or losing things[b], Health of family member[b], Physical Illness, Bodily functions	45.0
News events, Physical illness, Children[b]	40.0		

a   % figures represent the percentage of people who checked the item.
b   Items unique to each group.

Two environmental factors (noise and troublesome residents), one personal concern (regrets over past decisions) and one family matter (children) were unique to the institution group. One health concern (difficulties seeing/hearing), one environmental factor (weather), two practical matters (wasting time and misplacing things), three personal concerns (being a burden, being restricted and feeling ignored), and one family matter (health of family member) were specific to the community group. Employment and finance related problems are absent from the table.

At the end of the Hassles Scale participants were asked if any hassles had been missed. Table 6.3 lists hassles identified as 'missed' and the domains under which they can be categorised. The majority of missed hassles were personal concerns. Service issues appeared as a new category of hassles.

Table 6.3
Hassles identified by participants as missing from the hassles scale*

HASSLE	CATEGORY
Learning to live with MS	(personal)
Feeling conspicuous	(personal)
Frustration	(personal)
Superstition	(personal)
Lack of intimacy	(personal)
Dependency on others	(personal)
Special equipment	(services)
Pressure to take part in group activities	(services)
Nursing personnel	(services)
Watching other people with MS deteriorate	(health)
MS symptoms	(health)
Self-care	(practical)
Unable to do what want to do	(practical)
Access	(environmental)
People generally inconsiderate	(social)

* Participants were also asked if any uplifts had been missed from the Uplifts Scale but apart from seasonal dates (e.g. Christmas) no new uplifts were identified.

155

Table 6.4
Most frequently reported uplifts by multiple sclerosis groups

TOTAL MS GROUP (N=40)	%[a]
Music	85.0
Praying/meditating	72.5
Spending time with family	67.5
Relating well with friends	62.5
Being visited, phoned etc.	62.5
Gossiping	60.0
Laughing	57.5
Fresh air	55.0
Getting love	55.0
Giving love	55.0

MS - INSTITUTION (N=20)	%	MS - COMMUNITY (N=20)	%
Being visited, phoned etc.	85.0	Music	90.0
Music	80.0	Gossiping[b]	75.0
Praying/meditating	75.0	Spending time with family	70.0
Spending time with family	65.0	Praying/meditating	70.0
Relating well with friends	60.0	Being well prepared[b]	70.0
Being rested[b]	60.0	Relating well with friends	65.0
Giving a compliment[b]	60.0	Getting love[b]	65.0
Having privacy/being alone[b]	55.0	Giving love[b]	65.0
Laughing	55.0	Fresh air, Having someone to listen to you[b], Laughing, Having fun[b], Giving good advice[b], Practising your hobby[b]	60.0
Feeling safe in neighbourhood	50.0	Children's accomplishments[b]	55.0

[a] % figures represent the percentage of people who checked the item.
[b] Items unique to each group.

In Table 6.4 the most frequently reported uplifts are listed for multiple sclerosis groups, along with the percentage number of respondents endorsing each item. Uplifts were consistently reported across four domains: personal/private concerns, social activities, family and environmental matters. Personal/private concerns were prevalent in the samples (in particular, music, praying and laughing). Certain personal concerns (giving a compliment and having privacy) were unique to the institution group; others (getting and giving love, having fun and practising a hobby) were specific to the community group. Additionally, one environmental matter (feeling safe in the neighbourhood), one social activity (being visited) and one health matter (being rested) were reported by the institution group only. Two social activities (gossiping and having someone to listen to you), one family matter (children's accomplishments) and two practical matters (being well prepared and giving good advice) were unique to the community group. Health matters were unreported for the community group, whereas practical matters were not frequently mentioned by the institution group. Uplifts in the domains of finance and employment do not feature in the table. Differences between the two groups concerning the most frequently reported hassles and uplifts, suggests contrasting daily experiences.

Method and Focus of Coping

Participants were asked to identify the most stressful event or situation that had happened to them during the last month. In Table 6.5 these events are categorised for the two multiple sclerosis groups. Both groups identified a similar number of health related events (e.g. deterioration in health, double vision and balance, bedsores and pain). The institutional group reported more service type stressors (e.g. lack of privacy, noise, waiting lists and routines), whereas the community group experienced more family related stresses (e.g. carer's health, separation/divorce, sexual problems and relationship with children), and performance related stresses (e.g. unable to do housework, problems with walking/falling, and driving). Differences between the two groups were not statistically significant.

157

Table 6.5

The most stressful type of event for participants during the last month by two groups

MS - INSTITUTION	N	MS - COMMUNITY	N	TOTAL
Health (symptoms)	7	Health (symptoms)	8	15
Family relationships	4	Family relationships	7	11
Services	8	Services	2	10
Performance/functioning	1	Performance/functioning	3	4
TOTAL	20		20	40

Table 6.6 orders coping items from the most to least frequently used coping strategies, and categorises them according to method and focus of coping. At least 50% of the sample used the first four items on the list (kept feeling to myself, took one step at a time, prayed for guidance and strength and talked with a relative about the problem). These four items represent both emotion-focused and problem-focused strategies and cognitive, behavioural and avoidance methods of coping. Exercised more scored least and was used by only three people in the sample.

158

Table 6.6
Rank order of coping items scored for total multiple sclerosis group

ITEM	N	METHOD/FOCUS
Kept my feelings to myself	32	Avoidance/Emotion
Took things one step at a time	30	Cognitive/Problem
Prayed for guidance and strength	28	Cognitive/Emotion
Talked with relative about the problem	23	Behaviour/Problem
Talked with professional person about situation	19	Behaviour/Problem
Got busy with things to keep mind off problem	18	Avoidance/Emotion
Didn't worry about it	18	Cognitive/Emotion
Prepared for the worst	17	Avoidance/Emotion
Tried to see the positive side	16	Cognitive/Emotion
Drew on my past experience	16	Cognitive/Problem
Took some positive action	16	Behaviour/Problem
Took it out on other people when I felt angry	15	Avoidance/Emotion
Tried to step back and be objective	15	Cognitive/Problem
Tried to find out more about the situation	13	Behaviour/Problem
Talked with a friend about the situation	13	Behaviour/Problem
Considered alternatives for handling problem	12	Cognitive/Problem
Tried to reduce tension by eating more	09	Avoidance/Emotion
Tried to reduce tension by smoking more	09	Avoidance/Emotion
Exercised more	03	Behaviour/Emotion

Demographic and illness characteristics appeared to be associated with individual coping items. Significant associations can be summarised as follows:

Residential status

i) Of the 16 individuals who reported using try to see the positive side, 12 were from the community group (chi-square = 6.67, $p < 0.01$).

159

ii)   Of the 15 individuals who reported using take it out on other people when they felt angry or depressed, 11 were from the community group (chi-square = 5.23, p < 0.05).

Sex

i)   Of the 16 individuals who reported using try to see the positive side, 12 were female (chi-square = 6.67, p <0.01).

ii)   Of the 28 individuals who used pray for guidance and strength, 17 were female (chi-square = 4.29, p < 0.05).

iii)   Of the 9 people who reported using eat more, 8 were female (chi-square = 7.02, p < 0.01).

iv)   Of the 17 individuals who used prepared for the worst more, 14 were male (chi-square = 12.38, p < 0.001).

Marital status

i)   Of the 23 individuals who reported using talk with a spouse or relative about the problem, 14 were married (chi-square = 3.88, p < 0.05).

Age

i)   Of the 15 individuals who reported using step back from the situation and be more objective, 12 were from the older age-group (chi-square = 8.64, p < 0.005).

ii)   Of the 30 individuals who reported using took things one at a time, 18 were from the younger age-group (chi-square = 4.80, p < 0.05).

Duration

i)   Of the 15 individuals who reported using step back from the situation and be more objective, 7 were from the 10 - 19 years of illness group (chi-square = 8.78, p < 0.01).

Reported use of coping items appear to be more strongly associated with the sex of subjects than with any other demographic or illness characteristic. The mean number of coping items scored per individual was 8.05 (SD: 2.87) (possible range: 0 - 19). No significant differences were found between number of coping items used and demographic and illness characteristics.

All the measures of coping were used moderately often, as Table 6.7 shows. Cognitive strategies were the most frequently used coping strategy, followed by avoidance and lastly behavioural strategies. Problem-focused coping was used more than emotion-focused coping. The community group reported significantly more behavioural coping strategies (t = 2.21, p < 0.05 (two-tailed)), and emotion-focused coping (t = 2.06, p < 0.05 (two-tailed)) than the institution group. Sex, age, marital status and duration variables had no significant impact on coping measures.

Table 6.7
Mean percentage of coping response by residential status

COPING MEASURES	INSTITUTION (%)		COMMUNITY (%)	
	Mean	SD	Mean	SD
Method of Coping:				
Cognitive (% yes of 7)	46.4	26.2	50.0	22.5
Behaviour (% yes of 6)	29.2	19.4	43.3*	23.8
Avoidance (% yes of 6)	36.7	10.8	46.67	23.9
Focus of Coping:				
Problem (% yes of 8)	41.2	22.6	47.5	21.7
Emotion (% yes of 11)	35.4	13.8	46.4*	17.2

* p < 0.05.

The relationship between type of stressful event and coping response is shown in Table 6.8. Results should be treated with caution owing to the small number of events in the performance category. Performance events appear to elicit significantly more and family-related problem significantly less behavioural and problem-focused coping than did most other categories.

161

There is no clear coping measure preference for health related stressful events. Family events are associated with more cognitive, avoidance and emotion-focused measures. Service related events are related to cognitive and problem-focused coping.

Table 6.8
Mean percentage of coping responses for each type of stressful event

COPING MEASURES	Health		Family		Services		Performance		F Value
	X^a	SD	X	SD	X	SD	X	SD	
Method of Coping:									
Cognitive (% yes of 7)	46.7	27.8	41.6	22.6	52.8	20.3	60.7	24.4	0.77
Behaviour (% yes of 6)	40.0	24.2	21.2	15.1	40.0	19.6	54.2	25.0	3.13*
Avoidance (% yes of 6)	47.8	16.5	47.0	24.5	26.7	19.6	41.7	16.7	2.65
Focus of Coping:									
Problem (% yes of 8)	45.8	20.9	29.6	15.1	50.0	19.5	65.3	29.5	3.79^b
Emotion (% yes of 11)	44.2	18.5	42.2	18.8	33.6	11.4	43.2	8.7	0.91
No. of events	15		11		10		4		

a X = Mean   b $p < 0.05$

Self-Esteem

Table 6.9 presents mean self-esteem scores for the multiple sclerosis groups on a scale from 10-40. Higher scores represent positive self-esteem. The mean self-esteem scores for the total sample was 26.18 (range: 12 - 38), which is close to the conceptual mid-point score of 25. This score suggests that individuals tended to give an intermediate response to each item in the scale (i.e. 'agree' or 'disagree' rather than 'strongly' agree or disagree). The sample appears to have a relatively balanced or middle-of-the-road attitude towards their own self-worth. Residential status, age, sex, marital status and duration of illness variables had no significant impact on self-esteem scores.

Table 6.9
Mean self-esteem scores by residential status

GROUP	MEAN (range 10 - 40)	SD
Total (N=40)	26.18	6.81
Institution (N=20)	25.30	7.31
Community (N=20)	27.05	6.34

Table 6.10 displays responses to individual items on the self-esteem scale. At least half of the sample had negative perceptions of themselves on half of the items and were inclined to feel that: they were failures; they were no good at all; they had nothing to be proud of; they weren't able to do things as well as most other people; and they wished they could have more respect for themselves. On the positive side, at least half of the sample believed that: they were people of worth, on an equal basis with others; they had a number of good qualities; they took a positive attitude towards themselves; they were

satisfied with themselves; and they generally didn't feel useless at times. No significant differences were associated with demographic and illness variables.

Table 6.10
Responses to individual items on the self-esteem scale

	Item	(%) Agreeing
1.	I feel that I'm a person of worth, at least on an equal basis with others	87.5
2.	I feel that I have a number of good qualities	87.5
3.	I take a positive attitude toward myself	70.0
4.	On the whole I am satisfied with myself	60.0
5.	All in all I am inclined to feel that I am a failure	60.0
6.	At times I think I am no good at all	52.5
7.	I feel I do not have much to be proud of	50.0
8.	I wise I could have more respect for myself	50.0
9.	I am able to do things as well as most other people	40.0
10.	I certainly feel useless at times	20.0

Satisfaction with Life and Health

The next set of tables present responses to the Satisfaction with Life and Health Scales, which are measures of adaptation in the study. Before rating their lives and health, (on a 0 - 10 scale), participants were asked to describe their hopes and fears and then, good and bad health. In Table 6.11 participants' hopes and fears have been categorised under four major headings which relate to health, family life, state of mind and performance.

Table 6.11
Most common hopes and fears as reported by
multiple sclerosis sample (N=40)

HOPES	N*	FEARS	N
Health	21	Family Life	21
Family Life	14	Health	16
Performance	13	State of Mind	12
State of Mind	12		
TOTAL	60		49

* N refers to number of people who reported a concern in each of the categories. Total scores are not equal to sample size because more than one response was allowed.

Sources of hope were as follows:

1. Health - e.g. cure for multiple sclerosis, regain functioning in certain parts of body, and maintain current state of health.

2.	Family life - e.g. children succeed in life and become decent citizens, family protected from serious worries, family members have good health and prosperity.

3.	State of mind - e.g. be happy, feel secure, at peace with oneself, and maintain dignity.

4.	Performance - e.g. be able to walk, travel, read and write, go shopping, take part in hobbies and work.

Less frequent were hopes relating to financial matters (e.g. financial independence, prosperity and material possessions) and to service needs (e.g. own room in hospital, more comfortable wheelchair, able to live in own home, and more physiotherapy and day-care).

Reported fears were as follows:

1.	Health - e.g. deterioration in health, pain, blindness, incontinence and confinement to bed.

2.	Family life - e.g. relationships deteriorate, dependency on family, restrictions on other family member, lose contact with relations, children's health and marriage difficulties.

3.	State of mind - e.g. become dull, confused, or unhappy, suicidal, feel a failure, defeatist, mentally disordered and 'twisted'.

Less common were fears about performance abilities, financial matters and service needs. Some of the reported fears are similar to events identified as most stressful in the last month (see Table 6.5). Fears, therefore, often represented immediate concerns rather than hypothetical situations. Twelve people explicitly stated that they had neither hopes nor fears for the future, but after probing, all were able to think of personal wishes or dreads.

Definitions of good and bad health were categorised and are shown in Table 6.12. State of mind and performance matters were also integral to participants' perceptions of health and were similar to the examples given above. Definitions of good health were also associated with physical attributes and autonomy.

Table 6.12
Representations of good and bad health as reported by
multiple sclerosis sample (N=40)

GOOD HEALTH	N*	BAD HEALTH	N
Performance	31	Physical Symptoms	27
State of Mind	30	State of Mind	24
Physical Attributes	21	Performance	13
Autonomy	12	Autonomy	12
TOTAL	94		76

*   N refers to number of people who reported a concern in each of the categories. Total scores are not equal to sample size because more than one response was allowed.

Descriptions of good health were as follows:

1. Performance - e.g. able to carry out self-care needs, able to work, travel, pursue leisure interests, socialise, walk, able to get about and be active.

2. State of mind - e.g. feel happy and content, good about self, enjoy life, feel calm and mentally alert.

3. Physical attributes - e.g. good appetite, feeling strong and energetic, fitness, good heart, chest and nerves and absence of specific symptoms/illnesses.

167

4.   Autonomy - e.g. a normal and full life, independence, able to live in own home and able to participate in life.

Bad health was described in the following terms:

1.   Performance - e.g. unable to use hands, sitting in one position, inactivity and unable to do anything.

2.   State of mind - e.g. depression, feeling miserable, unhappy, hopelessness, frustration, unable to concentrate, suicidal thoughts, loss of interest in things and worry.

3.   Physical symptoms - e.g. tiredness, stiffness and soreness, pain and suffering, cancer, broken limbs, asthma, multiple sclerosis, being breathless, terminal illness, and dependent on medicines.

4.   Autonomy - e.g. dependent on others, living in hospital, confinement, feeling powerless, not having a normal life and lifestyle restricted.

Good and bad health were also connected to family life, in particular to relationships with spouse. References to health drew on personal experiences of multiple sclerosis (i.e. specific symptoms) and more universal representations of health and illness (i.e. physical attributes and prevalent diseases).

Participants' own descriptions of their hopes and fears and representations of good and bad health were used to define the top and bottom rungs of a ladder marked from 0 - 10. Mean ratings of life and health are shown in Figure 6.1. The sample perceived the time before multiple sclerosis as being very happy (mean = 8.4). This changed dramatically during the first few years of multiple sclerosis which were perceived to be the worst - people were generally discontented (mean = 4.0). Perceptions of life had improved since then, and their present life was rated as reasonable (mean = 5.6). People were hopeful about the future (mean = 7.5), although levels of happiness were not expected to reach previous attainments, before multiple sclerosis.

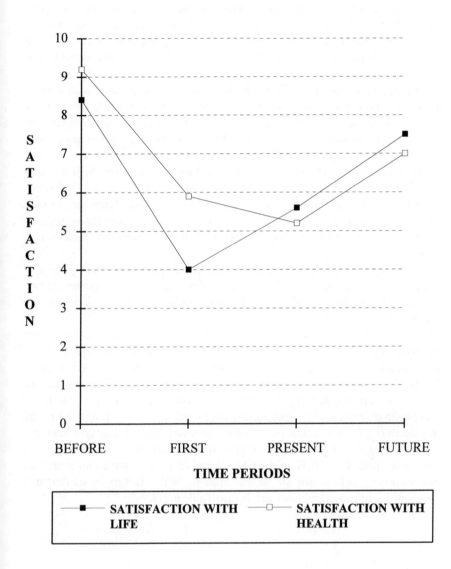

Figure 6.1   Mean ratings of satisfaction with life and health for multiple sclerosis group

The pattern for ratings of health is slightly different. Health was perceived to be very good before multiple sclerosis (mean = 9.2), but had worsened during the first years of illness (mean = 5.9) and had reached its lowest point at the present time (mean = 5.2). Again people were hopeful about the future (mean = 7.0), but aspirations for the future were lower than perceived health before multiple sclerosis.

Significant differences in mean rating scores were associated with a range of demographic and illness variables. People living in institutional settings were found to be significantly *less* satisfied with life at present, compared to people living at home (t = 2.17, p < 0.05 (two-tailed)). Satisfaction with health at present was also significantly different between men and women and between single and married people: men were less satisfied with their health (t = 2.25, p < 0.05 (two-tailed), as were married people (t = 2.04, p < 0.05 (two-tailed)). Younger people were more optimistic about their future health than older people (t = 2.11, p < 0.05 (two-tailed)). No statistically significant differences were found between people with longer or shorter durations of illness.

Ratings on health and happiness with life appear to be closely related. There is more variation in scores across the time periods than between the two ratings. Correlations within and between ratings of life and health are presented in Table 6.13.

Within scales, there are significant but relatively weak to moderate positive correlations between ratings of life at present and future life (r = 0.39, p < 0.01), and between health at present and future health (r = 0.44, p < 0.01). Moderate to strong positive correlations were found *between* the two scales for ratings of: life and health before multiple sclerosis (r = 0.41, p < 0.01); life and health during the first years of illness (r = 0.56, p < 0.001); life and health at present (r = 0.70, p < 0.001): and life and health in the future (r = 0.50, p < 0.001). A significant but weak correlation was found between life at present and future health (r = 0.39, p < 0.01). Correlations across the two scales are not surprising considering the prominence of health factors in participants' descriptions of hopes and fears in life (see Table 6.11).

170

Mean rating scores were categorised into three groups: scores from 0 - 4 were interpreted as indicators of dissatisfaction; a score of 5 was interpreted as an undecided/neither satisfaction nor dissatisfaction; and scores from 6 - 10 indicated satisfaction. Percentage levels of satisfaction and dissatisfaction among the multiple sclerosis sample are shown in Figures 6.2 and 6.3 (a scoring of 5 (undecided) is not included in the Figures). The majority of people (87.5%) were satisfied with their lives before multiple sclerosis became apparent. This fell to 25% of the sample during the first years of their illness. However, at the time of the study, the percentage of people satisfied with their lives had increased to 50%. The majority of people (77.5%) were optimistic about the future. Dissatisfaction was recorded by the largest proportion of people during the first years of illness (55%). At the time of the study approximately one third of the sample were dissatisfied with their lives.

In terms of health, most people (92.5%) were satisfied with their health before multiple sclerosis (see Figure 6.3). The majority of people (60%) were also satisfied with their health during the first years of the illness, but this had since declined to only 37.5% of the sample at the time of the study. Once again, the majority of people (65.5%) were optimistic about their health in the future. Equal proportions of the sample were dissatisfied with health during the first years of illness and present day - approximately one third of the sample were discontent. No-one had claimed to be dissatisfied with their health before multiple sclerosis.

Chi-square tests on the proportions of people who were either satisfied, undecided/neutral or dissatisfied with their lives and health across the four time periods did not reach statistical significance for any of the background variables apart from sex. Men were more likely to be dissatisfied with their health at present than women (chi-square = 9.09, p < 0.01).

In Chapter Four adaptation was interpreted as a situation in which satisfaction with present life compares favourably with past standards and future aspirations. According to the results presented in Figure 6.1, present lives compare unfavourably with lives before multiple sclerosis and future aspirations, particularly so for people living in institutions. However, ratings of life at present do compare favourably to ratings of life in the more recent past, (i.e. the first years of illness). This result suggests that a number of people are adapting to their condition. Indeed, 50% of the sample are satisfied with their lives at present compared to 25% during the first years of the illness (see Figure 6.2). Satisfaction with health at present, at 37.5%, on the other hand, has diminished considerably since the first years of illness when 60% of the sample were satisfied with their health. The role of daily life-events and coping on present day levels of satisfaction will be explored in the final part of this chapter, in order to understand this process of adaptation.

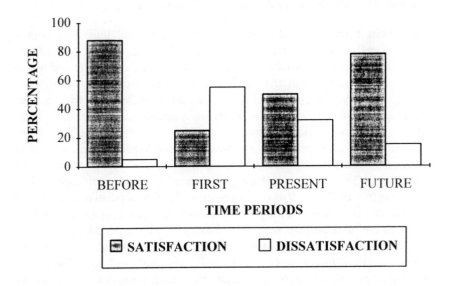

Figure 6.2   Satisfaction and dissatisfaction with life among multiple
sclerosis group

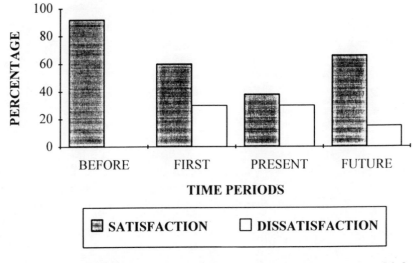

Figure 6.3   Satisfaction and dissatisfaction with health among multiple
sclerosis group

The Role of Daily Events and Coping on Adaptation

Correlations between hassles and uplifts (frequency and intensity), coping strategies, self-esteem and ratings of life and health at present are shown Table 6.14. There are strong positive correlations between ratings of life and health at present and self-esteem (r = 0.72 and 0.64 respectively, p < 0.001). A moderate positive correlation exists between life at present and frequency of uplifts (r = 0.42, p < 0.01). A moderate positive correlation also exists between self-esteem and frequency of uplifts (r = 0.51, p < 0.001). Three styles of coping are significantly but weakly related to self-esteem: a positive correlation with problem-focused coping (r=0.39, p < 0.01) and cognitive coping (r = 0.38, p < 0.01); and a negative correlation with avoidance method of coping (r = 0.37, p < 0.01). Frequency of hassles is positively correlated with hassle intensity (r = 0.39, p < 0.01), emotion-focused coping (r = 0.48, p < 0.001) and avoidance coping (r = 0.49, p < 0.001). Moderate positive correlations were found between frequency of uplifts and two coping measures: problem-focused coping (r = 0.47, p < 0.001) and behaviour coping (r = 0.41, p < 0.01). Strong correlations among measures of coping are spurious because the same individual coping items appear in both focus and method of coping measures.

174

Table 6.14

Pearson correlation coefficients for multiple sclerosis group (N=40)

		1	2	3	4	5	6	7	8	9	10	11	12	13
1.	Life Present	-												
2.	Health Present	.70b	-											
3.	Self-Esteem	-.72b	-.64b	-										
4.	Hassle Frequency	.27	-.21	-.25	-									
5.	Hassle Intensity	-.03	-.17	-.03	.39a	-								
6.	Uplift Frequency	.42a	.23	.51b	.26	-.09	-							
7.	Uplift Intensity	.20	.16	.32	-.16	.15	.08	-						
8.	Problem	.16	.12	.39a	.05	-.18	.47b	.32	-					
9.	Emotion	-.19	-.19	-.15	.48b	.16	.09	-.04	.30	-				
10.	Cognitive	.20	.10	.38a	.06	-.21	.32	.15	.68b	.54b	-			
11.	Behaviour	.03	.95	.18	.17	.07	.41a	.36	.81b	.35	.35	-		
12.	Avoidance	-.36	-.34	-.37a	.49b	.18	-.08	-.19	.03	.75b	.01	.10	-	
13.	Coping	-.03	-.05	.15	.33	-.01	.35	.17	.80b	.81b	.76b	.72b	.49b	-

1-tailed significance: a $p < .01$ b $p < .001$

The results suggest that uplift frequency is related to satisfaction with life and health at present more so than any other variable, apart from self-esteem. Different relationships were found between coping measures and frequency of either hassles or uplifts: problem-focused and behaviour coping strategies were related to the uplifts; whereas emotion-focused coping and avoidance strategies were related to hassles. Positive self-esteem is related to problem-focused and cognitive coping and limited use of avoidance coping. No significant correlations were found between ratings on life and health scales and coping measures. Hassles also appears to be unrelated to life and health ratings. Hassles and uplifts frequency and intensity scores correlate with each other but not at any significant level.

The strong positive relationship between self-esteem and satisfaction scores suggests that the scales may be measuring similar concepts. Indeed state of mind and autonomy factors (which incorporate important personal needs and standards concerning oneself), featured as important dimensions in descriptions of hopes and fears in life and definitions of good and bad health. As a result, self-esteem, in further statistical tests, was treated as an outcome measure. Thus, Satisfaction with Life and Health Scales and Self-Esteem Scale were used as indicators of adaptation.

Having established a relationship between uplifts frequency and satisfaction with life and self-esteem, the next step entailed comparing the respective ability of hassles, uplifts, and coping styles to predict ratings on these scales. To do this uplifts, hassles, and coping measures were each separately regressed step-wise onto the Satisfaction with Life and Health and Self-Esteem Scales. Table 6.15 reports only those variables which were significantly able to predict outcome scores.

Regression analysis shows that uplifts frequency was a considerably better predictor of satisfaction with life at present and self-esteem than any other variable. Hassles frequency also added significantly to the first-order relationship between uplifts and life satisfaction and self-esteem. Avoidance coping was the only variable to significantly predict satisfaction with health at present. Uplifts frequency predicted 18% of the variance in satisfaction with life at present score and 26% of the variance in self-esteem score. Higher levels of uplifts predicted greater levels of satisfaction with life and positive self-esteem. In both outcome measures hassles frequency predicted a further 15% of variance in scores. Lower levels of hassles predicted greater levels of satisfaction with life and positive self-esteem. Avoidance coping predicted 12% of the variance in satisfaction with health at present score. Lower levels of avoidance coping predicted greater satisfaction with health. Apart from avoidance coping, coping styles did not predict any significant variance in scores for the three outcome measures.

Table 6.15
Stepwise multiple regression analysis

		DEPENDENT VARIABLES					
		Life present		Health present		Self-Esteem	
INDEPENDENT STEP VARIABLES		B^a	R2	B^a	R2	B^a	R2
Uplift (frequency)	1.	.12	$.18^d$			.29	$.26^d$
Hassles (frequency)	2.	-.09	$.33^c$			.22	$.41^c$
Avoidance (coping)	1.			-.76	$.12^b$		

a   Regression coefficients
b $p < .05$
c $p < .01$
d $p < .001$

Summary

The major findings are as follows:

1.   The frequency of hassles and uplifts are similar for the institution   and community groups, although the community group perceived hassles to be significantly more severe than the institution group.

177

2.   A comparison of institution and community groups on their most frequent hassles and uplifts yielded "themes" unique to each sample. Hassles related to health and practical matters were similar in both groups. Different personal, environmental and family hassles were reported by two groups. Only the institutional groups reported a health related uplift and only the community group reported uplifts related to practical matters. Both groups reported similar environmental, social and family uplifts. There were differences in the sorts of personal uplifts identified. Employment and financial hassles and uplifts were not reported.

3.   A number of hassles specific to the multiple sclerosis sample were identified as missing from the Hassles Scale. A new category of hassles - service hassles - was identified.

4.   The most stressful events to occur in the last month fell into four categories: health, family relationships, service and performance problems.

5.   Difference between scores on individual coping items were associated with sex of individuals in particular. Accommodation status, age, marital status and duration of illness characteristics also accounted for some associations.

6.   All the measures of coping were used moderately often by the sample. Cognitive coping was used the most and behavioural coping the least. The community group reported significantly more behavioural and emotion-focused coping strategies than the institution group.

7.   The type of stressful events identified influenced the type of coping strategies reported. Family-related problems appeared to be associated with significantly fewer behaviour and problem-focused coping strategies.

8.   Self-esteem scores were moderate. There were no significant differences across demographic, accommodation status and illness variables.

9.   Descriptions of hopes and fears in life were related to health, family-life, performance and state of mind factors. Definitions of good and

bad health were related to performance, state of mind, autonomy and physical attribute/symptoms factors.

10. Ratings of happiness with life and health were much lower at present compared with the time before multiple sclerosis and with future aspirations. Ratings of happiness with life at present were significantly lower for the institution group than for the community group. The percentage satisfied at present life had increased since the first years of illness. This suggests that a proportion of the sample have adapted to their condition. Ratings of health at present compared unfavourably to all the other time periods. This suggests that state of health was a continual disappointment, even if people's lives had improved since the early years of illness.

11. At present, 50% of the sample were satisfied with their lives and 35% were satisfied with their health. There were no significant associations between residential status and level of satisfaction. Men were significantly more dissatisfied with their health at present than women.

12. There were strong positive correlations between ratings of life and health at present and self-esteem. Self-esteem, along with ratings of life and health at present, were treated as measures of adaptation. Moderate positive correlations were found between uplifts frequency and two of the outcome measures. Styles of coping were weakly to moderately associated with self-esteem, and frequency of hassles and uplifts.

13. Adaptation, in terms of higher levels of satisfaction and positive self-esteem, was significantly predicted by the reported frequency of uplifts and hassles experienced and use of avoidance coping. Higher levels of uplifts and lower levels of hassles predicted greater satisfaction with life at present and positive self-esteem. Uplifts frequency was a better predictor of satisfaction with life and perceived self-esteem than any other variable. Lower levels of avoidance coping predicted greater satisfaction with health at present and was the only significant such predictor.

Notes

1. Single group included never married, widowed, divorced and separated categories.

2. People under 58 years of age (the mean age of the participants) were classified as the younger age group; 58 year olds and over as the older age group.

3. Duration of illness was calculated from time of diagnosis. Three groups were distinguished: under 10 years, 10 - 19 years, and 20 years and over.

7 Integrating qualitative and quantitative results

Introduction

The insiders' perspective and the transactional model of stress are both concerned with subjective perceptions of illness; the types of problems people with chronic illness experience on a daily basis; the ways in which they manage to live with their illness; and the process of adaptation (see Chapter Three). This chapter builds on these similarities by integrating the findings from Chapters Five and Six. The role of perceptions of illness as well as hassles, uplifts and coping in adaptation is assessed. Responses to the general questions included at the end of the interview schedule (the Overview), are included to supplement findings from the semi-structured interviews and the psychometric scales. This combined methodological approach provides a more thorough analysis of personal experiences of multiple sclerosis than a single approach would have achieved. The psychometric scales were a useful means of measuring variables and their effects on adaptational outcomes, but they revealed little about the process of adaptation and individual life histories. Semi-structured interviews were used to elucidate these processes by encouraging participants to describe their own experiences of multiple sclerosis from the time of diagnosis. Both approaches reveal that adaptation to multiple sclerosis entails dealing with the physical, psychological and social consequences of the condition.

Responses to the psychometric scales were compared with personal accounts of illness as follows:

i)   Perceptions of stress - reported hassles with key problems in living with illness and participants' perceptions of stress and strain in their lives as a result of illness.

ii)   Positive events - reported uplifts with long-term gains/benefits arising from the experience of illness.

iii)   Coping strategies - coping strategies with the management of illness and perceived coping efficacy.

iv)   Adaptation - self-esteem with identity problems and whether participants felt they had changed as a person because of their illness; and ratings of satisfaction with life and health with participants' interpretation of adaptation to illness.

The chi-square test was used to assess associations between personal accounts of illness and adaptation. Comparisons between the institutional and community groups were kept to a minimum and are reported only where noticeable differences were apparent.

At the end of the chapter a diagram of the interconnections between the qualitative and quantitative results and the relationship between the variables (hassles, uplifts, coping strategies, self-esteem and satisfaction with life and health) are presented.

Perceptions of Stress

The psychometric measurements of stress and coping used in the study (Hassles Scale and Method and Focus of Coping Measure) were concerned with participants' experience of stress in the last month. During the semi-structured interviews it was evident that stressful events in the distant past were as important, and sometimes more vivid, to participants than more recent incidents. For example, stressful events were connected to the onset of the illness itself (see Chapter Five). Consequent life-stories were often recounted as a series of upsetting events, experienced from the first unfamiliar signs of illness and the diagnosis of multiple sclerosis to the gradual loss of customary roles in personal and public lives, as the illness progressed. Grievances concerning treatment during the early years of illness did not always lose their strength over time; for some they continued to influence current relationships with professionals. A passing comment could leave a lasting impression on some participants. For example, one man recalled that when he first visited his GP with an aching knee, his GP had said:

'You want to thank God, it's not MS' He came out with that comment 'You want to thank God, it's not MS.'

From the time of diagnosis this remark symbolised the tragedy of his situation and gave him a rationale for "giving up".

Table 7.1
Themes from personal accounts of illness
and most frequently reported hassles

THEMES FROM PERSONAL ACCOUNTS	HASSLES
1. UNDERSTANDING OF ILLNESS	(PHYSICAL ILLNESS)
Course	Declining physical abilities
Symptoms	Not enough energy
	Bodily functions
	Difficulties seeing/hearing
Complications	Concerns about weight
2. CONSEQUENCES OF ILLNESS	
Disability	Trouble reading/writing
Handicap	Being a burden
	Being restricted
	Having to wait
	Health of family member
3. EMOTIONAL IMPACT	
Sadness	Regrets over past decisions
Hopelessness	Feeling ignored
4. OPINIONS ABOUT CARE	
Dissatisfaction with services	Noise
	Troublesome residents

The sorts of problems people most frequently described during the semi-structured interview were compared to the most frequently reported hassles. Table 7.1 shows that the long-term strains associated with multiple sclerosis recurred as hassles in everyday life. The majority of hassles were either directly related to characteristics of the diseases (symptoms, course and complications) or the consequences of chronic illness (disability and handicap, the emotional impact of illness and problems with available care). Hassles which were common but appeared to have no bearing on personal accounts of illness were unpredictable events or concerns, such as news events, the weather, and misplacing or losing things, over which participants had little control.

The most frequently reported hassles were distributed across five life domains (health, environment, practical, family and personal matters). These domains were integral to the themes covered in personal accounts of illness (understanding of illness, consequences of illness, opinions about care and emotional impact of illness).

The scarcity of hassles reported in the domains of employment and finance requires an explanation. In terms of employment, it is difficult to establish, from the results of the hassles scale alone, whether people were employed but did not experience hassles at work, or whether they were unemployed. Ambiguities such as these were discussed whilst completing the scale or had already been dealt with in the semi-structured interview. As a result, the absence of employment-related hassles was known to be a direct effect of unemployment. None of the participants was currently employed. Although many had reached the age of retirement (40% of the sample), all who had previously been employed, but one, said they became unemployed as a result of their illness.[1] Analysis of the semi-structured interviews revealed that participants were still disappointed that their working lives had come to a premature end before the usual age of retirement. The very absence of hassles in one domain of life was often perceived to be an injustice or misfortune rather than an advantage. Lack of stimulation was as frustrating as pressures at work.

Financial concerns were relatively scarce in participants' personal accounts of illness and reports of hassles. The most frequently reported financial hassles were, concerns about the rising prices of common good (11 people), housing (8 people) and electricity bills (8 people). These concerns were particularly pertinent for people living at home, although for people living in hospital, apart from their families, household finances were still a worry. Financial matters were more evident in participants' descriptions of their hopes and fears for the future. Increasing disability and the concurrent expense this might entail, together with the strain this could place on family income, were

184

worrying possibilities. Nevertheless, health, family life, performance and state of mind matters were more pertinent to participants than financial concerns. Considering the amount of reliable evidence documenting the relationship between disability and financial hardship (Martin and White 1988; and Barnes 1991), these results are surprising. The ways in which participants managed their illness, as discussed in the semi-structured interviews, provide a possible explanation. Many of the coping strategies referred to throughout participants' accounts of illness entailed personal restraint, resilience and stoicism; for example, the themes of Perseverance, Accept it/face facts, Get on with things/Get used to things, Careful planning/Be prepared, Discipline, Maintain independence, Minimise, Fund-raising and Keep busy. Set against the paucity of rehabilitation services, these strategies could be described as both necessary and the most appropriate. Participants were accustomed to financial constraints, personally and within the health care system. It was perceived to be a fact of life and participants could be philosophical about it, as one man said of the time before he moved into hospital:

It's not as if I was well-off financially like. [My Friends] were probably carrying me rather than me carrying them.

One woman was proud of being frugal with the provisions she was entitled to:

They supply me with a thickish towel. There are people who use four to six a day but I do not. I don't waste them like. I keep them and make the month's supply I have last me for a month. Even the nurses say 'Angie, you destroy nothing.' Even if one takes a tear I don't throw them out, you never know, it will do me at night.

Although a number or participants were relatively secure financially, the majority were dependent on social security benefits. Despite limited funds, participants appeared to minimise financial difficulties. The low-key role attributed to financial problems appeared to be related to specific coping strategies and a matter of personal pride and privacy.[2] Opportunities to spend 'disposable income' was limited by mobility difficulties. Hobbies and pastimes tended to be relatively inexpensive (e.g. reading, listening to music, stamp collecting and knitting).

Finally, participants identified a number of hassles which were missing from the Hassles Scale (Chapter Six, Table 6.3). Most of these hassles were related to personal concerns; many of these had been talked about in the semi-structured interview (dependency on others, problems with new identity and problems in managing illness). Problems with services, not mentioned in the Hassles Scale, were also reported and were directly related to dissatisfaction

185

with care. Themes from the personal accounts of illness were, therefore, replicated in reports of daily hassles.

When participants were asked at the end of their interview whether they felt there was a lot of stress in their lives, 60% felt there was and related stress to family matters, disability, hospital surroundings, self-esteem, "battling" with multiple sclerosis, social isolation, boredom and tension. When asked whether their condition had led to an ongoing strain in their lives, 78% responded in the affirmative. Reasons for strain were more wide-ranging, and included the examples given above, as well as loss of choice, unemployment, being more sensitive, small problems were magnified, vivid imagination, losing faith in people, being a nuisance and feeling like a "shell" of one's former self. There was a significant difference in the mean number of hassles reported between respondents who felt there was a lot of stress in their lives as a result of their condition and respondents who felt there was not (t-test = 3.86, $p < 0.001$ (two-tailed)). Respondents who felt there was a lot of stress in their lives reported more hassles than respondents who felt that their condition had not lead to a lot of stress. Participants' perceptions of stress were consistent using qualitative and quantitative methods.

A significant association was found between self-reports of stress and only one measure of adaptation - satisfaction with health at present. Of the 15 people who scored above the median, suggesting greater satisfaction with health, 10 reported that there was not a lot of stress in their lives (chi-square = 5.44, $p < 0.05$). It appears then, that lower levels of stress are associated with greater satisfaction with present health. Participants' perceptions of stress appear to be more closely connected to health outcomes than self-esteem and life-satisfaction.

Positive Events

The Uplifts Scale provided a record of the sorts of positive events participants experienced and how often they occurred on a daily basis. The focus in the semi-structured interview was slightly different; participants were asked if anything positive had come out of the illness experience. So, although 45% of the sample reported a mean of 27 or more uplifting events in the last month and that uplifts occurred moderately often, only 43% of the sample felt that they had gained something as a result of their condition. People living at home were twice as likely to report benefits as people living in an institutional setting.

There were similarities, however, between the most frequently reported uplifts and the sorts of benefits participants were able to identify, as shown in Table 7.2.

Table 7.2
Positive outcomes of illness and most frequently reported uplifts

PERSONAL OUTCOMES	UPLIFTS
1. PERSONAL	
Faith	Praying/meditating
New hobbies	Practising your hobby
2. RELATIONSHIPS	
Closer to family	Spending time with family
More time for people	Relating well with friends
Good listener	Having someone to listen to you
More sociable	Gossiping Being visited, phoned etc.
3. PRACTICAL	
Give good advice	Giving good advice
Help others	

The most frequently reported uplifts were distributed across four life domains (personal/private, social, family and environmental matters). As Table 7.2 shows, the gains which people attributed to the experience of illness were connected to three of these domains. Uplifts which were frequently

187

reported, but not identified as a direct benefit of the illness were: music, laughing, fresh air, being rested, giving a compliment, having privacy, feeling safe in neighbourhood, being well prepared, getting and giving love, having fun and children's accomplishments. Positive outcomes of illness not captured by the Uplifts Scale were: appreciating the important things in life, learning about one's own personal strengths and weaknesses, the companionship of other people with multiple sclerosis, a greater awareness of people with disabilities and more understanding of disability issues. Participants who referred to these sorts of benefits believed that the experience of multiple sclerosis, although unwelcome, was an educative one:

> *It's made me realise just what sort of things people have to come through. When you're able-bodied you don't seem to... you take too much for granted. I think it's left me, like I don't take things for granted now. It kind of way opens your eyes more to what other people come through, you know.*

> *Just learning how other people cope with it. Before you have it you don't really think about it. I suppose that's the same with a lot of other illnesses. Until you have either seen someone or have it yourself you don't realise what it entails. You have more sympathy for other people, especially others in wheelchairs. I know how difficult it is to cope and try and get through doors and that sort of thing with a wheelchair.*

Table 7.2 and the quotations above show that relationships and the companionship of others with multiple sclerosis are important for raising participants' perceptions of their circumstances. Both factors relate to social support, which is known to have an important role in coping with stressful events.[3] The positive affects of social support are associated with perceptions of social integration, satisfying relationships, and the helpfulness and supportive behaviour of others. However, results from the hassles scale and the semi-structured interview have shown that many of these positive affects of social support are lost as a result of illness (participants reported isolation, unequal relationships, stigma and lack of understanding from others). Social support had a slightly different meaning for participants, and was more closely aligned to social comparison, equity and reciprocity. Participants' use of social comparison as a coping strategy was reported in Chapter Five. By comparing themselves to people less fortunate than themselves (downward comparison), participants were able to enhance their own perceptions of themselves. Attendance at the MS Society day-centre was largely based on the companionship of other people with multiple sclerosis. These relationships were supportive because of their equity (people at the centre shared similar experiences) and their reciprocity (participants both sought and offered advice). As Table 7.2 shows, giving advice was an important positive experience for participants. This is understandable if giving advice was also perceived to be a means of reciprocating the aid given by non-disabled people, particularly in area of self-care needs. In this way 'asymmetrical helping relationships' based on participants' dependency on others were made a little more equal.[4]

The frequency of uplifts reported was found to be positively correlated with behavioural and cognitive coping strategies (although not significantly in the latter case (See Chapter Six, Table 6.14), and with satisfaction with life at present and self-esteem. However, believing that something positive had come out of the illness experience was neither statistically associated with the coping strategy, 'Tried to see the positive side', nor the measures of adaptation (satisfaction with life and health at present and self-esteem). The lack of association between perceptions of positive outcomes of illness and adaptation is possibly related to the "double-edged" nature of positive outcomes. Participants who acknowledged the educative benefits of illness also recognised the concomitant personal hardships endured. Perceived hardships may negate favourable perceptions of adaptation.

Coping Strategies

The semi-structured interview, the Overview and the Method and Focus of Coping Measure all dealt with the ways in which participants managed stressful situations. Each participant used a variety of coping strategies (cognitive, avoidance and behavioural), although cognitive strategies tended to be the most frequently reported and behavioural ones the least.

Table 7.3
Reported coping strategies

REPORTED WAYS OF MANAGING ILLNESS	ITEMS FROM COPING SCALE
Keep feelings to myself/Contain feelings	Kept my feelings to myself
Take one day at a time	Took things one step at a time
Faith	Prayed for guidance and strength
Asked for help/advice and Talk to other people with illness	Talked with relative/friend/ professional about the problem
Keep busy and Think of other things	Got busy with things to keep mind off problem
Get on with things/get used to it	Didn't worry about it; figured everything would work out fine
Careful planning/be prepared	Prepared for the worst
Positive thinking/bright side of life	Tried to see the positive side
Write about experience, Fund-raising, Self-help, Try alternative therapies, Stopped going to doctor/taking medicine, Attend day-centre, Design tool/aid, try Special diet	Took some positive action
Accept it/face facts	Tried to step back from the situation and be more objective
Read/collect written information	Tried to find out more about the situation
Get drunk and Smoke	Tried to reduce tension by eating more/smoking more
Exercise	Exercise more

The coping strategies identified by participants during their accounts of illness were similar to the coping items included in the coping scale (see Table 7.3).

Two items in the coping scale (Took it out on other people when I felt angry and Considered alternatives for handling the problem) were not reported as coping strategies in participants' own accounts of their illness. Although participants coped with problems in many different ways, many felt that for some of the major problems in their life (e.g. moving into hospital, early redundancy and using a wheelchair), only one option had been available to them. If there had been alternatives they would have taken them (e.g. extra community services, retraining opportunities and preventive therapies). Taking it out on other people was perceived to be a sign of distress rather than a way of coping with stress. This strategy was, in fact, antithetical to most people's way of dealing with stress, as demonstrated by the most frequently used strategy reported by participants: Kept my feelings to myself (coping scale) and Keep my feelings to myself/Contain feelings (response to Q1. in the Overview).

An association was found between reported use of this strategy (Kept my feelings to myself) and satisfaction with life at present. Of the 8 people who did *not* use this strategy, 7 scored above the median score (median = 5.5), suggesting greater satisfaction with life (chi-square = 3.91. p < 0.05). No significant associations were found between this strategy and satisfaction with health at present and self-esteem.

The second most frequently used strategy on the coping scale was Took things one step at a time (Chapter Six, Table 6.6). This strategy seemed to be directly related to two fundamental physical properties of multiple sclerosis - its lack of certainty and control - which make it difficult for participants to plan for the future. A similar strategy, Take one day at a time, was identified by participants as a strategy for coping with illness during the semi-structured interviews. Prayed for guidance and strength was the third most frequently used strategy on the coping scale. The semi-structured interviews revealed that faith helped in others ways too, by providing social support and sustaining personal identity. In contrast, the item Exercised more was perceived to be inappropriate by all but three participants in the study because of their levels of disability. When exercise was identified as a coping strategy in the interviews, this was always in relation to physiotherapy activities.

Many coping strategies mentioned by participants were not directly included in the coping scale: Perseverance/maintain control, Maintain independence, Fight it, New Perspective, Adjust and learn to live with it, Minimise, Humour, Social comparison, Discipline, Self-blame, Set standards/example, Maintain hope, Talk to self, Monitor illness, Take rests,

Keep to routine, Fate, Pass illness off, Don't ask questions, Let illness take over/Nature take its course, Give up, Avoid contact with other people, Avoid family discussions, Wishful thinking/escapism, Try not to think about the future or/and past, and Deny that illness is really happening. Although some of the most prevalent coping strategies were captured by the coping scale, the variety of coping strategies used by the participants was not. The list of coping strategies collected does not claim to be exhaustive. It does demonstrate, however, that participants spontaneously cope with their illness in a multitude of ways.

Once participants had described how they coped with their illness, they were asked how well they thought these strategies worked. The majority of the sample (67.5%) believed that they coped well with their illness. The remainder (32.5%) either replied that they were not coping very well or they were just about coping or only coping at times. No significant association was found between perceived efficacy of coping strategies and satisfaction with life and health at present. A significant association was found between self-esteem score and perceived efficacy of coping strategies: of the 21 people who scored greater than or equal to the self-esteem median (indicating a more favourable self-esteem), 18 were from the group of people who felt they were coping well with their illness (chi-square = 5.05, p < 0.05). This relationship between coping efficacy and self-esteem is interesting because it suggests that participants' evaluations of their own coping abilities is related to perceptions of self-worth.[5]

Adaptation

Self-esteem and satisfaction with life and health were used as indicators of adaptation to illness. Participants' perceptions of self-worth were depicted in personal accounts of illness and directly assessed in the Self-Esteem Scale. Participants were also asked, at the end of the interview, whether they felt they had become a different person as a result of their condition, and if so, for better or for worse. Responses to these questions were compared. Satisfaction with life and health was measured with the use of Cantril's Ladder. In the Overview, participants were also asked whether they felt they had adapted to their condition. Responses given to this single question were compared to satisfaction ratings.

Self-esteem

In their personal accounts of illness, the sample referred mainly to the negative impact of illness on self-esteem. Stigma had a powerful influence on participants' perceptions of themselves; not only did they refer to being "labelled" as 'mentally deficient' by other people, they also "labelled" themselves as 'cripples' and 'useless'. As the research project progressed, participants sought reassurances that their own accounts of illness were not at odds with other participants' experiences. Lack of confidence, social embarrassment and feeling 'a fool' or 'stupid' were associated either with being treated differently:

> *Being in the wheelchair, very few will come to help you. I think it's fear. I think to them it's going to the unknown. They don't understand so they shy away from it.*

or an awareness that multiple sclerosis could affect mental functioning. For example, one man in the study spent a lot of time completing crosswords in order to keep his mind active, but he continued to worry about becoming 'mentally dull' and not 'fitting in'. Sometimes, participants themselves found it hard to adjust to their own public image:

> *Sometimes, if I'm going past a window or a mirror I hardly know myself. At times I think, oh crikey, that isn't me, but it is me, you know. You kid yourself.*

The loss of important social roles (provider for family, employee, parent, partner etc.) and the acquisition of new but less valued identities were detrimental to positive self-esteem. Maintaining positive self-esteem was difficult when social rejection was compounded by private doubts about themselves.

Participants were generally non-committal when evaluating their own self-esteem on the Self-Esteem Scale. Moderate ratings were preferred over categorically positive or negative ratings. When individuals were asked whether they had become a different person as a result of their condition, their responses were varied: 28% felt they were basically the same person as they had been before multiple sclerosis; 32% felt they had changed for the worse; 20% felt they had changed for the better; and a further 20% felt that they had changed both for the better and worse - that they were essentially the same but better or worse in certain departments! Many of the beneficial outcomes of illness discussed above recurred as reasons for feeling better as a person. For example, participants felt that they were more understanding and tolerant, they appreciated what was important in life, they were more thoughtful, they had developed a new and more balanced perspective on life, they were more sociable and they had learnt how to "fight".

Reasons for feeling worse as a person were related to loss of abilities and social roles, not being the same person, being dependent, feeling "out of it", being a burden and being confined. All of these problems had been referred to before. Some participants felt that they had developed fundamental character flaws as a result of their illness, such as turning into nasty, critical, obnoxious, impatient, irritable or opinionated people. Loss of faith in God, social withdrawal, not being able to "mix", and concerns about physical appearance were also associated with becoming a bad person and feelings of shame.

Few people explicitly referred to themselves as 'disabled' or 'handicapped'. Participants preferred to be more precise and identified themselves as people with a specific disease - multiple sclerosis. When participants were asked whether they often woke up in the morning and thought about their disability, only 15% answered affirmatively. For these people, mornings were perceived to be the worst part of the day: a time when they asked themselves "Why me?", and "What will the day bring?" The effort it took physically to get out of bed, for some, meant that it was impossible for them not to think about their disability. As a result, two people said they often felt like not getting up at all. One person thought about his disability in a constructive way in the mornings: this part of the day was assigned to writing up his journal and monitoring his illness.

For the majority of people who did not think about their disability when they woke up (75%), the following explanations were given: it would be too depressing to do so; I never think about my disability; too busy getting organised to think about disability; usually feel good in the mornings; and would go "mad" if thought about such things. Participants added that in the first years of their illness they had frequently been preoccupied with their disabilities, but over the years, they had "got used to" their condition and it had ceased being the foremost concern for them at the start of each day.

Participants appeared to emphasise their greater awareness of disability issues as a result of their own experiences, and yet downplay their own disability and dissociate themselves from other disabled people. This apparent contradiction appeared to be useful in sustaining positive perceptions of themselves. In the first instance, participants were able to identify the educative influence that first hand experience of illness continued to have on their lives. In a sense they felt they had become better people as a result of illness. Identifying oneself as disabled, however, was perceived to be a threat to positive self-esteem and consequently avoided. This discrepancy was dealt with by developing friendships with other people with multiple sclerosis, thus acknowledging their disabilities, but avoiding contact with people living with different illnesses, thus distancing themselves from disabled people generally. Participants' choice of day-care illustrates such manoeuvres: 75% of the sample attended the MS Society day-centre, but only 28% attended day-centres for physically disabled people. As mentioned in Chapter Five, companionship with other people with multiple sclerosis was one of the main benefits of attending the MS Society day-centre. The low attendance at other day-centres could be interpreted as a sign that alternative day-care was not required; that it was inappropriate; and/or that it did not offer the same companionship as MS society day-centres. Evidence of social isolation and unemployment suggest that day-care services were required. There were indications that day-centres, particularly those with an emphasis on handicraft activities, were inappropriate for people with multiple sclerosis.[6] Participants often felt uncomfortable mixing with people with other illnesses:

> *I go to the X day-centre but I'm not mad keen on it because I think MS people can communicate better between ourselves. MS to me feels like a totally separate disease and in the X day-centre it's all different things - cerebral palsy, and the results of accidents, and Parkinson's. There's a couple in there who are MS and I would find myself drawn to them more. It seems awful to me to be drawn to them more [but] there's more to talk about with them.*

Perceiving oneself to be a 'person with MS' or a 'MS patient' was preferable, or at least more tolerable, than perceiving oneself to be a 'disabled person'. There was a fear that in mixing with other disabled people who were sometimes more stigmatised, they to would be tainted with the same brush. By keeping to themselves, participants felt they had obtained a certain respectability for their condition which was important for their own self-image and for favourable public conceptions of multiple sclerosis. Only one person in the study sought out the company of people with different illnesses and disabilities and commented on the mutual benefit this had for both parties:

> *I went to a disabled holiday in England with the Red Cross. I found living with people with different illnesses, laughing and coping in their own way, they're all enjoying themselves, wasn't half a good experience. I found that very good, you have a whole new attitude. You want to help yourself and you're definitely going to help others. It's the experience of being among... you're not alone. You're part of this world and it's not just multiple sclerosis, there's other illnesses too.*

Umbrella organisations *of* disabled people rather than organisations *for* disabled people, have emerged in England. They attempt to empower disabled people as well as challenge social restrictions and negative attitudes towards disabled people (Oliver 1990). The absence of similar organisations in Northern Ireland may explain why the majority of participants in the study perceived no advantage, at a personal or political level, in associating with other disabled people. Indeed umbrella organisations for disabled people were sometimes perceived to compromise participants' strategy of dealing with their already threatened identities.

The negative feelings participants had towards the term 'disabled' unearthed a fundamental difference between the ICIDH's definition of the term and participants' understanding of the term. 'Disability' was defined in the coding frame as any problems participants had in performing activities. It followed that disabled people were people who experienced these difficulties. On the other hand, the word 'disabled' was value laden for participants. On a personal level, 'disabled' was interpreted as a sign of weakness in character. On a social level, being defined as 'disabled' meant losing one's individuality and being counted as an unfortunate national statistic. On both levels, the term had an unfavourable affect on participants' self-esteem. The precision required in defining a coding frame has its disadvantages when personal meanings are lost or unaccounted for. The ICIDH's definition of disability does not address emotional and cultural consequences of illness. Respondents' understanding of 'disabled' is more in line with the ICIDH's definition of 'handicapped'.

Satisfaction with life and health

At the time of the study, 50% of the sample were satisfied with their lives, and 38% were satisfied with their health. At the same time, approximately one-third of the sample were dissatisfied with their lives and health. The remainder were neither satisfied nor dissatisfied and gave mid-point ratings on these two dimensions. Although only half the participants were satisfied with their lives, 85% felt they had adapted to their condition (in response to question in Overview). Participants interpreted adaptation as a process of 'accepting and re-accepting' their condition rather than contentment per se. An important philosophy underpinning participants' lives was 'doing as well you can'. Such a philosophy did not involve making comparisons between the current situation and previous attainments or future aspirations. Adaptation was perceived to be a process of adjusting to problems on a daily basis. It was, therefore, tied to the present and dependent on current circumstances. As a result, adaptation was described as a 'lengthy' 'gradual' and 'ongoing' process rather than an end product or something attained after many years of experience. Participants pointed out that current levels of adaptation were no guarantee of future levels of adaptation, especially if the illness progressed and caused additional problems.

For the 15% of the sample who felt they had not adapted to their condition, the reasons given were feelings of resignation and shame, of being lazy and worrying unduly. Perceived adaptation was dependent on personal values rather than objective criteria. Thus, what was interpreted as resignation by one person was interpreted as acceptance by another. As already mentioned, the latter was generally associated with adaptation. Resignation was associated with 'giving in' to the illness or 'giving up' on life. Feelings of hopelessness (see Chapter Five) were common to participants who believed they had not adapted to their condition. In both instances self-blame was typical:

> *I haven't the ability now and that's where I feel cheated by the MS. I blame myself. Now it's got me into such a position that I think to myself I wouldn't be able to do [anything]. I just think to myself 'Why bother? Why should I bother?' I've convinced myself that I couldn't do it anyway, so why should I bother. I'm missing out in that respect, you know. It sort of makes me mad, not only with myself but with [others], through no fault of [their] own. I think my mind's cracked up. Sometimes I can't see the sense unless you blame yourself or someone else you know.*

As mentioned previously, participants who had contemplated suicide felt their lives were hopeless.

The majority of participants, however, were optimistic about the future: 78% hoped that their lives would be happy in the future and 66% that their health would be good. These findings are far more positive than responses in the semi-structured interview, where only 25% of the sample felt they had maintained a sense of pride and contentment. This disparity might be related to different methodological approaches. In the Satisfaction with Life and Health Scales participants were directly asked to state what their hopes and fears were. The semi-structured interview was much more open-ended and depended, to a great extent, on participants volunteering their feelings.

The Satisfaction with Life and Health Scales proved to be the most difficult measures to complete. Thirty percent of the sample said they had no hopes and fears when first asked. Further probing was needed before participants were willing to make some suggestions. In effect, participants were asked to confront their hopes and fears and to evaluate their current lives - a difficult task for anyone to do. This research demand might also have conflicted with participants' ways of coping with illness (e.g. Keep feelings to myself, Put illness to the back of my mind/don't think about it). There was a fine balance between facing facts about their lives (and health in particular), and remaining hopeful; both were perceived to be necessary in the process of accepting and adapting to multiple sclerosis. A variety of coping strategies are required to deal with the problem (illness orientated), to deal with emotional distress (person orientated) and to maintain life goals (motivation orientated). When completing the Satisfaction with Life and Health Scales, tensions between these different demands were made more visible.

State of mind was the only category to appear in participants' definitions of what would make them happy *and* unhappy and what good *and* bad health represented to them. This category consisted mainly of references to emotional states from happiness, security, peace, contentment and joy to unhappiness, feelings of failure, misery, hopelessness, and depression. Cognitive states were also included, but less common (e.g. mental alertness, mental disorder and difficulties in concentrating). Satisfaction with Life and Health was, therefore, closely associated with feelings. The categories of health, performance/abilities, family life, autonomy, physical attributes and symptoms were also regarded as important. These categories appear to be central to participants' own assessments of what successful and unsuccessful adaptation to illness entails.

These aspects of adaptation recurred throughout the interviews - in accounts of illness (in terms of disability and handicap, common fears and feelings of hopelessness and sadness), in reports of daily hassles and uplifts, and in ways of coping with stress and self-esteem. The relationship between these variables appeared to be reciprocal; perceived adaptation was dependent on perceptions of stress, coping strategies, emotional responses and understanding of illness, and conversely, perceptions of stress, coping strategies, emotional responses and understanding of illness were dependent on perceived adaptation.[7]

Figure 7.1 summarises the relationships between these variables and their equivalents in the quantitative and qualitative data. The quantitative part of the study was concerned with measuring interactions between variables and adaptation outcome. The arrows in the diagram illustrate these interactions. The frequency of uplifts and hassles and the use of avoidance coping significantly predicted levels of satisfaction with life and health and self-esteem (Chapter Six, Table 6.15). Correlations were also found between the frequency of hassles and uplifts and coping strategies (Chapter Six, Table 6.14). Participants who reported greater numbers of hassles tended to use more emotion-focused coping and avoidance coping strategies. Participants who reported greater numbers of uplifts tended to use more problem-focused coping and behavioural coping strategies.

The qualitative part of the study was concerned with the process of adaptation to illness from the time of diagnosis, as reported in personal experiences of illness. Interrelations between the research variables remains unclear, but personal accounts of illness suggest mediating, dynamic and reciprocal relationships between long-term problems/hassles, uplifts, management of illness, emotional states and adaptation, rather than moderating, static and unidirectional relationships. Participants perceived adaptation to be a continuous process. Figure 7.1 shows that the emotional aspect of adaptation, as recorded in the semi-structured interviews, was not measured quantitatively, which points to a shortcoming in the design of the project. Folkman and Lazarus (1988) describe the relationship between emotion and coping as dynamic and mutually reciprocal. Adaptation was a matter of 'getting used to' multiple sclerosis and making sense of the disease, personal beliefs, emotional responses and social values.

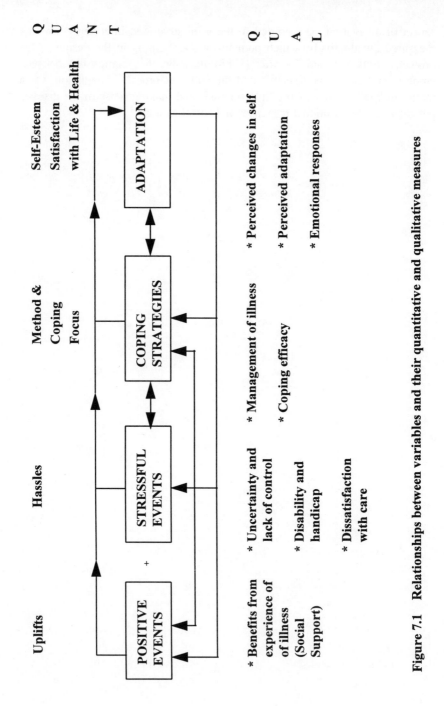

Figure 7.1 Relationships between variables and their quantitative and qualitative measures

Summary

Results from the semi-structured interviews, questionnaires and Overview were compared to identify common themes in participants' experiences of multiple sclerosis. Chapter Five identified five themes (under the broad headings of understanding of illness, consequences of illness, emotional impact of illness, management of illness and opinions about care) which were consistent with participants' perceptions of the hassles, uplifts, coping strategies and adaptation, presented in Chapter Six. Quantitative methods were used to measure outcomes and qualitative methods to describe the personal stories of adaptation. The results can be summarised as follows:

1. The role of stress on participants' lives was recorded from as far back as childhood events (where stress was believed to be responsible for causing multiple sclerosis) to present day hassles (where stress was believed to influence adaptation to the illness). Daily hassles were connected to more long-term strains arising from participants' understanding of illness, the consequences of illness, the emotional impact of illness and opinions about care. It was suggested that under-reporting of financial hassles was related to specific coping strategies. The absence of employment-related hassles was a result of high unemployment amongst the sample. Hassle frequency and reports of stress were significantly related to measures of adaptation.

2. The positive consequences of illness were assessed in terms of incidental daily uplifts and the more sustaining benefits or lessons derived from the personal experience of illness. Uplifting events were associated with long-term gains (on personal, relationship and practical levels), but unlike uplifts, the benefits of illness were not significantly associated with adaptation. Positive outcomes of illness were largely educational or developmental, involving greater personal awareness of disability issues. Participants living in institutions were less likely to suggest that anything positive had come out of their experience of illness. The role of social support was discussed in terms of social comparison, equity and reciprocity.

3. The semi-structured interview and Overview questions drew out participants' own strategies for managing stress related to their illness. Many of these strategies were not included in the Method and Focus of Coping Measure. Participants could be extremely inventive, resourceful, tenacious or even flippant in dealing with stressful

situations. The majority felt they were coping well with their illness. The popularity of the coping strategy took things one step at a time was related to the uncertain nature of the disease. There was a strong tendency for participants to keep their feeling to themselves. This avoidance coping strategy was associated with lower levels of satisfaction with life at present. Participants used a variety of coping strategies, but used cognitive ones the most and behavioural ones the least. An association was found between self-esteem and perceived efficacy of coping strategies.

4. Responses to the Self-Esteem Scale were generally non-committal. Discussions during the semi-structured interview and Overview uncovered an apparent reservation concerning self-esteem. Stigma and the loss of important social roles were detrimental to participants' positive self-esteem. On the other hand, the development of friendships with other people with multiple sclerosis had a positive affect on self-esteem. Approximately one-third of the sample believed that they had changed for the worse as a person as a result of their condition. The remainder either felt that they had not changed at all, or they felt that they were better people, or gave mixed responses. Participants preferred not to associate with people with different illnesses and disabilities. It was suggested that the term 'disabled person' was threatening to self-esteem, whereas 'person with multiple sclerosis' was not. Limitations in the ICIDH's definition of disability was discussed and compared to participants' understanding of the term, which embraced the emotional and cultural significance of illness.

5. The majority of participants felt they had successfully adapted to their condition, but not all of these participants were satisfied with their lives. Adaptation was perceived to be an ongoing process and dependent on current circumstances. Poor adaptation was associated with self-blame, hopelessness and 'giving in' to the illness. Good adaptation was associated with acceptance, doing one's best, and maintaining hope. The characteristics of multiple sclerosis (e.g. uncertainty) made adaptation an ongoing process, which could only be understood in terms of present circumstances. Adaptation to illness was closely associated with emotional states. Personal accounts of illness, reports of stressful and uplifting events, coping strategies and perceptions of adaptation appeared to be mutually dependent on one another (Figure 7.1). Adaptation entailed constructing a life with multiple sclerosis which was personally meaningful.

Notes

1. Larocca et al (1985) interviewed 312 people with multiple sclerosis and found that only 23% were employed. Older, more educated and less disabled males were more likely to be employed. Sex, age, degree of disability, duration of illness and education level variables only accounted for 14% of the variation in employment status.

2. Similar attitudes have been recorded among elderly Aberdonians regarding their own health (Williams 1990 (see Chapter Two)).

3. For example, Norbeck et al (1991) found that the family carers of psychiatric patients needed four types of social support: emotional (acceptance, commitment, social involvement, affective and mutuality); feedback (affirmation, listening and talking); informational (illness information, behaviour management, coping, decision and perspective); and instrumental (resources, respite, care-help, backup and household).

4. See Buunk and Hoorens (1992) for a theoretical discussion on the role of social comparison and social exchange processes in social support.

5. Schonpflug and Wolfgang (1988) discuss the benefits and costs of coping. Although researchers have concentrated on the benefits of coping, the authors point out that coping can be costly or have negative effects. Problems may arise out of the use of certain coping strategies and this can cause further stress.

6. For example, woodwork and picture framing were the main occupations available at one day-centre. Owing to their increasing disability, participants who attended this centre could no longer take part in these activities. Despite the demoralising affect this had on them, they continued to attend because it was an opportunity to get out for the day.

7. Bandura (1989) describes psychosocial functioning in terms of "triadic reciprocal causation" or "reciprocal determinism". In other words, he believes that cognitive, behavioural and environmental events interact and influence each other "bi-directionally".

8 Discussion

Introduction

This chapter will start by relating the main findings of the project to the original aims of the research. The outcome of integrating qualitative and quantitative approaches will be summarised. The results will then be compared to the research reviewed in the first three chapters of the book. Shortcomings and recommendations for further research will be suggested. Finally, the implications of the findings for people with multiple sclerosis and health and social care practices and policies will be discussed.

Relating the Results to the Aims of the Research

There were two major research aims: the first was concerned with collecting individual accounts or stories of illness from the perspective of people with multiple sclerosis; the second was concerned with assessing the role of stress in adaptation to multiple sclerosis. The insiders' perspective was used to gather personal accounts of illness and the transactional model of stress to test the role of stress in adaptation to multiple sclerosis. Both approaches were used to complement one another and to gain a richer understanding of the physical, personal and social implications of multiple sclerosis in adaptation. The research was also concerned with people with multiple sclerosis who lived in institutional settings and how their lives compared to affected people living at home.

Personal accounts of multiple sclerosis were collected using semi-structured interviews which were guided by five research questions: What does multiple sclerosis mean to participants? What sort of problems do they experience? How do they cope with or manage their illness? What is the emotional impact of their illness? And what help have they received from health care professionals and services? Participants' accounts of multiple sclerosis were similar whether they lived in institutions or at home. Discussions of institutional life, however, had a different slant for each group: people living in places of long-term care spoke from direct experience, whereas people living at home spoke about the potential threat of institutional care in the event of a change in circumstances. Answers to each of these five questions are provided in Chapter Five and can be summarised as follows:

Understanding multiple sclerosis The meanings of multiple sclerosis were related initially to the physical aspects of the disease - its aetiology, diagnosis, prognosis, course and symptoms. The cause of multiple sclerosis was tied to personal life-histories which took into account an individual's susceptibility to the disease and the role of stressful events in promoting the onset of the disease. Many participants felt that the disease had lain dormant inside them for many years without having any noticeable affect. This concept appears to derive from slow viral theories of multiples sclerosis popular within current scientific research.

The diagnosis of multiple sclerosis was a source of frustration for many of the participants. Five complaints were common: the length of time it took to make a diagnosis; the manner in which a diagnosis was conveyed; the lack of information given; the use of euphemisms; and never having been formally diagnosed. Some participants had already guessed their diagnosis before it was given. Others were either overwhelmed, shocked, relieved or puzzled when a diagnosis was eventually conveyed.

The majority of people were able to make a favourable prognosis of their own illness by comparing themselves to people who were less fortunate than themselves or by minimising the severity of their own illness. Participants were more likely to refer to the gradual progression of their disease over the years rather than draw attention to dramatic relapses and remissions. Other diseases (e.g. diabetes and arthritis) and the ageing process were often implicated in the course of the disease and could be viewed as more troubling to participants than multiple sclerosis itself.

The most frequently reported symptoms were related to problems with fatigue, vision, sensations, spasms, pain, weakness, control of movements, balance and memory. Secondary symptoms were equally problematic (e.g. infections, bedsores, drowsiness, weight gain, loss of appetite, vomiting, circulatory disturbance, impotence, posture problems and contractures). It was sometimes difficult for participants to differentiate between the symptoms of multiple sclerosis, secondary symptoms arising from treatments, therapies or unsuitable aids and the symptoms of other diseases.

Uncertainty underpinned many of the physical aspects of the disease: its aetiology, diagnosis, prognosis, course and symptoms. These uncertainties influenced participants' perceptions of control. Distinctions were made between having physical, psychological and social control over multiple sclerosis. Participants often emphasised that they had psychological control over their illness, but little control over the physical and social consequences of their illness.

Consequences of illness The concepts disability and handicap provided a useful means of assessing the consequences of multiple sclerosis. Disabilities were interpreted as difficulties in performing normal activities. The five most frequently reported disabilities were mobility, self-care, activities/hobbies, housework and movement. Participants found disabilities frustrating because the most simple tasks became major exertions. A particularly difficult aspect of disability was dependency on others to help with personal self-care needs. Participants mentioned that their illness had an impact on the activities of the whole family and not just themselves. Marital strains were a concern.

Handicap was defined as socio-cultural disadvantage which stemmed from disabilities and impairments and environmental constraints. The five most frequently reported handicapping problems were employment, environmental restrictions, stigma, social roles and institutional care. Unemployment was the most common outcome of illness and a source of regret for many. Stigma was particularly damaging to participants' perceptions of themselves. Participants also missed the loss of important social roles such as being a worker, a colleague, a parent, a partner, friend or member of a club. Being disabled or handicapped was a new but unwelcome identity. However, participants also mentioned role changes for the better which were associated with personal development and insight. Leaving home to live in an institutional setting was one of the most obvious consequences of chronic illness. It was rarely a positive choice, more a sign of not being able to manage at home. For participants living at home, institutional care was a reminder of what could lie ahead of them if their own health or the health of their carers deteriorated and community services were unable to meet the additional needs of the individual and his/her family.

Managing illness Participants used a variety of methods to cope with their illness. No one strategy (cognitive, behavioural or avoidance) or combination of strategies appeared to be preferred over another. Nineteen cognitive, 18 behavioural and 15 avoidance coping strategies were identified. When faith was referred to as a coping strategy it often played a central role in participants' lives and in the day to day management of their illness. Participants were inclined to keep their feelings to themselves; to put their illness to the back of their mind; to use positive thinking; to ask for help and advice; and to try and accept their illness or face the facts.

Emotional impact of illness The most obvious emotional consequences of illness were feelings of hopelessness and sadness. Participants' fears were discussed. Feelings of contentment and pride were also apparent. Hopelessness, for five men, was closely associated with contemplations of suicide - the feeling that life was not worth living. Sadness was tied to the grieving process - dealing with the loss of former identities, abilities, and lifestyles. Fears, on the other hand, were a product of trying to predict the future and the possibility of further deterioration, greater dependency and family problems. Pride and contentment were related to feeling useful, maintaining a sense of achievement and sustaining hope in the face of illness.

Opinions about care Participants were especially dissatisfied with the help they had received from their doctors. General practitioners were criticised for their lack of knowledge concerning multiple sclerosis and neurologists for their often abrupt and seemingly uncaring manner. Lack of information was a common complaint. In terms of community services, some participants felt they had learnt how to fight the system rather than be helped by it. The paucity of community services was mentioned as a reason for living in institutional settings. Although grateful for full-time care, participants were unhappy with many aspects of institutional life, in particular the lack of privacy, unappetising food and the monotony of daily routines in the absence of organised activities. Participants had mixed feelings about the MS Society: the Society provided valuable information and organised a day-centre where people could meet other people with the illness, but the centre was also described as a dull and dispiriting place to visit and there was disquiet about the proportion of funds spent on research as opposed to improving people's quality of life. Although participants were in contact with a variety of health and social services the concept 'rehabilitation' was absent from their accounts. There was little evidence of participants being involved in constructive goal-oriented rehabilitation programmes. The lack of rehabilitation may suggest to people with multiple sclerosis that professionals see the lack of certainty about future physical abilities as a 'reason' for not offering rehabilitation. This would serve to reinforce affected people's fears for the future and feelings of worthlessness.

Transactional model of stress

Psychometric scales were used to measure hassles, uplifts, coping strategies, self-esteem and satisfaction with life and health. There were two main objectives: firstly to compare the scores of participants living at home with those of participants living in institutional settings; and secondly, to assess the role of hassles, uplifts, coping and self-esteem on adaptation. The results will be related to the ten hypotheses (listed in Chapter Four).

Hypothesis 1: People living in institutional settings report fewer hassles and uplifts than people living at home.

As expected, the institution group reported fewer hassles and uplifts than the community group, although this did not reach statistical significance. This result suggests that institutional environments may protect participants from the stresses of community living, but the benefits of community life are lost too. Institutional environments, for the participants, were characterised by inactivity; the complexity and diversity of everyday life was curtailed within such settings.

Hassles were perceived to be significantly more severe for the community group than for the institutional group. Although preferable, living at home appeared to be more demanding for participants than living in institutions. Participants living in institutions felt that residential care relieved families of the strains of illness. Participants living at home were still having to juggle with the difficulties their illness imposed on their families and friends, feelings of guilt and inadequacy and environmental barriers which prevented them from taking part in community life.

Hypothesis 2: People living in institutional settings report different types of hassles and uplifts to people living at home.

Hassles relating to noise, troublesome residents, regrets over past decisions and children were unique to the institutional group. The hassles being a burden, feeling ignored, difficulties seeing/hearing, being restricted, weather, and health of a family member were unique to the community group. Hassles peculiar to participants living in institutions reveal the deficiencies of institutional care and the disruption it causes to family life. These participants had regrets about their decision to move into hospital: they worried that they

209

had given in or given up to soon; that they had taken the easy option; that they had not pursued alternative options; or that they had not been assertive enough in securing their own wishes. Participants living at home were more worried about their diminishing role in the family and the extent to which their illness imposed restrictions on family life. Concerns about physical and environmental limitations and the burden their condition places on carers point to underlying fears which may eventually convince a person that institutional life is the only available option.

Uplifts relating to giving a compliment, being rested, having privacy/being alone and feeling safe in neighbourhood were unique to the institution group. The uplifts gossiping, being well prepared, getting love, giving love, having someone to listen to you, giving good advice, practising your hobby and children's accomplishments were unique to the community group. Despite their disadvantages, institutions were perceived to be places of retreat or shelter. Professionals were at hand and the physical environmental was relatively secure. As a result, participants felt protected, safe, attended to and cared for within institutions. They were often grateful for these aspects of institutional life. Although lack of privacy is a problem associated with institutional life, participants were able to report that they enjoyed being alone at times. Uplifts for the community group, in contrast, were based largely on interactions with others. The community group benefited from maintaining relationships with family and friends and being a part of the local community. These participants were also able to preserve their independence and pursue personal interests and hobbies.

Hypothesis 3: People living in institutional settings use more emotion-focused coping strategies than people living at home.

If a situation is perceived to be uncontrollable emotion-focused coping, aimed at making the situation more tolerable, is thought to be more appropriate than problem-focused coping (see Chapter Three). It was anticipated, therefore, that participants living in institutions would use more emotion-focused coping because they would have less control over their environment than participants living at home.

Contrary to the hypothesis, however, the community group reported significantly more emotion-focused coping strategies than the institutional group. This might partly be explained by the types of stressful events reported. The institutional group reported more service-related problems (e.g. lack of privacy, noise, waiting for attention and routines), whereas the community group reported more family-centred problems (carer's health, separation/divorce, sexual problems and relationship with children). Family-centred events were associated with emotion-focused coping and service-related concerns to problem-focused coping.

The community group were significantly more likely than the institution group to report using two emotion-focused strategies in particular - trying to see the positive side and take it out on other people when they felt angry or depressed. Living in an institution was often regarded, by participants, as the end of the road; a last resort; or a point of no return. It was difficult, therefore, for participants living in an institution to see the positive side of things. The institution group also appeared to have fewer opportunities to take out their anger on other people; they had less contact with their families and friends and they rarely felt that they could take out their feelings on professional carers or other residents. Indeed emotional restraint was more apparent in institutional settings than at home.

The only emotion-focused strategies that were frequently reported by participants living in institutional settings were also frequently used by the community group (e.g. kept feelings to myself and prayed for guidance and strength). Many of the emotion-focused strategies in the coping scale, (e.g. tried to see the positive side and took it out on other people (as mentioned above), eating more, smoking more, got busy to keep mind off problem and prepared for the worst) were antipathetic to institutional regimes and approaches to illness. However, the institution group also reported fewer problem-focused coping and cognitive, behavioural and avoidance coping strategies than participants living at home, although the only other statistically significant result was in relation to behavioural coping. Institutions appear to take complete control over the management of illness and, in so doing, limit the opportunities for residents to develop their own ways of coping with their illness.

Hypothesis 4: People living in institutional settings have poorer self-esteem than people living at home.

Participants living in institutions had poorer self-esteem scores than people living at home, but this difference was not statistically significant. On the whole, participants felt that they were people of worth, on an equal basis with others; that they had a number of good qualities and that they did not feel useless at times. On the other hand, they were more inclined to feel they were a failure; and that they were not able to do things as well as most other people.

Hypothesis 5: People living in institutions are less satisfied with their lives and health than people living at home.

The institutional group were significantly less satisfied with their life at present, than the community group. They were also less satisfied with their health at present than the community group, although this result was not statistically significant. The average rating of satisfaction with life at present was around the mid-point - indicating that participants were neither particularly satisfied nor dissatisfied with their lives. Ratings of satisfaction with health at present were slightly lower, indicating that people were, on average, dissatisfied. The upturn in ratings of satisfaction with life from the first years of the illness to present day suggests a degree of adaptation to a lower level of health and an acceptance of this level (see Figure 6.1).

Satisfaction with life across the life-span followed a similar pattern for both groups: life satisfaction was highest before the diagnosis of multiple sclerosis; lowest during the first years of the illness; around the middle mark at present time; and nearly as high as before illness in terms of hoping what the future might bring. Satisfaction with health followed a similar pattern except that the lowest point was at the present time rather than during the first years of the illness. Only 50% of the sample were satisfied with their lives at present and 38% with their health at present.

Satisfaction with life for both groups was closely tied to health, family life, performing normal activities and state of mind. Financial matters and service needs played a secondary role. Satisfaction with health was related to performing normal activities, state of mind, physical attributes, physical symptoms and maintaining autonomy. Family life was less important in definitions of good and bad health.

Hypothesis 6: High levels of hassles are associated with low levels of satisfaction.

The frequency of hassles reported predicted 15% of the variance in adaptation; a greater number of hassles predicted lower levels of satisfaction with life at present and poorer self-esteem. The hassles concerns about weight, declining physical abilities and not enough energy were reported by more than half of the sample.

Hypothesis 7: Low levels of uplifts are associated with low levels of satisfaction.

The frequency of uplifts reported predicted between 18% and 26% of the variance in adaptation: a greater number of uplifts predicted higher levels of

212

satisfaction with life at present and better self-esteem. Uplifts' frequency was a better predictor of adaptation than any other variable. Uplifts reported by more than two-thirds of the sample were music, praying/meditating and spending time with family.

Hypothesis 8: Coping strategies are influenced by demographic and illness characteristics and the type of problem reported.

Females were more likely to see the positive side, pray for guidance and strength and eat more, whereas men were more likely to prepare for the worst; married people were more likely to talk with a spouse or relative about the problem; and older people were more likely to step back from the situation and be more objective, whereas younger people were more likely to take things one at a time. However, demographic and illness variables had no significant impact on the overall type of coping strategy used (i.e. emotion- or problem-focused, behavioural, cognitive and avoidance).

Coping strategies were related to the type of problem reported. Behavioural and problem-focused coping was rarely reported when family-centred problems were identified, but were prominent when difficulties performing activities were mentioned. Coping strategies were also related to the frequency of hassles and uplifts reported. There was a significant positive correlation between emotion-focused and avoidance coping and the frequency of hassles reported; and between problem-focused and behavioural coping and the frequency of uplifts reported. The direction of causality in these relationships is unclear. For example, participants who report greater numbers of uplifts may be encouraged to use coping strategies characterised by dealing with the source of the problem and direct action. On the other hand, problem-focused coping and direct action may lead to a more positive outlook on life and the perception that uplifts occur frequently.

Hypothesis 9: Problem-focused coping and avoidance coping are associated with lower levels of satisfaction.

The first part of the hypothesis was not supported, but the second part was. As expected, there was a significant negative correlation between avoidance coping and self-esteem score. Avoidance coping predicted 12% of the variance in adaptation: the greater the reported use of this strategy the lower the level of satisfaction with health at present. There were significant positive correlations between self-esteem and problem-focused and cognitive coping, but neither coping strategy predicted any variance in levels of adaptation. Although emotion-focused coping strategies correlated negatively and behavioural coping strategies positively with measures of adaptation, these

213

relationships were not statistically significant. Hassles and avoidance coping strategies appear to be related to poorer adaptation, whereas uplifts and problem-focused coping appear to be related to better adaptation.

Hypothesis 10:   Positive self-esteem is associated with high levels of satisfaction.

There were significant positive correlations between self-esteem and satisfaction with life and health at present. Participants with a positive self-esteem were also more satisfied with their life and health. Self-esteem was also treated as a measure of adaptation rather than a personal resource because of the strong correlations between these variables.

Integrating the Results from Qualitative and Quantitative Approaches to the Project

In chapter Seven, results from the Chapters Five and Six were compared to gain a better understanding of the roles of perceptions of illness and stress variables (hassles, uplifts and coping strategies) in adaptation to multiple sclerosis. Combining both approaches revealed that accounts of illness and perceptions of stress, coping and adaptation were intricately inter-linked. Physical, psychological and social aspects of illness were implicated in participants' attempts to adapt to their illness.

Hassles and problems with illness

There were similarities between the types of hassles reported on a daily basis and themes evolving out of the personal accounts of illness associated with more long-term problems (e.g. disability and handicap). The absence of hassles in certain domains (e.g. finance and employment) was found to be as important to participants as common sources of stress (e.g. health, environment, practical, family and personal matters). Inactivity and learning how to manage spare time could be as problematic as the extra demands associated with illness such as tending to secondary symptoms, the effort and extra time required to deal with self-care activities and the organisational skills needed to maintain a social life.

The majority of participants felt there was a lot of stress and strain in their lives as a result of illness. Stress was also connected to the onset of illness. Although participants had spoken to and received help from various professionals about specific problems and consequent hassles in daily life relating to health, environmental and practical matters, there was little evidence that family and personal problems had been discussed with professionals and dealt with in a constructive way.

Uplifts and the benefits of illness

The majority of participants felt that nothing positive had come out of the experience of illness. For the 42% who felt they had gained something as a result of their illness, benefits were largely perceived to be educative, such as learning about their own strengths and weaknesses, appreciating the important things in life, and being more aware and understanding of disability issues. These long-term gains were associated with personal development. Daily uplifts, on the other hand, derived from a variety of sources (e.g. personal, social, family and environmental circumstances) and were more easily attainable than the path towards personal development (participants, on average, reported 27 uplifts each). There were similarities between reports of positive outcomes and daily uplifts. For example, some participants said they had found faith in God as a result of their illness and many reported praying as an uplift. Some participants said they had developed new hobbies and 60% of the community group reported practising your hobby, as an uplift. Some participants said they had become closer to their family as a result of illness and 68% of the sample reported spending time with the family, as an uplift.

The Uplifts Scale also demonstrates the importance of social support in participants' daily lives. The uplifts gossiping, relating well with friends, getting love and giving love were reported by over 50% of the sample. Social support in these instances often derived from family relationships and pre-illness friendships.[1] The semi-structured interviews demonstrated another source of social support: other people with multiple sclerosis. This was not surprising because the community sample was drawn from the register of the MS Society day-centre (i.e. people who regularly meet others who have the same disease). Friendships with other people with multiple sclerosis enabled participants to be grateful for their situation (there were always people worse off than themselves); gave them the companionship of others who really understood, rather than just sympathised; and were based on mutual support, reciprocity and equality. The most severely disabled people with multiple sclerosis did not attend the day-centre. Therefore, future possibilities are not all seen. It is surprising that others less well off were not the object of fear for representing personal futures. Those not able to manage such fear would possibly avoid the day-centre. Indeed, it was often said, by participants and staff at the day-centre, that the day-centre was not suitable for those newly diagnosed with multiple sclerosis. Some participants felt that similar friendships with non-disabled people were more difficult to achieve because

215

'mixed' interactions were often unequal and based on participants' dependency and non-disabled people's generosity.

Coping with stress and managing illness

The semi-structured interviews revealed that participants were much more inventive in dealing with their illness than indicated by the Method and Focus of Coping Measure. Fifty-two coping strategies were identified in personal accounts of illness compared to 19 items in the coping measure. The most popular coping strategies were: keep my feelings to myself; take one step/day at a time; pray for guidance and strength; talk to someone about the problem; and keep my mind off the problem. Participants seemed to talk to other people about specific problems, but did not necessarily confide in them their feelings. Faith, on the other hand, often provided an emotional outlet for participants' feelings: God was the focus of people's anger and bitterness, but also brought peace and compassion into some participants' lives. Taking one step at a time for many participants was a practical and realistic method of dealing with an unpredictable disease like multiple sclerosis. Trying to put the illness to the back of their minds was also functional; it enabled participants to get with their lives rather than be held back by fears for their future. Participants had to balance the danger of the MS Society day-centre in presenting this against the positive aspects of social support that it offers.

Participants were less likely to turn to the comforts of overindulgence (alcohol, nicotine or food) and the benefits of exercise. Medical professionals often advised against the taking of stimulants such as alcohol and nicotine and recommended special diets instead. The opportunity to exercise was curtailed by participants' disabilities and the availability of informal and formal carers when help was required to perform exercises. Physical and socio-environmental factors could, therefore, limit the range of coping strategies available to participants. Nevertheless, the majority of participants (approximately two-thirds) felt they were coping well with their illness.

The meanings and measurement of adaptation to multiple sclerosis

Subjective evaluations of self-esteem and satisfaction with life and health were used as measures of adaptation. Participants' scores on the Self-Esteem Scale were moderate and seemed to be a result of conflicting processes. On the one hand, participants recounted identity problems (i.e. loss of social roles, stigma, self-doubt and feelings of shame associated with not being 'normal'); on the other hand, two-thirds of the sample felt they were fundamentally the same people they had always been or that they had changed in some way for the better. Most participants had retained their non-disabled identities. Feelings of pride or the belief that they had become wiser as a result of their condition also suggests that some participants were able to maintain their self-esteem by integrating their disabled identities with their non-disabled identities. However, it was still difficult for some participants to accept their disabilities, as the distinction between being more aware of disability issues without wanting to associate with other disabled people implies. These ambiguities and discrepancies may explain participants' ability to maintain reasonable self-esteem scores.

Although only 50% of the sample were satisfied with their lives at present, 78% hoped that they would be satisfied with their lives in the future and 85% felt they had adapted to multiple sclerosis. Adaptation was associated with acceptance rather than satisfaction. Acceptance was characterised by resignation (that life with multiple sclerosis was not going to be as easy as life before it) and processes of negotiation or bargaining (doing deals with oneself or with others or setting manageable short-term goals rather than more risky long-term plans). Resignation without negotiation appeared to be more common among participants who believed they had not adapted to their illness. Resignation on its own offered no hope because participants were overwhelmed by their condition and pessimistic about their future. State of mind was central to participants definition of good and bad health, and underpinned descriptions of hopes and fears. On the positive side, state of mind was related to enjoying life, feeling happy, calm, secure, good, alert and at peace with oneself. On the negative side, it was linked to being unhappy, depressed, miserable, hopeless, suicidal, frustrated, confused, dull, mentally disordered, twisted, defeatist, a failure, worrying, loss of interest in things and lack of concentration. Feelings were central to this concept. Performing activities, family life, autonomy, physical attributes and symptoms were also associated with health and happiness. Satisfaction with life and health, as measured in the project, was, therefore, an emotional as well as a cognitive construct.

Relationships between perceptions of illness, hassles, uplifts, coping strategies, self-esteem and satisfaction with life and health appeared to be reciprocal rather than causal. It was apparent that adaptation was a dynamic process rather than a fixed outcome. It was associated with participants feelings and perceptions about themselves, their illness, their daily lives and the personal and community resources available to help them to cope with their condition.

The Findings and Other Research

The disease and health care

Participants' theories about the cause of multiple sclerosis were founded on an understanding of biomedical knowledge[2] and extrapolating from their life-histories those events which they perceived to be important. Stress was a particularly useful concept in this context because it met social approval (within medical and lay populations), and could be used to link biographical events to the onset of the disease and subsequent relapses. Pollack (1984) suggested that stress theories enabled people with multiple sclerosis to absolve themselves from any responsibility for causing the illness, but gave them a means of exerting control over its future course.

In terms of the future, most participants were optimistic about their prognosis despite medical uncertainty. There were both favourable and unfavourable aspects to uncertainty: it kept hope alive (the disease could get better or stabilise or a treatment might be found); but it also cast a shadow over any future plans (the disease could worsen at any time). Participants generally minimised the severity of their illness. This was sometimes achieved by comparing themselves to others less fortunate than themselves; since making downward comparisons enabled participants to enhance their self-perceptions. This strategy has also been found among people with arthritis and cancer (Buunk and Hoorens 1992). Although distinctions have been made between benign, mild, progressive, severe and asymptomatic forms of multiple sclerosis, participants tended to describe the course of their illness as one of gradual deterioration. In this sense the disease was under control rather than rather than out of control.

Participants' understanding of multiple sclerosis was tied closely to appraisals of control. An external locus of control has been associated with poorer adaptation among people with multiple sclerosis and other chronic diseases (see Chapter Three). In institutional settings, however, an external locus of control, in the form of a significant other ('a champion'), was found to be more appropriate since elderly residents had little say in the way homes were run. Appraisals of control are closely linked to perceptions of blame and responsibility. Participants were willing to accept personal responsibility for their own attitude towards multiple sclerosis, but they were less prepared to accept responsibility for the negative physical and social consequences of their disease. The advantage of an internal locus of control over an external locus of control was, therefore, dependent on the aspect of the disease referred to.

Participants' dissatisfaction with the way in which a diagnosis was conveyed was not surprising. Previous studies have documented

218

communications problems between doctors and patients during the stages of diagnosis (Brunel ARMS Research Unit 1983b; Radford and Trew 1987; McLellan et al 1989). These studies have consistently found that around 25% of people with multiple sclerosis are not told of their diagnosis by a doctor. Equivalent findings were found in this study: 75% of the sample had received a diagnosis from a doctor (neurologist or GP). The remainder found out their diagnosis by chance or had never been given a formal diagnosis and a small proportion found it difficult to recall exactly how a diagnosis had been made. More recently, guidelines have been written for doctors on how to give a diagnosis of multiple sclerosis to patients (Royal College of Physicians 1990; and British Society for Rehabilitation Medicine 1993).

Another common complaint reported by people with multiple sclerosis in this study and in the above mentioned surveys was a lack of information provided by doctors about the nature of the disease. This practice may be related to doctors' unease with changing doctor-patient relationships; the difficulties they experience in conveying bad news; and the feeling that they can offer little in helping people adapt to their illness (these issues were raised in Chapter Two). Consumerism, within health care policy, has encouraged the development of working partnerships between doctors and patients. Authoritarianism and submissiveness have become outdated models for doctors and patients respectively. It may take longer, however, for patients and doctors to change accustomed patterns of interaction to fit contemporary ideas about the correct way to conduct such relationships. Doctors may only play lip service to the idea of a partnership (in practice, they continue to retain power over patients by withholding information or using specialised medical jargon), and patients may feel more comfortable remaining within the 'sick role', although its application is limited in the field of chronic illness (they may prefer to follow doctors' orders in the hope of getting better rather than accept joint responsibility for the management of their illness). Both traditional and modern-day doctor-patient interactions were described in participants' accounts of illness. Lack of information was partly related to bad practice and partly, to patients' and doctors' adherence to the conventional 'sick role'. Doctors played a central role in participants' accounts of illness, from conveying the diagnosis and monitoring the disease to providing information, or not, about the services available. There is a need for participants to be realistic about the help doctors can provide and for doctors to admit their limits, relinquish their control over patients' care and to work as a member of a team of rehabilitation professionals rather than assume authority and expertise. Other professionals are more experienced in dealing with some of the personal and social consequences of multiple sclerosis.

Doctor-patient relationships were fraught with problems, arising not only from communication problems, but from alternative representations of illness. For example, a doctor may treat muscular weakness as a physical limitation which can be alleviated with special treatment/aids, but a participant's concerns may focus on how these symptoms bring about the loss of a hobby, being dependent on others and feeling frustrated, inferior and unattractive. The doctor may focus on the problem and how to rectify it, whereas the patient may focus on the consequences and how to live with them.

Participants found it difficult to talk to professionals about the more personal aspects of their illness and were often too embarrassed to mention sexual problems. When this matter was raised with one of the four neurologists in Northern Ireland (personal communication), he replied that patients in Northern Ireland were, as yet, too conservative to discuss such problems with their doctors! It would probably be more accurate to suggest that both doctors and patients feel uneasy about discussing sexual problems during clinical appointments. Counsellors and therapists are believed to be better qualified to deal with these issues. Participants also felt inhibited about discussing their feelings with medical personnel, particularly their feelings of depression and hopelessness, in case their doctors felt that they were not coping; that they were inadequate; that they were wasting a professional's time; or that they were hypochondriacs. These worries reflect how the moral undertones of lay concepts of health and illness may hinder communication processes. The time limited nature of clinical appointments, their intermittent occurrence and the variety of doctors seen also does little to encourage participants to confide in the professionals. Indeed, the needs of participants are not necessarily best met by rehabilitation services led by the medical profession. Participants reported many personal and social problems which lay outside the medical domain.

Participants living in institutions found it no easier to discuss their feelings with health care professionals despite their close proximity to health care services. An uncomplaining attitude was fostered among participants living in institutions, especially statutory hospitals. It was easier to criticise the business-like approach of private residential homes than to complain about the services provided by an under-resourced National Health Service committed to the care of patients. Participants expressed their gratitude towards the care received, but were more reserved about showing their unhappiness in case they appeared ungrateful, self-pitying, critical of the personnel or likely to upset informal carers.

The concept of 'rehabilitation' was conspicuous by its absence in participants' accounts of their illness. Health care services focused on the treatment of symptoms as they arose and the provision of aids and adaptations as disabilities began to intrude into people's lives. There was little evidence of participants and professionals working together towards agreed goals, whether they were as vague as improving a person's quality of life or as precise as finding a person alternative employment. Participants suggested that the services available responded to crises rather than prepared a person for a life with chronic illness. Although professionals were sensitive to specific symptoms (e.g. pain, spasticity and incontinence), secondary complications (e.g. pressure sores and weakness) and disabilities (e.g. mobility and movement and problems in daily living), the provision of equipment and contact with specialised rehabilitation personnel were restricted by resource shortages. For example, some participants' sole reason for going to the MS Society day-centre was to see the part-time physiotherapist employed by the society. Without this service, few participants had contact with the physiotherapy services.

Participants' unfamiliarity with the concept of rehabilitation reflects professionals' own concerns with the low profile of rehabilitation medicine in Northern Ireland and the low priority given to physical disability generally (Royal College of Physicians 1986; Swallow 1990; Swallow and Darragh 1991). In 1959 and 1960 a 'social report' on people with multiple sclerosis in Northern Ireland was conducted (Gruber 1962). Information on 698 people with multiple sclerosis was obtained. The author summarised the gaps in service provision as follows: lack of suitable employment; inadequate financial benefits; poor or unsuitable housing; lack of aids and gadgets; insufficient help for the families of the severely disabled; austere standards in hospitals and Homes; unfulfilled demand for more frequent medical attention and for ancillary services; and lack of human contact, particularly with informed professional workers.

Although health and social services have improved since Gruber's report was written, her findings are pertinent to the situation in Northern Ireland thirty years on. However, the work carried out by the PPRU on the prevalence of disability in Northern Ireland (McCoy and Smith 1992) and the priority given to physical and sensory disabilities in the most recent Regional Strategy report for Northern Ireland Health and Personal Social Service (DHSS(NI), 1991), suggest that there is a commitment to providing better services for disabled people in the future. It is to be hoped that these services will ensure that people with disabilities are able to participate fully in community life.

221

The lack of progress in service provision for people with multiple sclerosis is mirrored by the stability of negative social attitudes and discriminatory practices towards disabled people (see Chapter Two). Against this context, participants' reports of stigma and loss of social roles were unsurprising. Despite social disadvantage and problems with new, unwanted identities, participants' self-esteem scores (mean = 26.18) are comparable with those of a community population (mean = 29.4) (Baumeister et al 1989) and people with Parkinson's disease (mean = 26.87) (MacCarthy and Brown 1989). Participants appeared to maintain a sense of their own worth by maintaining their non-disabled identities and attempting to accept their disabled identities. Personal developments compensated for personal losses. Participants' satisfaction with life scores were moderate (mean = 5.6 out of 10 points), but comparable to other people with chronic illnesses (mean = 5.28 and 6.65 out of 9 points)[3] (Brown et al 1981), although slightly lower than community samples' (mean = 7.1 out of 9 points) (Palmore and Kivett 1977). Only 50% of the participants in the study were satisfied with their lives at present compared to 65% of a sample who had had a stroke (Anderson 1988). Participants' scores on satisfaction with health at present (mean = 5.2 out of 10 points) were similar to satisfaction with life scores and comparable to other people with chronic illness (mean = 5.22 and 3.88 out of 9 points) (Brown et al 1981), but lower than a middle-aged community sample (mean = 5.96 out of 7 points) (Medley 1980).

Participants' definitions of happiness and health were similar to those identified by Baumann (1961) among people with chronic illnesses and medical students. Conceptions of health and happiness were closely related to feelings of well-being, the absence of symptoms, and the ability to carry out activities. In this study, family life, autonomy and physical attributes were also important in participants' ratings of satisfaction and dissatisfaction. Taylor et al (1989) suggest that most people have unrealistically positive, rather than accurate, views of themselves, the world and their future. They also argue that positive illusions or biases are conducive to adaptation. Positive illusions, it is suggested, enable people to be realistic about the threat of negative information, whilst remaining optimistic about their ability to control negative events.

Positive illusions may also be associated with participants' perceptions of hassles and uplifts in their daily lives. The numbers of uplifts and hassles reported by participants were shown to be the only variables to significantly predict satisfaction with life and self-esteem. Reports of many uplifts and few hassles were favourable to adaptation. Participants, on average, reported slightly more uplifts than hassles. However, the number of uplifts reported by participants (mean = 27.0) is noticeably lower than that reported by a community sample (mean = 69.5) (Kanner et al 1981) and that reported by another multiple sclerosis population (mean = 46.5) (Warren et al 1991). The lack of uplifts reported is not explained by accommodation status: although participants living in institutions reported fewer uplifts than participants living at home, the difference between the two groups was not statistically significant. However, the occurrence of uplifts was similar among participants (mean = 1.77 out of 3), a community sample (mean = 2.14) (Kanner et al 1981) and a multiple sclerosis sample (mean = 1.72)(Warren et al 1991).

Out of the ten most frequently reported uplifts only spending time with family and relating well with friends were reported by participants and a community sample (Kanner et al 1981). Participants had more uplifts in common with elderly residents living in residential settings, such as praying, gossiping, getting love, giving love, and laughing. The uplift feeling safe, was shared by elderly residents and participants living in institutions only. The high frequency of the uplifts music, fresh air, and being visited, phoned etc. appear to be characteristic of participants in the study.

Unlike uplifts, the number of hassles reported by participants (mean = 20.6) is consistent with that of a community sample (mean = 22.4) (Kanner et al 1981) and other people with multiple sclerosis (mean = 22.1) (Warren et al 1991). Hassles, however, were perceived to be more severe for participants (mean 1.96 out of 3) than for a community sample (mean = 1.56) (Kanner et al 1981) and the other multiple sclerosis sample (mean = 1.39) (Warren et al 1991). Among the ten most frequently reported hassles reported by participants,[4] only two hassles - concerns about weight, and not having enough personal energy - were also reported by community samples (Kanner et al 1981; and Chamberlain and Zika 1990).[5] Again, participants had more in common with elderly people: the hassles declining physical abilities, news events, physical illness/health and difficulties seeing and hearing were reported by both groups. The high frequency of the hassles being a burden, having to wait, trouble reading, writing etc. and being restricted appear to be unique to participants in the study.

These results suggest that participants' levels of stress are comparable to unaffected people's reports of stress. The difference appears to lie more with the severity and type of hassles reported and the number and type of uplifts experienced. Compared to community samples, participants' appear to be more circumspect about the prevalence of uplifts in their lives. Participants and elderly people report similar types of hassles and uplifts which suggests common patterns in their everyday worlds. In fact 40% of the sample had reached retirement age and were, therefore, dealing with the problems of illness and old age. For participants, life with multiple sclerosis was characterised by relatively low levels of positive events rather than elevated levels of stressful events.[6] Maintaining positive illusions may be more responsible for minimising the effects of negative effects rather than maximising perceptions of positive events.

Social sanctions influence the ways in which people with multiple sclerosis cope with their illness. Self-help practices and philosophical approaches to illness which focus on coming to terms with the illness, fighting it and being positive, are generally regarded as socially acceptable responses to chronic illness (see the insiders' perspective in Chapter Three). Goffman (1963) observed that stigmatised people often manage social interactions by either minimising their problem, passing as normal or withdrawing into the company of people who are similarly disadvantaged. These cultural standards reflect a bias towards cognitive and behavioural coping strategies as opposed to emotional expression and avoidance coping strategies. Participants' preference for problem-focused (mean = 41.2%) rather than emotion-focused coping (mean = 35.4%) is comparable to scores obtained from a community sample (means = 49.9% and 38.0% respectively) (Billings and Moos 1981) and from another study on people with multiple sclerosis (means = 73.3% and 61.6%) (Hickey and Greene 1989). Although problem-focused coping was significantly correlated with self-esteem in this study, it did not significantly predict variance in adaptation. Hickey's and Greene's (1989) study of people with multiple sclerosis suggested that problem-focused coping was associated with higher levels of depression and hopelessness. Participants and community populations also appear to use cognitive coping strategies the most (mean = 46.4% and 62.7% respectively). However, participants reported using behavioural strategies the least (mean = 29.2%), whereas the community group reported avoidance strategies the least (mean = 24.0%).

Participants' coping biases generally reflect cultural biases, apart from their tendency to use more avoidance strategies. Out of a possible 19 coping strategies, one avoidance coping strategy - kept feelings to myself - was the most frequently reported of all. The evidence above suggests that this strategy, unlike other avoidance strategies, is socially supported if not encouraged. Unfortunately, there was a significant negative correlation between avoidance strategies and self-esteem and avoidance coping predicted poor satisfaction with health at present. Research has shown that avoidance, wishful thinking and self-blame strategies are associated with poor adaptation (Bombardier et al 1990; and Felton et al 1984). Coping strategies that meet social approval, therefore, are not always the best methods of dealing with the stresses of chronic illness. The benefits of one coping strategy over another are obscured by cultural stereotypes of good and bad coping.

Shortcomings and Recommendations for Further Research

One of the most obvious shortcomings of the research project is its cross-sectional design. A longitudinal research design would have been more appropriate to study the ongoing process of adaptation to multiple sclerosis. Unfortunately, resource constraints and time limitations made a cross-sectional design the only feasible option. A cross section of participants could have been selected according to the duration of illness, but there is no conclusive evidence that there are stages of adaptation and that these stages relate to time from diagnosis. A priority was given to comparing adaptation among people living in different environmental settings since the experiences of people with multiple sclerosis living in institutional settings have been largely unrecorded.

Personal accounts revealed how participants cope with their illness in the context of their personal and social lives. Retrospective accounts of illness are obviously influenced by memory distortions and perceptual biases. Personal accounts of illness, however, were not used to collect factual information systematically. The emphasis was on allowing people to tell their own stories from their perspective - the insiders' perspective. The accounts provided biographical information and descriptions and explanations of the events leading up to the diagnosis of multiple sclerosis and the aftermath. Participants constructed and developed stories about their illness which enabled them to make sense out of their current circumstances. These stories were based on facts, social conventions and personal characteristics. The researcher was also involved in the interpretation of personal accounts of illness and determined, to a large extent, the presentation of the findings. Any account can have multiple interpretations. Previous research findings and theoretical models were used to guide content analysis procedures which were designed to maximise consistency in the analyses of transcripts. The excerpts provided can give the reader only a flavour of some of the pertinent issues in participants' lives. Biographical information about the participants could have been explored further using narrative analysis and case histories.

The psychometric scales, in contrast, were concerned only with the present and the immediate past.[7] The focus on daily hassles and uplifts, rather than major life-events proved to be fitting when participants themselves revealed that they approached their illness by taking one day at a time. The minor alterations made to the Hassles and Uplifts Scales created problems in terms of comparing the research findings to other studies. For example, the hassles being a burden and being restricted were among the most 10 most frequently reported hassles in the study. It is difficult to assess whether these hassles are unique, or not to participants because these items are additions to the original Hassles Scale. If these items had not been included, however, an important aspect of participants' daily lives would have been missed. The Hassles and Uplifts Scale cannot claim to be an exhaustive list of daily events. Additions are sometimes necessary to improve its sensitivity to different populations. Nevertheless service-related hassles and the more educative aspects of uplifts were still unaccounted for in the revised Hassles and Uplifts Scales. There were similar limitation to the Method and Focus of Coping Measure, although content analysis of the semi-structured interviews suggests that the main coping strategies are captured by the scale.

The failure to measure the emotional consequences of multiple sclerosis using a standardised instrument was an oversight. The Hope Scale (Synder 1989), the Affect-Balance Scale (Bradburn 1969) or the Purpose-in-Life Test (Crumbaugh and Maholick 1964) might have provided useful information on participants' emotions, which could have been compared to the feelings described in their personal accounts of illness. However, the Satisfaction with Life and Health Scales were not totally lacking in an affective component. Definitions of hopes and fears and good and bad health included emotional states.

Finally, even though perceptions of illness, stress and coping seem to be integral to the adaptation process, hassles and uplifts and coping strategies accounted for only approximately 30% of the variance. Seventy percent of the variance in adaptation is still unaccounted for. The role of social support, impairments, disabilities and handicaps, emotional states, socio-economic variables and rehabilitation services need to be explored further to assess the contributions they make to people's ability to adapt to a life with multiple sclerosis.

Implications of the Research Findings

It is hoped that the findings from this project provide useful information for rehabilitation personnel. There is a dearth of research on the effectiveness of rehabilitation services and how to improve the quality of life of people with chronic illness. This project makes a small contribution to the field by describing the ordinary, day-to-day lives of people with multiple sclerosis and highlighting the problems people experience and the expertise they hold. The final part of this chapter will discuss the policy implications of the research findings.

Throughout the book, the daily lives of people with multiple sclerosis have been described and related to the process of adapting to chronic illness. The focus of the book has been on the perceptions of people with multiple sclerosis themselves, but these have been set against the physical characteristics of the disease and the social (lay and medical) concepts of chronic illness. Gaps in biomedical and social science research, social disadvantages and problems with health care practices and policies have been referred to in the literature reviews provided in the first three chapters of the book. Findings from this study have confirmed many of these issues and have implications, therefore, not only for people with multiple sclerosis, but for people with other chronic illnesses as well.

The personal accounts of illness emphasised the ordinary, common-sense reports of individuals experiencing problems with multiple sclerosis. They also demonstrated participants' desire to understand and to share personal stories with interested others. Personal accounts generally enable people to express their feelings, to justify their actions and to regain a sense of control over their lives. Participants' own distinction between having psychological as opposed to physical or social control over their illness, seems to confirm the importance of account-making. By telling their own stories, participants demonstrated how they coped with one of life's major stresses - chronic illness. Personal accounts of illness helped participants clarify some of their thoughts and feelings about their illness. Presenting these accounts may also help others facing similar problems and provide 'inside' information for planners and policy makers concerned with developing appropriate care packages for disabled individuals.

The Hassles and Uplifts Scales were sensitive to the context of participants' lives in institutions and at home and were also responsive to the effects of the more long-term strains in people's lives relating to disability and handicap. The absence of hassles in certain life domains and the preponderance of hassles in others point to areas for intervention in rehabilitation. For example, participants appear to receive little help in finding suitable employment or adapting their employment to meet their needs. Retraining opportunities appear to be non-existent. Participants in institutions tended to report environmental hassles and participants at home family-related hassles. Developing health care services which are responsive to central problems in different people's daily environments could dramatically improve the quality of people's lives.

Similarly, the lack of uplifts in participants' lives suggests the need to develop alternative, but equally stimulating, lifestyles for people with multiple sclerosis. Uplifts may be important for people with multiple sclerosis by sustaining coping strategies, self-esteem and hopes for the future; by providing a breather from stressful events; and by restoring energy. Segregation and social isolation limited participants' opportunities to experience the good as well as the bad things in life which make life interesting and worthwhile for most of us. Participants living in institutions were more likely than the

227

community group to feel safe and rested in their environment. Institutional care offered few uplifts but fewer hassles. The benefits of institutional care stem from the provision of 24-hour nursing care, but only one participant within the institutional group appeared to be in need of constant nursing care. The costs of institutional care - loss of autonomy, separation from family and friends and stagnation - appeared to outweigh the benefits of full-time care.

Both institutional and community groups, however, missed the spontaneity and freedom a life without chronic illness offers. The uplifts reported by participants represent some of the fundamentals of human life - getting love, giving love and fresh air - whereas the uplifts reported by a community sample (Kanner et al 1981) reflect the more frivolous, materialistic and functional aspects of human life - eating out, home (inside) pleasing to you and completing a task - which, it could be argued, are important, but not indispensable aspects of human life. Most participants had the essentials in life, but had to do without the additional extras - the perks or bonuses which motivate many of us. The scarcity of uplifts in participants' lives was more important than any other variable in predicting adaptation to illness. Creating opportunities for people with multiple sclerosis to enjoy uplifts is as important, if not more so, than alleviating the stresses in their lives. In the same way that Schnurr (1992) advises people with cancer in hospital to be a little rebellious, rehabilitation programmes need to be a little more adventurous and enterprising and less hard-boiled and utilitarian. It may sound trite, but wheelchairs, therapies and diets need not be completely joyless subjects; they can also offer independence and self-confidence. A good rehabilitation service consists of professional people who are understanding and attentive to people's losses, but also help motivate disabled people and others so that working together is a positive and enjoyable experience for both partners. Although the disease played an important part in their lives, participants also needed help with general life processes, such as unemployment and old age, which were just as problematic.

Rehabilitation programmes should focus on the social environment and each individual's circumstances. Thus, a public education programme aimed at tackling negative attitudes and discriminatory practices towards disabled people is as important as developing the expertise of people living with chronic illness. Participants, even if they did not always realise it, were experts on coping with multiple sclerosis.[8] Rehabilitation programmes need to build on those strengths and also advise on alternative coping strategies when necessary. Cultural coping biases also need to be addressed in order to find a compromise between society's discomfort with people showing their feelings and an individual's need sometimes to release these feelings.[9] A greater honesty is needed so that feelings of powerlessness, jealousy, shame, misery and anger are not interpreted as signs of weakness. Bravery and stoicism, although admirable, can be overrated virtues which put unnecessary pressures on people with chronic illness in terms of what society interprets as acceptable or respectable responses to their condition.

Participants' definitions of hopes and fears and good and bad health provide useful targets for rehabilitation programmes and standards for the evaluation of institutional care. The criteria participants used for rating their own happiness and health could be used to measure changes in an individual's quality of life at home and in institutional settings. In this study, hopes and fears were tied to health, state of mind (feelings and cognition), family life and being able to perform activities. Good and bad health were also related to state of mind and the ability to perform activities, along with personal autonomy, physical attributes (e.g. good appetite, good heart, feeling strong and energetic) and physical symptoms. Given that one of the main aims of the 1990 NHS and Community Care Act is to put the needs of service users and carers first, the priorities of participants in this study in rating their own health and happiness should be of some interest to service providers and purchasers. The outcome of community care policies for disabled and elderly people is dependent, to a large extent, on the successful implementation of care management. Only fifty percent of the participants in this study indicated that they were satisfied with their lives at present. This proportion may increase in the future if care managers and service users are able to work together to make real choices about service needs (e.g. paying friends, relatives and neighbours to come in at odd hours rather than using day centres or residential care) and have the financial resources to make this possible.

The study has shown that people with multiple sclerosis residing in institutions are less satisfied with their lives than people living at home. A policy of care in the community which simply replaces one form of institutional care (hospitals) with another (private residential homes) should be criticised because it does little to promote individual autonomy and is insensitive to individual needs. All of the participants living in institutions in this study, with one exception, could have lived in their homes. However, the necessary care in the community was not available to them or was not flexible enough to deal with changing needs.

The process of adapting to multiple sclerosis is continuous and, therefore, as relevant in old age as it is to young adults; to people with a long duration of illness as well as those recently diagnosed; and to people living in institutional settings as well as those people living at home. Information, advice, encouragement and reassurance may be the most sought after but least attainable help a person with multiple sclerosis needs. Dealing with the stresses of chronic illness is a daily task most people with multiple sclerosis do on their own or with the help of their families and friends. This book has focused on these individual achievements despite physical and social disadvantages. It ends, therefore, with an excerpt from one of the interviews which reinforces the personal significance of multiple sclerosis on the lives of people with the disease:

You can put strangers at their ease if you have a sense of humour. If you can make them smile, conversation comes more naturally. They're sort of confused and I've found that humour always helps. They can say "Well, I can talk to this guy, he's human." And if you talk with them, they find that I've got a lot of experience in my life and I can relate to them and get conversation going. But communication is the problem sometimes - not in here (hospital) because there are a lot of people with wheelchairs. I've found people in wheelchairs help each other. It's not forced, it's being there and being natural and appreciating. One thing I don't want is sympathy. That's no good to anybody, particularly to me. I just need understanding 'cos some people think "Aah poor fella" - they think they have to almost talk down to you. As I said, if they talk naturally I will talk naturally.

There's a sort of myth that when you're in a wheelchair you're grounded - you're not useful for anything, you know. You just have to sit there and, as you do as a child, "Be seen and not heard". But, ah, I don't believe that. Some things I have initiated myself. I suppose partly, it's self-belief, you know. Believing and knowing what you can do and what you used to be able to do. Although part of me can't function right, you know, there's other parts. The brain's still the same. It's probably sharper now than it was 'cos you've got to compensate for more things. It's more your quality of life, you know, not quantity.

Notes

1. Pre-morbid personality, family size, structure and dynamics would presumably be influencing the extent to which some people with multiple sclerosis were able to experience these uplifts. For example, single participants are less likely to than married participants with children.

2. Towards which participants contributed financially in terms of fund raising activities.

3. People with coronary artery disease and chronic obstructive pulmonary disease respectively.

4. Results from the total sample rather than the two separate groups (see Table 6.2).

5. Although participants living at home, like the community samples, also reported hassles relating to health of a family member, misplacing or losing things and the weather.

6. Zautra and Reich (1980) also found that positive life events had a greater influence in enhancing well-being than negative life events had in diminishing it. There has been relatively little research on the impact of positive psychological states and events on physical health and well being compared to negative states and events (Edwards and Cooper 1988).

7. The satisfaction scales were the exception. Participants were asked to rate satisfaction according to life before and during the first years of illness as well as in the present and future.

8. Prior to the completion of this book, an article in the journal Social Science and Medicine by McLauglin and Zeeberg (August 1993) looked at the role of self-care practices in the management of multiple sclerosis during periods of non-medical contact in two different cultures. The article focused on people's self-care responses to specific symptoms of the disease as well as changes in employment and in living environment and loneliness. These self-care practices revealed people's ingenuity in coping with the stresses of illness. Knowledge about self-help skills was gained largely through people's own experience or from magazines and books, family and mutual aid groups. Respondents felt that self-initiated self-care practices were empowering. The authors suggest that health professionals can assist in this adaptive process and advise when dangers exist.

9. The role of 'expressed emotion' in the management of illness has received more attention in the field of mental illness (Vaughn and Leff 1976). This work has concentrated on the negative aspects of expressed emotion in the family life of people with schizophrenia. They found that the relapse rate was much higher in people with schizophrenia who lived with relatives rated as high in hostility, over-involvment and expressed criticism. Moos and Moos (1981) developed the Family Environment Scale (FES) to measure the characteristics of all types of families. The FES consists of 10

subscales (cohesiveness, expressiveness, conflict, independence, achievement, intellectual-cultural and active-recreational orientation, moral-religious emphasis, organisation and control). This scale has been useful in understanding the family environment of runaway adolescents, alcoholics and people with depression. Distressed families were found to be lower on cohesion, expressiveness, independence, and intellectual and recreational orientation and higher on conflict and control. It may also be useful in understanding the family background of people who have problems in adapting to their illness.

Bibliography

Abberley, P. (1992), 'A critique of OPCS disability surveys', *Radical Statistics,* 51, pp. 7-20.

Abram, H.S. (1972), 'The psychology of chronic illness', *Journal of Chronic Disease,* 25, pp. 659-64.

Aldwin, C.M. and Revenson, T.A. (1987), 'Does coping help? A reexamination of the relation between coping and mental health', *Journal of Personality and Social Psychology,* 53, pp. 337-48.

Alpert, D. and Culberton, A. (1987), 'Daily hassles and coping strategies of dual-earner and nonduel-earner women', *Psychology of Women Quarterly,* 11, pp. 359-66.

Anderson, R. (1988), 'The quality of life of stroke patients and their carers' in Anderson, R. and Bury, M. (eds.), *Living with chronic illness. The experience of patients and their families,* Unwin Hyman, London.

Anderson, R. and Bury, M. (1988), *Living with chronic illness. The experience of patients and their families,* Unwin Hyman, London.

Antonovsky, A. (1987), *Unravelling the Mystery of Health,* Jossey-Boss, San Francisco.

Argyle, M. (1987), *The Psychology of happiness,* Methuen, London.

Armstrong, D. (1984), 'The Patient's view', *Social Science and Medicine,* 18, pp. 737-44.

Asch, A. (1984), 'The experience of disability. A challenge for psychology', *American Pyschologist,* 39, pp. 529-36.

Ashitey, G.A. and Miller, J.H.D. (1970), 'Multiple sclerosis in Northern Ireland. A study of the date and place of birth of patients', *Ulster Medical Journal,* 39, pp. 55-63.

233

Atkinson, J.M. (1993), 'The patient as sufferer', *British Journal of Medical Psychology*, 66, pp. 113-20.

Audit Commission (1986), *Making a Reality of Community Care*, HMSO, London.

Auerbach, S.M. (1989), 'Stress management and coping research in the health care setting: an overview and methodological commentary', *Journal of Consulting and Clinical Psychology*, 57, pp. 388-95.

Bandura, A. (1982), 'Self-efficecy mechanism in human agency', *American Psychologist*, 37, pp. 122-47.

Bandura, A. (1989), 'Perceived self-efficacy in the exercise of personal agency', *The Psychologist*, 10, pp. 411-24.

Baric, L. (1969), 'Recognition of the 'at-risk' role: a means to influence health behavior', *International Journal of Health Education*, 12, pp. 24-34.

Barnes, C. (1991), *Disabled people in Britain and discrimination. A case for anti-discrimination legislation*, Hurst and Company, London.

Barton, R. (1959), *Institutional neurosis*, John Wright, Bristol.

Bauer, H.J. and Hanefeld, F.A. (1993), *Multiple sclerosis. Its impact from childhood to old age*, W.B. Saunders Company, London.

Baumann, B. (1961), 'Diversities in conceptions of health and physical fitness', *Journal of Health and Human Behavior*, 2, pp. 39-46.

Baumeister, R.F., Tice, D.M. and Hutton, D.G. (1989), 'Self-presentational motivations and personality differences in self-esteem', *Journal of Personality*, 57, pp. 547-79.

Beardshaw, V. (1988), *Last on the list. Community services for people with physical disabilities*, King's Fund Institute, London.

Beebe, G., Kurtzke, J.F., Kurland, L.T., Auth, T.L. and Nazler, B. (1967), 'Studies on the natural history of multiple sclerosis in U.S. veterans', *Neurology*, 17, pp. 2-17.

Beckham, J.C., Keefe, F.J., Caldwell, D.S. and Roodman, A.S. (1991), 'Pain coping stratagies in rheumatoid arthritis: relationships to pain, disability, depression and daily hassles', *Behavior Therapy*, 22, pp. 113-24.

Benner, P. and Wrubel, J. (1989), *The primacy of caring. Stress and coping in health and illness*, Addison Wesley, Menlo Park.

Ben-Sira, Z. (1984), 'Chronic illness, stress and coping', *Social Science and Medicine*, 18, pp. 725-36.

Benz, C. (1988), *Coping with MS. Multiple sclerosis*, Optima, London.

Bernat, J.L. and Vincent, F.M. (1987), *Neurology: Problems in primary care*, Medical Economic Books, Oradell.

Biklen, D. and Bogdana, R. (1977), 'Media portrayal of disabled people: a study of stereotypes', *Inter-Racial Children's Books Bulletin*, 8, 6 and 7, pp. 4-9.

Billings, A.S. and Moos, R.H. (1981), 'The role of coping responses and social resources in attenuating the stress of life events', Journal of Behavioral Medicine, 4, pp. 139-57.

Blankstein, K.R., Flett, G.L. and Koledin, S. (1991), 'The brief college student hassles scale: development, validation, and relation with pessimism', Journal of College Student Development, 32, pp. 258-64.

Blaxter, M. (1976), The meaning of disability, Heinemann, London.

Blaxter, M. (1983), 'The causes of disease. Women talking', Social Science and Medicine, 17, pp. 59-69.

Blaxter, M. (1990), Health and lifestyles, Tavistock/Routledge, London.

Bloor, M. (1978), 'Shorter report on the analysis of observational data: a discussion of the worth and uses of inductive techniques and respondent validation', Sociology, 12, pp. 545-52.

BMP DDB Needham (1993), The Multiple Sclerosis Society, BMP DDB Needham, London.

Bogdan, R. and Taylor, S.J. (1989), 'Relationships with severely disabled people: the social construction of humanness', Social Problems, 36, pp. 135-48.

Boker, W., Brenner, H.D., Gerstner, G., Keller, F., Muller, J. and Spichtig, L. (1984), 'Self-healing stratagies among schizophrenics: attempts at compensation for basis disorders', Acta Psychiatrica Scandinavica, 69, pp. 373-78.

Boker, W., Brenner, H.D. and Wurlger, S. (1989), 'Vulnerability-linked deficiencies, psychopathology and coping behaviour of schizophrenics and their relatives', British Journal of Psychiatry, 155, pp. 128-35.

Bombardier, C.H., D'Amico, C. and Jordon, J.S. (1990), 'The relationship of appraisal and coping to chronic illness adjustment', Behaviour Research Therapy, 28, pp. 297-304.

Bourhis, R.Y., Roth, S. and MacQueen, G. (1989), 'Communication in the hospital setting: a survey of medical and everyday language use amongst patients, nurses and doctors', Social Science and Medicine, 28, pp. 339-46.

Bowling, A. (1991), Measuring health. A review of quality of life measurement scales, Open University Press, Milton Keynes.

Breakwell, G. (1986), Coping with threatened identities, Methuen, London.

Breir, A. and Strauss, J.S. (1983), 'Self-control in psychotic disorders', Archive of General Psychiatry, 40, pp. 1141-5.

British Society of Rehabilitation Medicine (1993), Multiple Sclerosis: A Working Party Report of the British Society of Rehabilitation Medicine, B.S.R.M., London.

Brooks, N.A. and Matson, R.R. (1982), 'Social-psychological adjustment to multiple sclerosis', Social Science and Medicine, 16, pp. 2129-35.

Brown, G.W. and Harris, T.O. (1978), *Social origins of depression: a study of psychiatric disorder in women,* Tavistock, London.

Brown, J.S., Rawlinson, M.E. and Hilles, N.C. (1981), 'Life satisfaction and chronic disease: exploration of a theoretical model', *Medical Care,* 19, pp. 1136-46.

Brunel ARMS Research Unit. (1982), *Talking about MS,* General Report Number 1, Department of Human Sciences, Brunel, University of West London.

Brunel ARMS Research Unit. (1983a), *MS People: a demographic profile,* General Report Number 2, Department of Human Sciences, Brunel, University of West London.

Brunel ARMS Research Unit. (1983b), *Discovering the diagnosis of MS,* General Report Number 3, Department of Human Sciences, Brunel, University of West London.

Brunel ARMS Research Unit. (1986), *Measuring effects,* General Report Number 4, Department of Human Sciences, Brunel, University of West London.

Brunel ARMS Research Unit. (1986), *Doing justice to MS symptoms,* General Report Number 5. Department of Human Sciences, Brunel, University of West London.

Budd, R.W. (1971), *Content analysis of communications,* Macmillan, New York.

Bulman, R.J. and Wortman, C.B. (1977), 'Attributions of blame and coping in the 'real world': severe accident victims react to their lot', *Journal of Personality and Social Psychology,* 35, pp. 351-63.

Burks, N. and Martin, B. (1985), 'Everyday problems and life change events: ongoing versus acute sources of stress', *Journal of Human Stress,* 11, pp. 27-35.

Burnfield, A. (1985), *Multiple sclerosis: a personal exploration,* Souvenir Press, London.

Bury, M.R. (1982), 'Chronic illness as biographical disruption', *Sociology of Health and Illness,* 4, pp. 167-82.

Buunk, B.P. and Hoorens, V. (1992), 'Social support and stress: the role of social comparison and social exchange processes', *British Journal of Clinical Psychology,* 31, pp. 445-57.

Calnan, M. (1987), *Health and illness: The lay perspective,* Tavistock, London.

Cameron, P., Titus, D.G., Kostin, J. and Kostin, M. (1973), 'The life satisfaction of nonnormal persons', *Journal of Consulting and Clinical Psychology,* 41, pp. 207-14.

236

Campbell, A., Converse, P.E. and Rogers, W.L. (1976), *The quality of American life*, Russell Sage, New York.

Campling, J. (1981), *Images of ourselves. Women with disabilities talking*, Routledge and Kegan Paul, London.

Cantril, H. (1965), *The pattern of human concerns*, Rutgers University Press, New Brunswick.

Carey, M.A. and Smith, M.W. (1992), 'Enhancement of validity through qualitative approaches. Incorporating the patient's perspective', *Evaluation and The Health Care Professionals*, 15, pp. 107-14.

Cassileth, B.R., Lisk, E.J., Strouse, T.B., Miller, D.S., Brown, L.L., Cross, P.A. and Tenaglia, A.N. (1984), 'Psychosocial status in chronic illness. A comparative analysis of six diagnostic groups', *The New England Journal of Medicine*, 311, pp. 506-11.

Chamberlin, K., Zika, S. (1990), 'The minor events approach to stress: support for the use of daily hassles', *British Journal of Psychology*, 81, pp. 469-81.

Chamberlain, M.A. (1991), 'The way forward for rehabilitation medicine', in the Royal College of Physicians of London, *The National Concept of Rehabilitation Medicine*, RCP publications, London.

Charmaz, K. (1983), 'Loss of self: a fundamental form of suffering in the chronically ill', *Sociology of Health and Illness*, 5, pp. 168-95.

Charmaz, K. (1987), 'Struggling for a self: identity levels of the chronically ill', in Conrad, P. and Roth, J. (ed.), *The Experience and Management of Chronic Illness, JAI Press, Greenwich*, pp. 283-307.

Clark, P. and Bowling, A. (1990), 'Quality of everyday life in long stay institutions for the elderly. An observational study of long stay hospital and nursing home care', *Social Science and Medicine*, 30, pp. 1201-10.

Cohen, F. and Lazarus, R.S. (1979), 'Coping with the stresses of illness', in Stone, G.C., Cohen, F., Adler, N.E. and Associates (ed.), *Health psychology - a handbook*, Jossey-Bass, San Francisco, pp. 217-254.

Confavreux, C., Aimard, G. and Devic, M. (1980), 'Course and prognosis of multiple sclerosis assessed by the computerised data processing of 349 patients', *Brain*, 103, pp. 281-300.

Conrad, P. (1990), 'Qualitative research on chronic illness: a commentary on method and conceptual development', *Social Science and Medicine*, 30, 1257-63.

Cooley, C.H. (1902), *Human nature and the social order*, Scribner's, New York.

Cooper, C.L. (1988), 'Personality, life stress and cancerous disease', in Fisher, S. and Reason, J (ed.), *Handbook of life stress, cognition and health*, John Wiley and Sons, Chichester, pp. 369-81.

Cooper, C.L. and Faragher, E.B. (1992), 'Coping strategies and breast disorders/cancer', *Psychological Medicine,* 22, pp. 447-55.

Cooper, G.L. and Payne, R. (1991), *Personality and stress: individual differences in the stress process,* John Wiley and Sons, Chichester.

Coopersmith, S. (1967), *The antecedents of self-esteem,* W.H. Freeman, San Francisco.

Cornell, S. (1992), 'Multiple sclerosis under pressure', *Disability,* 6, pp. 3-5.

Cornwell, J. (1984), *Hard-earned lives. Accounts of health and illness from East London,* Tavistock, London.

Counte, M.A., Bieliauskas, L.A. and Pavlou, M. (1983), 'Stress and personal attitudes in chronic illness', *Archives of Physical Medicine and Rehabilitation,* 64, pp. 272-5.

Crnic, K.A. and Booth, C.C. (1991), 'Parenting across early childhood', *Journal of Marriage and Family,* 53, pp. 1042-50.

Dalos, N.P., Rabins, P.V., Brooks, M.D. and O'Donnell, P. (1983), 'Disease activity and emotional state in multiple sclerosis', *Annals of Neurology,* 13, pp. 573-7.

Daly, J., McDonald, I. and Willis, E. (1992), 'Why don't you ask them? A qualitative research framework for investigating the diagnosis of cardiac normality', in Daly, J., McDonald, I. and Willis, E. (ed.), *Researching health care. Designs, dilemmas, disciplines,* Tavistock/Routledge, London, pp. 188-206.

Darton, R.A. and Wright, K.G. (1993), 'Changes in the provision of long-stay care, 1970-1990', *Health and Social Care,* 1, pp. 11-25.

Davidson, L. and Strauss, J.S. (1992), 'Sense of self in recovery from severe mental illness', *British of Journal of Medical Psychology,* 65, pp. 131-45.

Deary, I.J., Smart, A. and Wilson, J.A. (1992), 'Depression and hassles in globus-pharyngis', *British Journal of Psyhiatry,* 161, pp. 115-17.

DHSS. (1990), *People First. Community care in Northern Ireland for the 1990s,* HMSO, Belfast.

DHSS, NI. (1991), *A regional Strategy for the Northern Ireland Health and Personal Social Services 1992-1997,* DHSS, Belfast.

DHSS, NI. (1991), *The Northern Ireland Census 1991: Summary Report,* HMSO, Belfast.

Department of Health. (1989), *Caring for people,* HMSO, London.

Department of Health. (1989), *Working for patients,* HMSO, London.

Department of Health. (1990), *Caring for quality. Guidance on standards for residential homes for people with a physical disability. A compilation of stadards and guidance developled by the Social Services Inspectorate,* HMSO, London.

Department of Health. (1992), *The patient's charter,* HMSO, London.

DeLongis, A., Coyne, J.C., Dakof, G., Folkman, S. and Lazarus, R.S. (1982), 'Relationship of daily hassles, uplifts and major life events to health status', *Health Psychology*, 1, pp. 119-36.

De Souza, L. (1990), *Multiple sclerosis. Approaches to management*, Chapman and Hall, London.

Devins, G.M. and Seland, T.P. (1987), 'Emotional impact of multiple sclerosis: recent findings and suggestions for future research', *Psychological Research*, 101, pp. 363-75.

Dimond, M. and Jones, S.L. (1983), *Chronic illness across the life span*, Appleton-Century-Crofts, East Norwalk.

Diener, E. (1984), 'Subjective well-being. *Psychological Bulletin*, 95, pp. 542-75.

Dingwall, R. (1992), 'Don't mind him - he's from Barcelona.', in Daly, J., McDonald, I. and Willis, E. (ed.), *Researching health care. Designs, dilemmas, disciplines*, Tavistock/Routledge, London, pp. 161-75.

Dittman, J. and Schutter, R. (1990), 'Disease consciousness and coping stratagies of patients with schizophrenic psychosis', *Acta Psychiatrica Scandinavica*, 82, pp. 318-22.

Dohrenwend, B.P. and Shrout, P.E. (1985), '"Hassles" in the conceptualization and measurement of life stress variables', *American Psychologist*, 40, pp. 780-85.

Duval, M.L. (1984), 'Psychosocial metaphors of physical distress among MS patients', *Social Science and Medicine*, 19, pp. 635-38.

Eastern Health and Social Services Board. (1992), *Making life Better. The Eastern Health and Social Services Board's charter for patients and clients*, EHSSB, Belfast.

Eckenrode, J. (1984), 'Impact of chronic and acute stressors on daily reports of mood', *Journal of Personality and Social Psychology*, 46, pp. 907-18.

Edwards, J.R. and Cooper, C.L. (1988), 'The impacts of positive psychological states on physical health: a review and theoretical framework', *Social Science and Medicine*, 27, pp. 1447-59.

Ehmann, T.S., Beninger, R.J., Gawal, M.J. and Riopelle, R.J. (1990), 'Coping, social support. and depressive symptoms in Parkinson's disease', *Journal of Geriatric Psychiatry and Neurology*, 3, pp. 85-90.

Eichler, A., Silverman, M. and Pratt, D. (1986), *How to define and research stress*, American Psychiatric Press, Washington.

Elian, M. and Dean, G. (1983), 'Need for and use of social and health services by multiple sclerosis patients living at home in England', *The Lancet*, pp. 1091-3.

Elliot, T.R., Witty, T.E., Herrick, S. and Hoffman, J.T. (1991), 'Negotiating reality after physical loss: hope, depression, and disability', *Journal of Personality and Social Psychology*, 61, pp. 608-13.

Endler, N.S. and Parker, J.D.A. (1990), 'Multidimensional assessment of coping: a critical evaluation', *Journal of Personality and Social Psychology*, 58, pp. 844-54.

Epstein, S. (1973), 'The self concept revisited, or a theory of a theory', *American Psychologist*, 41, pp. 404-16.

Erikson, E.H. (1963), *Childhood and society*, (2nd ed.), Norton, New York.

Euridiss (1990), 'European research on incapacitating diseases and social support', *International Journal of Health Sciences*, 1, pp. 217-28.

Evans, C.D. (1982), 'Progress in rehabilitation of multiple sclerosis', in Capildeo, R. and Maxwell, A. (ed.), *Progress in Rehabilitatiuon. Multiple Sclerosis*, The MacMillan Press, London, pp. 101-114.

Ewedemi, F. and Linn, M.W. (1987), 'Health and hassles in older and younger men', *Journal of Clinical Psychology*, 43, pp. 347-53.

Falloon, I.R.H. and Talbot, R.E. (1981), 'Persistent auditory hallucinations: coping mechanisms and implications for management', *Psychological Medicine*, 11, pp. 329-39.

Feldman, D.J. (1974), 'Chronic disabling illness: a holistic view', *Journal of Chronic Disease*, 27, pp. 287-91.

Felton, B. and Kahana, E. (1974), 'Adjustment and situationally-bound locus of control among institutionalized aged', *Journal of Gerontology*, 29, pp. 295-301.

Felton, B.J., Revenson, T.A. and Hinrichsen, G.A. (1984), 'Stress and coping in the explanation of psychological adjustment among chronically ill adults', *Social Science and Medicine*, 18, pp. 889-98.

Felton, B.J. and Revenson, T.A. (1987), 'Age differences in coping with chronic illness', *Psychology of Aging*, 2, pp. 164-70.

Finkelstein, V. (1980), *Attitudes and disabled people*, World Rehabilitation Fund Inc., New York.

Fisher, S. and Reason, J. (1988), *Handbook of life stress, cognition and health*, John Wiley and Sons, Chichester.

Fitts, W.H. (1965), *Tennessee self-concept manual*, Counselor Recordings and Tests, Nashville.

Fitzpatrick, R., Hinton, J., Newman, S., Scrambler, G. and Thompson, J. (1984), *The experience of illness*, Tavistock, London.

Flanagan, J.C. (1982), 'Measurement of quality of life: current state of art', *Archives of Physical Medicine and Rehabilitation*, 63, pp. 56-59.

240

Flaskerud, J.H. and Calvillo, E.R. (1991), 'Beliefs about AIDS, health and illness among low-income Latina women', *Research in Nursing and Health*, 14, pp. 431-8.

Fleishman, J.A. (1984), 'Personality characteristics and coping patterns', *Journal of Health and Social Behavior*, 25, pp. 229-44.

Fleming, R., Baum, A. and Singer, J.E. (1984), 'Toward an integrative approach to the study of stress', *Journal of Personality and Social Psychology*, 46, pp. 939-49.

Folkman, S. (1984), 'Personal control and stress and coping processes: a theoretical analysis', *Journal of Personality and Social Psychology*, 46, pp. 839-52.

Folkman, S. and Lazarus, R.S. (1985), 'If it changes it must be a process: study of emotion and coping during three stages of a college examination', *Journal of Personality and Social Psychology*, 48, pp. 150-70.

Folkman, S. and Lazarus, R.S. (1988), 'The relationship between coping and emotion: implications for theory and research', *Social Science and Medicine*, 26, pp. 309-17.

Fowles, D.C. (1992), 'Schizophrenia - diathesis-stress revisited', *Annual Review of Psychology*, 43, pp. 303-36.

Fylkesnes, K. and Forde, O.H. (1992), 'Determinants and dimensions involved in self-evaluation of health',. *Social Science and Medicine*, 35, pp. 271-9.

Gallagher, E.B. (1976), 'Lines of reconstruction and extension in the Parsonian sociology of illness', *Social Science and Medicine*, 10, pp. 207-18.

Gerhardt, U. (1990), 'Qualitative research on chronic illness: the issue and the story', *Social Science and Medicine*, 30, pp. 1149-59.

Gerson, E.M. (1976), 'The social character of illness: Deviance or politics?', *Social Science and Medicine*, 10, pp. 219-24.

Gething, L. (1991), 'Generality vs. specificity of attitudes towards people with disabilities', *British Journal of Medical Psychology*, 64, pp. 55-64.

Glouberman, S. (1990), *Keepers. Inside stories from total institutions*, King's Fund, London.

Glover, J. (1988), *I: the philosophy and psychology of personal identity*. London: Penguin.

Goffman, E. (1963). *Stigma. Notes on the management of spoiled identity*, Penguin, Harmondsworth.

Goffman, E. (1968), *Asylums. Essays on the social situation of mental patients and other inmates*, Penguin, Harmondsworth.

Goldberg, D.P. and Hillier, V.F. (1979), 'A scaled version of the General Health Questionnaire', *Psychological Medicine*, 9,pp. 139-45.

Gould, J. (1982), 'Disabilities and how to live with them', *The Lancet*, 2, pp. 1208-10.

241

Graham, J. (1987), *Multiple sclerosis. A self-help guide to its management*, Thorsons Publishing Group, Wellingborough.

Grant, I., McDonald, W.I., Patterson, T. and Trimble, M.R. (1989), 'Multiple sclerosis', in Brown, G.W and Harris, T.O. (ed.), *Life events and illness*, Unwin Hyman, London, pp. 295-311.

Gray, D.E. (1993), 'Perceptions of stigma: the parents of autistic children', *Sociology of Health and Illness*, 15, pp. 102-20.

Greene, J. and D'Oliveira, M.(1982), *Learning to use statistical tests in psychology. A student's guide*, The Open University Press, Milton Keynes.

Griffiths, R. (1988), *Community care: agenda for action*, DHSS, London.

Gruber, E. (1962), *Social report on a follow-up study of patients suffering from multiple sclerosis*, Graham and Heslip, Belfast.

Gruen, R.J., Folkman, S. and Lazarus, R.S. (1988), 'Centrality and individual differences in the meaning of daily hassles', *Journal of Personality*, 56, pp. 743-62.

Hall, J. A., Epstein, A.M., DeCianis, M.L. and McNeil, B.J. (1993), 'Physicians' liking for their patients: more evidence for the role of affect in medical care', *Health Psychology*, 12, pp. 140-6.

Hall, J.N. (1990), 'Towards a psychology of caring', *British Journal of Clinical Psychology*, 29, pp. 129-44.

Hammersley, M. (1990), 'What's wrong with ethnography? The myth of theoretical description', *Sociology*, 24, pp. 597-615.

Hannaford, S. (1985), *Living outside inside*, Canterbury Press, Berkeley.

Harper, A.C., Harper, D.A., Chambers, L.W., Cino, P.M. and Singer, J. (1986), 'An epidemiological description of physical, social and psychological problems in multiple sclerosis', *Journal of Chronic Disease*, 39, pp 305-10.

Hart, N. (1985), *The sociology of health and medicine*, Causeway Books, Ormskirk.

Hawkins, S and Kee, F. (1988), 'Updated epidemiological studies of multiple sclerosis in Northern Ireland', *Journal of Neurology*, 235 (suppl 1), pp. S86.

Heaton, R.K., Nelson, L.M., Thompson, D.S., Burks, J.S. and Franklin, G.M. (1985), 'Neuropsychological findings in relapsing-remitting and chronic-progressive multiple sclerosis. *Journal of Consulting and Clinical Psychology*, 53, pp. 103-10.

Henwood, K.L. and Pidgeon, N.F. (1992), 'Qualitative research and psychological theorizing', *British Journal of Psychology*, 83, pp. 97-111.

Hermanova, H. (1991), 'State of rehabilitation medicine in Europe in 1990 and targets for the year 2000', in RCP/DSA (ed.), *The National Concept of Rehabilitation Medicine. Proceedings of a conference of the Disablement Services Authority and the Royal College of Physicians,* RCP publications, London pp. 21-31.

Herzlich, C. (1973), *Health and illness. A social psychological analysis,* Academic Press, London.

Herzlich, C. and Pierret, J. (1987), *Illness and self in society,* The John Hopkins University Press, Baltimore.

Hetu, R., Riverin, L., Lalande, N., Getty, L. and St-Cyr, C. (1988), 'Qualitative analysis of the handicap associated with occupational hearing loss', *British Journal of Audiology,* 22, pp. 251-64.

Hetu, R., Riverin, L., Getty, L. Lalande, N.M. and St-Cyr, C. (1990), 'The reluctance to acknowledge hearing difficulties among hearing-impaired workers', *British Journal of Audiology,* 24, pp. 265-76.

Heyden, V. (1993), 'Never mind the quality', *Health Service Journal,* 103, pp. 21.

Hickey, A. and Greene, S.M. (1989), 'Coping with multiple sclerosis', *Irish Journal of Psychological Medicine,* 6, pp. 118-24.

Higgs, P.F., MacDonald, L.D. and ward, M.C. (1992), 'Responses to the institution among elderly patients in hospital long-stay care', *Social Science and Medicine,* 35, pp. 287-93.

Hildman, T.B., Ferguson, G.H. and Thompson, W.R. (1991), 'Daily hassles cause burnout', *Journal of Nursing Administration,* 21, pp. 44-5.

Hinkle, L.E. (1974), 'The concept of "stress" in the biological and social sciences', *International Journal of Psychiatry in Medicine,* 5, pp. 335-57.

Hobfoll, S.E. (1986), *Stress, social support and women,* Hemisphere Publishing Corporation, Washington.

Hobfoll, S.E. (1988), *The ecology of stress* Hemisphere, New York.

Holahan, C.J. and Moos, R.H. (1987), 'Personal and contextual determinants of coping strategies', *Journal of Personality and Social Psychology,* 52, pp. 946-55.

Humphries, S. and Gordon, P. (1992), *Out of sight. The experience of disability 1900-1950,* Northcote House, Plymouth.

Hunt, S.M., McKenna, S.P. and Williams, J. (1981) 'Reliability of a population survey tool for measuring perceived health problems: a study of patients with osteo-arthritis', *Journal of Epidemiology and Community Health,* 35, pp. 297-300.

Insel, P.M. and Moos, R.H. (1974) *Health and the social environment,* Lexington Books, Massachusetts.

Ivancevich, J.M. (1986), 'Life events and hassles as predictors of health symptoms, job performance, and absenteeism', *Journal of Occupational Behavior*, 7, pp. 39-51.

James, W. (1950), *The principles of psychology*, 2 Vols. Dover, New York.

Janisse, J.P. (1988), *Individual differences, stress, and health psychology*, Springer-Vertag, New York.

Joffe, R.T., Lippert, G.P. and Gray, T.A. (1987), 'Mood disorder and multiple sclerosis', *Archives of Neurology*, 44, pp. 376-8.

Kanner, A.D., Kafry, D. and Pines, A. (1978), 'Conspicuous in its absence: the lack of positive conditions as a source of stress', *Journal of Human Stress*, 4, pp. 33-9.

Kanner, A.D., Coyne, J.C., Schaefer, C. and Lazarus, R.S. (1981), 'Comparison of two modes of stress measurement: daily hassles and uplifts versus major life events', *Journal of Behavioral Medicine*, 4, pp. 1-39.

Kaplun, A. (1992), *Health promotion and chronic illness*, WHO Regional Publications, Copenhagen.

Kenealy, P. (1989), 'Children's strategies for coping with depression', *Behaviour Research Therapy*, 27, pp. 27-34.

Kinney, J.M. and Stephens, M.A.P. (1989), 'Hassles and uplifts of giving care to a family member with dementia', *Psychology and Aging*, 4, pp. 402-8.

Kleinman, A. (1980), *Patients and healers in the context of culture. An exploration of the borderland between anthropology, medicine and psychiatry*, University of California Press, Berkeley.

Kleinman, A. (1988), *The Illness Narratives*, Basic Books Inc., New York.

Kobasa, S.C. (1979), 'Stressful life events, personality and health: an inquiry into hardiness', *Journal of Personality and Social Psychology*, 37, pp. 1-11.

Krippendorff, K. (1980), *Content analysis. An introduction to its methodology*, Sage, Beverley Hills.

Kumar, S., Thara, R. and Rajkumar, S. (1989), 'Coping with symptoms of relapse in schizophrenia', *European Archive of Psychiatric and Neurological Sciences*, 239, pp. 213-15.

Kurtzke, J.F. (1983), 'Rating neurologic impairment in multiple sclerosis: an expanded disability status scale (EDSS)', *Neurology*, 33, pp. 1444-52.

Kurtzke, J.K. (1988), 'Multiple Sclerosis: What's in a name?', *Neurology*, 38, pp. 309-16.

Larocca, N., Kalb, R., Scheinberg, L. and Kendall, P. (1985), 'Factors associated with unemployment of patients with multiple sclerosis', *Journal of Chronic Disease*, 38, 203-10.

Lawson, A., Robinson, I. and Bakes, C. (1985), 'Problems in evaluating the consequences of disabling illness: the case of multiple sclerosis', *Psychological Medicine*, 15, pp. 555-79.

Lazarus, R.S. and Folkman, S. (1984), *Stress, appraisal and coping*, Springer Publishing Company, New York.

Lazarus, R.S. and Folkman, S. (1985), 'If it changes it must be a process: an analysis of emotion and coping during three stages of a college exam', *Journal of Personality and Social Psychology*, 48, pp. 150-170.

Lazarus, R.S., DeLongis, A., Folkman, S. and Gruen, R. (1985), 'Stress and adaptational outcomes. The problem of confounded measures', *American Psychologist*, 40, pp. 770-9.

Lazarus, R.S. (1986), 'Stress: appraisal and coping capacities', in Eichler, A., Silverman, M. and Pratt, D. (ed.), *How to define and research stress*, American Psychiatric Press, Washington, pp. 5-12.

Lazarus, R.S. (1992), 'Coping with the stress of illness', in Kaplun, A. (ed.), *Health promotion and chronic illness*, WHO Regional Publications, Copenhagen, pp. 11-29.

Lazarus, R.S. (1993), 'From psychological stress to the emotions: a history of changing outlooks', *Annual Review of Psychology*, 44, pp. 1-21.

Lepore, S.J., Palsane, M.N. and Evans, G.W. (1991), 'Daily hassles and chronic strains - a hierarchy of stressors', *Social Science and Medicine*, 33, pp. 1029-36.

Levick, P. (1992), 'The janis face of community care legislation: an opportunity for radical possibilities?' *Critical Social Policy*, 12, pp. 75-92.

Levine, A.M. (1985), Management of multiple sclerosis: how to improve the quality of life. *Postgraduate Medicine*, 77, pp. 121-27.

Lincoln, N.B. (1981), 'Discrepancies between capabilities and performance of activites of daily living in multiple sclerosis patients', *International Rehabilitation Medicine*, 3, pp. 84-8.

Linkowski, D.C. and Dunn, M.A. (1974), 'Self-concept and acceptance of disability', *Rehabilitation Counselling Bulletin*, 18, pp. 28-32.

Lipowski, Z.J. (1970), 'Physical illness, the individual and the coping processes', *Psychiatry in Medicine*, 1, pp. 91-102.

Locker, D. (1983), *Disability and disadvantage. The consequences of chronic illness*, Tavistock, London.

MacCarthy, B. and Brown, R. (1989), 'Psychosocial factors in Parkinson's disease', *British Journal of Clinical Psychology*, 28, pp. 41-52.

Mairs, N. (1988), 'On being a cripple', in Saxton, M. and Howe, F. (ed.), *With wings. An anthology of literature by women with disabilities*, Virago Press, London, pp. 118-127.

Marsh, G.G., Ellison, G.W. and Strite, C. (1983), 'Psychosocial and vocational rehabilitation approaches to multiple sclerosis', *Annual Review of Rehabilitation,* 3, pp. 242-67.

Martin, J., Meltzer, H. and Elliot, D. (1988), *The prevalence of disability among adults,* OPCS. London.

Martin, J. and White, A. (1988), *The financial circumstances of disabled adults living in private households,* OPCS, London.

Martin, J., White, A. and Meltzer, H. (1989), *Disabled adults: services, transport and employment,* OPCS, London.

Matthews, B. (1980), *Multiple sclerosis. The facts,* Oxford University Press, Oxford.

Matthews, W.B., Compston, A., Allen, I.V. and Martin, C.N. (1991), *McAlphine's multiple sclerosis* (2nd Edition), Churchill Livingstone, Edinburgh.

Matson, R.R. and Brooks, N.A. (1977), 'Adjusting to multiple sclerosis: an exploratory study', *Social Science and Medicine,* 11, pp. 245-50.

Mattingly, G., Baker, K., Zorumski, C.F. and Figiel, G.S. (1992), 'Multiple sclerosis and ECT: possible value of gadolinium-enhanced magnetic resonance scans for identifying high-risk patients', *Journal of Neuropsychiatry,* 4, pp. 145-51.

May, C. (1992), 'Individual care? Power and subjectivity in therapeutic relationships', *Sociology,* 26, pp. 589-602.

Maybery, C.P. and Brewin, C.R. (1984), 'Social relationships, knowledge and adjustment to multiple sclerosis', *Journal of Neurology, Neurosurgery, and Psychiatry,* 47, pp. 372-6.

McAdams, D.P. (1988), 'Biography, narrative, and lives: an introduction', *Journal of Personality,* 56, pp. 1-18.

McConkey, K.M., Roche, S.M. and Sheehan, P.W. (1989), 'Reports of forensic hypnosis: a critical analysis', *Austalian Psychologist,* 24, pp. 249-72.

McCoy, D. and Smith, M. (1992), *The prevalence of disability among adults in Northern Ireland,* Policy Planning and Research Unit, Belfast.

McCrae, R.R. (1984), 'Situational determinants of coping responses: loss, threat and challenge', *Journal of Personality and Social Psychology,* 46, pp. 919-28.

McCrae, R.R. and Costa, P.T. (1986), 'Personality, coping, and coping effectiveness in an adult sample', *Journal of Personality,* 54, pp. 385-405.

McDonald, I. (1992), 'Multiple sclerosis: diagnostic optimism', *British Medical Journal,* 304, pp. 1259-60.

McDowell, I. and Newell, C. (1987), *Measuring health. A guide to rating scales and questionnaires,* Oxford University Press, Oxford.

McFarlin, D.E. and McFarland, H.F. (1982), 'Medical progress. Multiple sclerosis', (part one), *The New England Journal of Medicine,* 307, pp. 1183-8.

McFarlin, D.E. and McFarland, H.F. (1982), 'Medical progress. Multiple sclerosis', (part two), *The New england Journal of Medicine,* 307, pp. 1246-51.

McGlashan, T.H., Levy, S.T. and Carpenter, W.T. (1975), 'Integration and sealing over: clinically distinct recovery styles from schizophrenia', *Archive of General Psychiatry,* 32, pp. 1269-72.

McIntosh-Michaelis, S.A., Wilkinson, S.M., Diamond, I.D., McLellan, D.L., Martin, J.P. and Spackman, A.J. (1991), 'The prevalence of cognitive impairment in a community survey of multiple sclerosis', *The Journal of Clinical Psychology,* 30, pp. 333-48.

McIver, G.P., Riklan, M. and Reznikoff, M. (1984), 'Depression in multiple sclerosis as a function of length and severity of illness, age, remissions, and perceived social support', *Journal of Clinical Pyschology,* 40, pp. 1028-33.

McLaughlin, J. and Zeeberg, I. (1993), 'Self-care and multiple sclerosis: a view from two cultures', *Social Science and Medicine,* 37, pp. 315-29.

McLellan, D.l., Martin, J.R., Roberts, M.H.W., Spackman, A., McIntosh-Michaelis, S. and Nichols, S, (1989), *Multiple Sclerosis in the Southampton District,* Rehabilation Research Unit and Department of Sociology and Social Policy, University of Southampton.

Mead, G.H. (1934), *Mind, Self, and Society,* Chicago University Press, Chicago.

Mechanic, D. (1972), 'Social psychologic factors affecting the presentation of bodily complaints' *New England Journal of Medicine,* 286, pp. 1132-9.

Medley, M.L. (1980), 'Life satisfaction across four stages of adult life', *International Journal of Aging and Human Development,* 11, pp. 193-209.

Miles, A. (1979), 'Some psycho-social consequences of multiple sclerosis: problems of social interaction and group identity', *British Journal of Medical Psychology,* 52, pp. 321-31.

Milgram, N.A. (1986), 'An attributional analysis of war-related stress: modes of coping and helping', in Milgram, N.A. (ed.), *Stress and coping in time of war,* Brunner/Mazel, New York.

Miller, E.J. and Gwynne, G.V. (1972), *A life apart,* Tavistock, London.

Miller, M.J., Wilcox, C.T. and Soper, B. (1984), 'Perceived hassles and uplifts among nursing home residents', *Psychological Reports,* 55, pp. 277-8.

Miller-Mair. (1988), *Telling psycological tales,* paper presented at the Forth Australasian Conference on Personal Construct Psychology, University of Wollongon, Australia.

Mitchell, R.E. and Hodson, C.A. (1986), 'Coping and social support among battered women: an ecological perspective', in Hobfoll, S.E. (ed.), *Stress, Social Support, and Women*, Hemisphere publishing corporation, Washington, pp. 153-69.

Miyaji, N.T. (1993), 'The power of compassion: truth-telling among American doctors in the care of dying patients', *Social Science and Medicine,* 36, pp. 249-64.

Monks, J. (1993), 'Think positive': moral issues in managing multiple sclerosis', paper presented at the International Conference on Social and Psychological Aspects of Multiple Sclerosis: Implications for Diagnsosis, Management and Rehabilitation, St. Catherines's College, Oxford.

Monroe, S.M. (1983), 'Major and minor life events as predictors of psychological distress: further issues and findings', *Journal of Behavioral Medicine,* 6, pp. 189-205.

Moos, R.H. (1974), *Evaluating treatment environments*, John Wiley and Sons, New York.

Moos, R.H. (1984), *Coping with physical illness. 2: New perspectives*, Plenum Medical Book Company, New York.

Moos, R.H. (1986), *Coping with life crises: an integrative approach*, Plenum, New York.

Moos, R.H. and Moos, B.S. (1981), *Family Environment Scale Manual*, Consulting Psychologists Press, California.

Moos, R.H. and Tsu, V. (1977), 'The crisis of physical illness: an overview', in R.H. Moos (ed.), *Coping with physical illness*, Plenum Press, New York, pp. 3-21.

Morris, J. (1989), *Able Lives. Women's experience of paralysis*, The Women's Press, London.

Morris, J. (1991), *Pride against prejudice*, The Women's Press, London.

Morris, J. (1992), 'Personal and political: a feminist perspective on researching physical disability', *Disability, Handicap and Society,* 7, pp. 157-66.

MS Society (1987), *Multiple Sclerosis: An Information Pack for Professional Carers, MS Society, London.*

Nachmias, C. and Nachmias, D. (1981), *Research methods in the social sciences*, St. Martin's Press, New York.

National Audit Office. (1992), *Health services for physically disabled people aged 16 to 64*, HMSO, London.

Norbeck, J.S., Chaftez, L., Skodol-Wilson, H. and Weiss, S.J. (1991), 'Social support needs of family caregivers of psychiatric patients from three age groups', *Nursing Research,* 40, pp. 208-13.

North, R.C., Holsti, O.R., Zaninovich, M.G. and Zinnes, D.A. (1963), *Content Analysis, a handbook with applications for the study of international crisis*, Northwestern University Press, Evanston.

Northern Ireland Health and Personal Social Services. (1992), *A charter for patients and clients*, DHSS, Belfast.

Nowack, K.M. (1989), 'Coping style, cognitive hardiness, and health status', *Journal of Behavioral Medicine*, 12, pp. 145-58.

Nunnally, J.C. (1961), *Popular conceptions of mental health*, Holt, Rinehart and Winston, New York.

Nuttall, P. (1988), 'Maternal responses to home apnea monitoring of infants', *Nursing Research*, 37, pp. 354-7.

O'Brien, S.J. and Conger, P.R. (1991), 'No time to look back: approaching the finish line of life's course', *International Journal of Aging and Human Development*, 33, pp. 75-87.

Oliver, M. (1990), *The politics of disablement*, Macmillan, London.

Oliver, M. (1992), 'Changing the social relations of research production?' *Disability, Handicap and Society*, 7, pp. 101-55.

Pappas, G. (1990), 'Some implication for the study of the doctor-patient interaction: power, structure, and agency in the works of Howard Waitzkin and Arther Kleinman', *Social Science and Medicine*, 30, pp. 199-204.

Parkes, K. (1986), 'Coping in stressful episodes: the role of individual differences, environmental factors, and situational characteristics'. *Journal of Personality and Social Psychology*, 51, pp. 1277-92.

Parker, C. (1988), *Medicine and culture. Varities of threatments in the United States, England, West Germany, and France*, Henry Holt and Company, New York.

Parsons, T. (1951), *The social system*, Routledge and Kegan Paul, London.

Patterson, T.L., Smith, L.W., Grant, I., Clopton, P., Josepho, S. and Yager, J. (1990), 'Internal vs. external determinants of coping responses to stressful life-event in the elderly', *British Journal of Medical Psychology*, 63, pp. 149-60.

Paulley, J.W. (1985), 'Psychosomatic aspects of multiple sclerosis', *Advances in Psychosomatic Medicine*, 13, pp. 85-110.

Pavlou, M. and Counte, M. (1982), 'Aspects of coping in multiple sclerosis', *Rehabilitation Counselling Bulletin*, 25, pp. 138-45.

Pearlin, L.I. and Schooler, C. (1978), 'The structure of coping', *Journal of Health and Social Behavior*, 19, pp. 2-21.

Pellman, J. (1992), 'Widowhood in elderly women: exploring its relationship to community integration, hassles, stress, social support, and social support seeking', *International Journal of Aging and Human Development*, 35, pp. 253-64.

Perry, S. (1993), 'Living with multiple sclerosis: the role of perceptions of illness, stress and coping on adaptation', unpublished doctoral dissertation, The Queen's University of Belfast, Belfast.

Peyser, J.M., Edwards, K.R. and Poser, C.M. (1980), 'Psychological profiles in patients with multiple sclerosis', *Archives of Neurology*, 37, pp. 437-40.

Phadke, J.G. (1990), 'Clinical aspects of multiple sclerosis in North-East Scotland with particular reference to its course and prognosis', *Brain*, 113, pp. 1597-628.

Pill, R. and Stott (1985), 'Choice or chance: further evidence on ideas of illness and responsibility for health', *Social Science and Medicine*, 20, pp. 981-91.

Pinder, R. (1990), *The management of chronic illness. Patient and doctor perspectives on Parkinson's disease*, Macmillan Press, London.

Pollitt, C., Harrison, S., Hunter, D. and Marnoch, G. (1990), 'No hiding place: on the discomforts of researching the contemporary policy process', *Journal of Social Policy*, 19, pp. 169-90.

Pollock, K. (1984), *Mind and Matter*, unpublished doctoral dissertation, Universiaty of Cambridge, Cambridge.

Pollock, K. (1988), 'On the nature of social stress: production of a modern mythology', *Social Science and Medicine*, 26, pp. 381-92.

Pollock, S.E. (1986), 'Human responses to chronic illness: physiologic and psychosocial adaption', *Nursing Research*, 35, pp. 90-5.

Pollock, S.E., Christian, B.J. and Sands, D. (1990), 'Responses to chronic illness: analysis of psychological and physiological adaptation', *Nursing Research*, 39, pp. 300-4.

Pope, C. and Mays, N. (1993), 'Opening the black box: an encounter in the corridors of health services research', *British Medical Journal*, 306, pp. 315-18.

Poser, C.M., Pary, D.W., Scheinberg, L., McDonald, I., Davis, F.A., Ebers, G.C., Johnson, K.P., Sibley, W.A., Silberberg, D.H. and Touretllotte, W.W. (1983), 'New diagnostic criteria for multiple sclerosis: Guidelines for reserch protocols', *Annals of Neurology*, 13, pp. 227-31.

Poskanzer, D.C., Schapira, K. and Miller, H. (1963), 'Epidemiology of multiple sclerosis in the counties of Northumberland and Durham', *Journal of Neurology, Neurosurgery and Psychiatry*, 26, pp.368-76.

Powell, S.S. and Drotar, D. (1992), 'Postpartum depressed mood - the impact of daily hassles', *Journal of Psychosomatic Obstetrics and Gynaecology*, 13, pp. 255-66.

Primomo, J., Yates, B.C. and Woods, N.F. (1990), 'Social support for women during chronic illness: the relationship among sources and types to adjustment', *Research in Nursing and Health*, 13, pp.153-61.

Prosser, G. (1992), 'Psychological issues when others mediate your life', *Educational and Child Pyschology*, 9, pp. 17-26.

Quine, L. and Pahl, J. (1991), 'Stress and coping in mothers caring for a child with severe learning difficulties: a test of Lazarus' transactional model of coping', *Journal of Community and Applied Social Psychology*, 1, pp.57-70.

Rabkin, J.G. and Struening, E.L. (1976), 'Life events, stress, and illness', *Science*, 194, pp. 1013-20.

Radford, I. and Trew, K. (1987). *Action for MS care. A survey of multiple sclerosis sufferers and their carers in Northern Ireland*, Multiple Sclerosis Action Group (Action MS), Belfast.

Rao, S. M., Huber, S.J. and Bornstein, R.A. (1992), 'Emotional changes with multiple sclerosis and Parkinson's disease', *Journal of Consulting and Clinical Psychology*, 60, pp. 369-78.

Register, C. (1987), *Living with chronic illness*, The Free Press, New York.

Riessman, C.K. (1990), 'Strategic uses of narrative in the presentation of self and illness: a research note', *Social Science and Medicine*, 30, pp. 1195-1200.

Roberts, H. (1985), *The patient patients. Women and their doctors*, Routledge and Kegan Paul, London.

Roberts, M.H.W., Martin,J.P., McLellan, D.L., McIntosh-Michawlis, S.A. and Spackman, A.J. (1991), 'The prevalence of multiple sclerosis in the Southamptom and South West Hampshire Health Authority', *Journal of Neurology Neurosurgery, and Psychiatry*, 54, pp. 55-9.

Robinson, F. and Gregson, N. (1992), 'The 'underclass': a class apart?', *Critical Social Policy*, 12, pp. 38-51.

Robinson, I. (1988a), *Multiple sclerosis*, Routledge, London.

Robinson, I. (1988b), 'Reconstructing lives: negotiating the meaning of multiple sclerosis', in Anderson, R. and Bury, M. (ed.), *Living with chronic illness. The experience of patients and their families*, Unwin Hyman, London, pp. 43-66.

Robinson, I. (1990), 'Personal narratives, social careers and medical courses: analysing life trajectories in autobiographies of people with multiple sclerosis', *Social Science and Medicine*, 30, pp. 1173-86.

Robson, P.J. (1988), 'Self-esteem - a psychiatric view', *British Journal of Psychiatry*, 153, pp. 6-15.

Rodin, J. and Salovey, P. (1989), 'Health psychology', *American Review of Psychology*, 40, pp. 533-79.

Roessler, R. and Bolton, B. (1978), *Psychosocial adjustment and disability*, University Park Press, Baltimore.

251

Romano, P.S., Bloom, J. and Smyme, S.L. (1991), 'Smoking, social support and hassles in an urban African-American community', *Journal of Public Health,* 81, pp. 1415-22.

Ron, M.A. (1986), 'Multiple sclerois: psychiatric and psychometric abnormalities', *Journal of Psychosomatic Research,* 30, pp. 3-11.

Ron, M.A. and Feinstein, A. (1992), 'Multiple sclerosis and the mind', *Journal of Neurology, Neurosurgery, and Psychiatry,* 55, pp. 1-3.

Rosenberg, M. (1965), *Society and the adolescent self image,* Princeton University Press, Princeton.

Rosenstiel, A.K. and Keefe, F.J. (1983), 'The use of coping strategies in chronic low back pain patients: relationship to patient characteristics and current adjustment', *Pain,* 17, pp. 33-44.

Rosenstock, I.M. (1974), 'Historical origins of the health belief model', *Health Education Monographs,* 2, pp. 328-35.

Roter, D. and Frankel, R. (1992), 'Quantitative and qualitative approaches to the evaluation of the medical dialogue', *Social Science and Medicine,* 34, pp. 1097-103.

Roth, J.A. and Conrad, P. (1987), *The experience and management of chronic illness,* JAI Press, Greenwich.

Rothschild, C.S. (1970), *Sociology and social psychology of disability and rehabilitation,* Random House, New York.

Royal College of Physicians. (1986), *Physical disability in 1986 and beyond,* Royal College of Physicians of London, London.

Royal College of Physicians. (1990), 'Standards of care for patients with neurological disease', *Journal of the Royal College of Physicians of London,* 24, pp. 90-7.

Rubinstein, R. (1989), *Take it and leave it,* Marion Boyars, London.

Ruch, L.O. and Leon, J.L. (1986), 'The victim of rape and the role of life change, coping, and social support during the rape trauma syndrome', in Hobfoll, S.E. (ed.), *Stress, Social Support, and Women,* Hemisphere publishing corporation, Washington, pp. 137-152.

Rutter, M. (1981), 'Stress, coping and development: some issues and some questions', *Journal of Child Psychology,* 22, pp. 323-56.

Safilos-Rothschild, C. (1970), *The sociology and social psychology of disability and rehabilitation,* Random House, New York.

Saltonstall, R. (1993), 'Healthy bodies, social bodies: men's and women's concepts and practices of health in everyday life', *Social Science and Medicine,* 36, pp. 7-14.

Saxton, M. and Howe, F. (1988), *With wings. An anthology of literature by women with disabilities,* Virago Press, London.

Scambler, G. and Hopkins, A. (1986), 'Being epileptic: coming to terms with stigma', *Sociology of Health and Illness,* 8, pp. 26-43.

Scambler, G. (1984), 'Perceiving and coping with stigmatising illness', in Fitzpatrick, R., Hinton, J., Newman, S., Scambler, G. and Thompson, J. (ed.), *The experience of illness,* Tavistock, Londo, pp. 203-26.

Scheff, T.J. (1966), *Being Mentally Ill: a sociological theory,* Aldine, Chicago.

Scherl, L.M. and Smithson, M. (1987), 'A new dimension to content analysis: exploring relationships among thematic categories', *Quality and Quantity,* 21, pp, 199-208.

Schiffer, R.B., Rudick, R.A. and Herndon, R.M. (1983), 'Psychologic aspects of multiple sclerosis', *New York State Journal of Medicine,* March, pp. 312-16.

Schnurre, M. (1992), 'Helping the patient sing his own song', in Kaplan, A. (ed.), *Health Promotion and Chronic Illness,* WHO Regional Publication, Copenhagen, pp. 388-95.

Schonpflug, W. and Battmann, W. (1988), 'The costs and benefits of coping', in Fisher, S. and Reason, J. (ed.), *Handbook of life stress, cognition and health,* John Wiley and Sons, Chichester, pp. 699-713.

Schulz, R. and Decker, S. (1985), 'Long-term adjustment to physical disability: the role of social support, perceived control and self-blame', *Journal of Personality and Social Psychology,* 48, 1162-72.

Schussler, G. (1992), 'Coping strategies and individual meanings of illness', *Social Science and Medicine,* 34, pp. 427-32.

Scull, A. (1984), *Decarceration: Community Treatment and the Deviant - A Radical View,* Polity Press, Cambridge.

Selye, H. (1983), 'The stress concept: past, present and future', in Cooper, C.L. (ed.), *Stress Research,* Wiley, New York.

Shotter, J. and Gergen, K.J. (1989), *Texts of identity,* Sage, London.

Simons, A. (1984), 'Perceptions of Health Care', in Simons, A.F. (ed.), *Multiple Sclerosis,* William Heineman Medical Books Ltd., London, pp.115-32.

Simons, A. (1984). 'Problems of providing support for people with multiple sclerosis and their families', in Simons, A.F. (ed.), *Multiple sclerosis,* William Heineman Medical Books Ltd., London, pp. 1-20.

Social Services Committee. (1985), *Second Report. Community care with special reference to adult mentally ill and mentally handicapped people,* HMSO, London.

Solomon, S., Greenberg, J. and Pyszczynski, T. (1991), 'Terror management theory of self-esteem', in Snyder, C.R. and Forsyth, P.R. (eds.), *Handbook of Social and Clinical Psychology,* Pergamon Press, New York, pp. 21-40.

253

Sontag, S. (1991), *Illness as metaphor, Aids and its metaphors*, Penguin, London.

Stacey, M. (1976), 'The health service consumer: a sociological misconception', *Sociological Review Monograph*, 22, pp. 194-200.

Stainton Rogers. W. (1991), *Explaining health and illness. An exploration of diversity*, Harvester Wheatsheaf, Hemel Hempstead.

Stanley, L. (1990), 'Doing ethnography, writing ethnography: a comment on Hammersley', *Sociology*, 24, pp. 617-27.

Stewart, D.C. and Sullivan, T.J. (1982), 'Illness behaviour and the sick role in chronic disease', *Social Science and Medicine*, 16, pp. 1397-404.

Stone, A.A. and Neale, J.M. (1984), 'New measure of daily coping: development and preliminary results', *Journal of Personality and Social Psychology*, 46, pp. 892-906.

Stone, G.C., Cohen, F., Adler, N.E. and Associates. (1979), *Health psychology - a handbook*, Jossey-Bass Publishers, San Francisco.

Strauss, A.L. and Glaser, B. (1975), *Chronic illness and the quality of life*, Mosby, St Louis.

Strauss, A.L. and Glaser, B. (1984), *Chronic illness and the quality of life*, (2nd ed.), Mosby, St Louis.

Strauss, A.L. and Corbin, J. (1990), *Basics of qualitative research, grounded theory procedures and techniques*, Sage, Newbury Park.

Strauss, A. (1990), 'Preface', *Social Science and Medicine*, 30, pp. v-vi.

Swallow, M. (1990), *Disability '90. A report on the first two years of the committee on services for people with physical disabilities*, EHSSB Medical Disability Committee, Belfast.

Swallow, M. and Darragh, P. (1991), 'Health services for adults with physical disability. A survey of provision by the Health and Social Boards in Northern Ireland in 1988-89', *The Ulster Medical Journal*, 60, Supplement.

Tajfel, H. (1978), *Differentiation between social groups*, Academic Press, London.

Taylor, S.E. (1983), 'Adjustment to threatening events', *American Psychologist*, 38, pp. 1161-73.

Templer, D.I., Trent, N.H., Spencer, D.A., Trent, A., Corgiat, M.D., Mortensen, P.B. and Gorton, M. (1992), 'Season of birth in multiple sclerosis', *Acta Neurologica Scandinavica*, 85, pp. 107-9.

Townsend, P. and Davidson, N. (1982), *The Black Report*, Penguin, London.

Tringo, J.L. (1970), 'The hierarchy of preference toward disability groups', *The Journal of Special Education*, 4, pp. 295-306.

Vaizey, J. (1986), *Scenes from institutional life and other writings*, Weidenfeld and Nicolson, London.

254

Vaillant, G.E. (1977), *Adaptation to life: how the best and the brightest came of age*, Little, Brown, Boston.

VanderPlate, C. (1984), 'Psychological aspects of multiple sclerosis and its treatment: towards a biopsychosocial perspective', *Health Psychology*, 3, pp. 253-72.

Vaughn, C.E. and Leff, J. (1976), 'The influence of family and social factors on the course of psychiatric illness', *British Journal of Psychiatry*, 129, pp. 125-37.

Veit, C.T. and Ware, J.E. Jr. (1983), 'The structure of psychological distress and well-being in general populations', *Journal of Consulting and Clinical Psychology*, 51, pp. 730-42.

Viney, L.L. and Westbrook, M.T. (1981), 'Psychological reaction to chronic illness-related disability as a function of its severity and type', *Journal of Psychosomatic Research*, 25, pp. 513-23.

Viney, L.L. and Westbrook, M.T. (1982), 'Coping with chronic illness: the mediating role of biographic and illness-related factors', *Journal of Psychosomatic Research*, 26, pp. 595-605.

Vingerhoets, A.J.J.M. and Marcelissen, F.H.G. (1988), 'Stress research: its present status and issues for future developments', *Social Science and Medicine*, 26, pp. 279-91.

Visscher, B.R., Clark, V.A., Detals, R., Malmgren, R.M., Valdiviezo, N.L. and Dudley, J.P. (1981), 'Two populations with multiple sclerosis. Clinical and demographic characteristics', *Journal of Neurology*, 225, pp. 237-49.

Vitaliano, P.P., Maiuro, R.D., Russo, J., Katon, W., DeWolfe, D. and Hall, G. (1990), 'Coping profiles associated with psychiatric, physical health, work, and family problems', *Health Psychology*, 9, pp. 348-76.

Wagner, G. (1988), *A positive choice: report of the independent review of residential care*, NISW/HMSO, London.

Waitzkin, H. (1990), 'On studying the discourse of medical encounters. A critiques of quantitative and qualitative methods and a proposal for reasonable compromise', *Medical Care*, 28, pp. 473-88.

Walker, C.L. (1988), 'Stress and coping in siblings of childhood cancer patients', *Nursing Research*, 37, pp. 208-12.

Wallston, K.A., Wallston, B.S. and De Vellis, R. (1978), 'Development of the multidimensional health locus of control (MHLC) scales', *Health Education Monographs*, 6, pp. 161-70.

Walton, C. (1989), *Essentials of Neurology*, (6th ed.), Churchill Livingstone, Edinburgh.

Waltz, M. and Badura, B. (1990), 'Social support and chronic illness; conceptual and methodological problems', *International Journal of Health Sciences*, 1, pp. 177-83.

Warren, S., Warren, K.G. and Cockerill, R. (1991), 'Emotional stress and coping in multiple sclerosis (MS) Exacerbations', *Journal of Psychosomatic Research*, 35, pp. 37-47.

Watson, L, Irwin, J. and Michalske, S. (1991), 'Researcher as friend: methods of the interviewer in a longitudinal study', *Qualitative Health Research*, 1, pp. 497-514.

Webb, H.E. (1992), 'Multiple sclerosis: therapeutic pessimism', *British Medical Journal*, 304, pp. 1260-1

Weber, R.P. (1985), *Basic content analysis*, Sage, Beverly Hills.

Weinshenker, B.G. and Ebers, G.C. (1987), 'The natural history of multiple sclerosis', *Canadian Journal of Neurology*, 14, pp. 255-61.

Weinshenker, B.G., Bass, B., Rice, G.P.A., Noseworthy, J., Carriere, W., Baskerville, J. and Ebers, G.C. (1989), 'The natural history of multiple sclerosis: a geographically based study', *Brain*, 112, pp. 133-46.

Westbrook, M.T. and Viney, L.L. (1982), 'Psychological reactions to the onset of chronic illness', *Social Science and Medicine*, 16, pp. 899-905.

Westbrook, M.T., Legge, V. and Pennay, M. (1993), 'Attitudes towards disabilities in a multicultural society', *Social Science and Medicine*, 36, pp. 615-23.

Whan, M.C. (1979), 'Accounts, narrative and case history', *British Journal of Social Work*, 9, pp. 489-99.

Wheaton, B. (1983), 'Stress, personal coping resources, and psychiatric symptoms: an investigation of interactive models', *Journal of Health and Social Behavior*, 24, pp. 208-29.

Whitehead, A. (1983), *Final Report: Outset 'Action on Handicap Survey' in Northern Ireland*, Outset, London.

Whitehead, M. (1988), *The Health Divide*, Penguin, London.

Williams, G. (1984), 'The genesis of chronic illness: narrative reconstruction', *Sociology of Health and Illness*, 6, pp. 175-200.

Williams, G.H. (1991), 'Disablement and the ideological crisis in health care', *Social Science and Medicine*, 32, pp. 517-24.

Williams, R. (1983), 'Concepts of health: an analysis of lay logic', *Sociology*, 17, pp. 185-205.

Williams, R. (1990), *A protestant legacy*, Clarendon, Oxford.

Williams, R., Zyzanski, S.J. and Wright, A.L. (1992), 'Life events and daily hassles and uplifts as predictors of hospitalization and outpatient visitation', *Social Science and Medicine*, 34, pp. 763-8.

Wineman, N.M. (1990), 'Adaptation to Multiple sclerosis: the role of social support, functional disability, and perceived uncertainty', *Nursing Research*, 39, pp. 294-9.

Wing, J.K. and Olsen, R. (1979), *Community Care for the Mentally Disabled*, Oxford University Press, Oxford.

World Health Organisation (1980), *International Classification of Impairments, Disabilities and Handicaps*, WHO, Geneva.

Wortman, C.B. and Silver, R.C. (1989), 'The myths of coping with loss', *Journal of Consulting and Clinical psychology*, 57, pp. 349-57.

Wright, J., Deary, I.J. and Geissler, P.R. (1991), 'Depression, hassles and somatic symptoms in mandibular dysfunction patients', *Journal of Denistry*, 19, pp. 352-6.

Wright, M. (1992) 'An alternative road to being healthily unwell', *The European*, 18-21 June, pp. 27.

Yoshida, K.K. (1993), 'Reshaping of self: a pendular reconstruction of self and identity among adults with traumatic spinal cord injury', *Sociology of Health and Illness*, 15, pp. 217-45.

Young, A. (1980), 'The discourse on stress and the reproduction of conventional knowledge', *Social Science and Medicine*, 14B, pp. 133-46.

Zautra, A. and Reich, J. (1980), 'Positive life events and reports of well-being: some useful distinctions', *American Journal of Community Psychology*, 8, pp. 657-70.

Zautra, A. and Hempel, A. (1984), 'Subjective well-being and physical health: a narrative literature review with suggestions for future research', *International Journal of Aging and Human Development*, 19. pp. 95-110.

Zola, I.K. (1993), 'Self, identity and the naming question: reflections on the language of disability', *Social Science and Medicine*, 36, pp. 167-73.